# THE ZADDIK

# ALSO BY ELAINE GRUDIN DENHOLTZ

### PLAYS

*Frozen*
*The Dungmen Are Coming*
*Hey Out There, Is Anyone Out There?*
*Some Men Are Good at That*
*The Highchairs*
*Love Games*
*Doggy Bag*

### FILMS

*Summerhill*
*Waiting . . . The Life of Styles of the Elderly*
*The Dental Auxiliary*
*What's Inside*
*Is That What You Want for Yourself?*
*Another Mother* (Eugene O'Neill adaptation for television)

### BOOKS

*Education, Where It's Been, Where It's At, Where It's Going*
(contributor)
*The Highchairs*
*How to Save Your Teeth and Your Money* (co-author)
*The Dental Facelift* (co-author)
*Having It Both Ways: A Report on Married Women with Lovers*
*Playing for High Stakes*
*Balancing Work and Love:*
*Jewish Women Facing the Family-Career Challenge*

# THE ZADDIK

*The Battle for a Boy's Soul*

ELAINE GRUDIN DENHOLTZ

**Prometheus Books**

59 John Glenn Drive
Amherst, New York 14228-2197

Cover image: *Boy with Earlocks*, Poland, ca. 1938
By Roman Vishniac
Gelatin silver print
© Mara Vishniac Kohn, courtesy of the
International Center of Photography

Published 2001 by Prometheus Books

Inquiries should be addressed to
Prometheus Books
59 John Glenn Drive
Amherst, New York 14228–2197
VOICE: 716–691–0133, ext. 207
FAX: 716–564–2711
WWW.PROMETHEUSBOOKS.COM

05 04 03 02 01    5 4 3 2 1

Library of Congress Cataloging-in-Publication Data

Denholtz, Elaine.
    The zaddik : the battle for a boy's soul / Elaine Grudin Denholtz.
        p. cm.
    ISBN 1–57392–920–4 (alk. paper)

Printed in the United States of America on acid-free paper

*In memory of my mother*

LILLIAN SACHS GRUDIN

*and*

*for* MEL *and* PEEPS

There Was a Child Went Forth

There was a child went forth every day;
And the first object he looked upon, that object he became;
And that object became part of him for the day, or a certain
    part of the day, or for many years, or stretching
    cycles of years.

Walt Whitman

# CONTENTS

# PART III.  BROOKLYN

# PART IV.  1993

# PART V.  1994

# PART VI.  THE TRIAL

# PART VII. 1995

# PART VIII. 1996

# THE PEOPLE

SHAI FHIMA, the boy
HANA FHIMA, his mother
JACKY FHIMA, his stepfather
MICHAEL REUVEN, his biological father
RABBI WEINBERG

RABBI SCHLOMO HELBRANS, head of yeshiva
MALKA HELBRANS, his wife
MORDECAI WEISS, yeshiva student
TOBIAS FREUND, follower of Helbrans

CHARLES "JOE" HYNES, Brooklyn District Attorney
CAPTAIN BILL PLACKENMEYER, Brooklyn NYPD

LARRY MEYERSON, Hana's attorney
STEVE RUBENSTEIN, Hana's attorney and senior partner of law
firm
ELAINE MEYERSON, head of Shelter Our Sisters and Larry's
wife

JUDGE STANGER, Rockland County Family Court, N.Y.
JUDGE SWEEN, Bergen County Family Court, N.J.
JUDGE SLOBAD, Rockland County Family Court, N.Y.

ERIC THORSEN, Shai's attorney
RABBI ARYEH ZAKS, Shai's appointed guardian
MITCHEL and BEN OSTRER, attorneys for Rabbi Zaks
LIEB WALDMAN, Rabbi Zaks's father-in-law

JUDGE THADDEUS OWENS, presiding at Brooklyn Supreme
 Court

ALAN VINEGRAD, Assistant U.S. Attorney, Eastern Division
MICHAEL VECCHIONE, District Attorney, Brooklyn

PAUL ROONEY, Rabbi Helbrans's defense attorney
JOYCE DAVID, Malka Helbrans's defense attorney

# FOREWORD

*I can only imagine the depth of her pain.*

That's what I was thinking the first time I met Hana Fhima on February 10, 1995. A petite young woman, early thirties, with long brown hair, her dark eyes brimmed as she spoke to me.

We sat across the table from each other at the Glenpointe Marriott restaurant in Teaneck, New Jersey, and talked and talked. Nearly five hours, through breakfast and lunch. Steve Rubenstein and Larry Meyerson, her lawyers, sat beside her. The story she told me was bone chilling.

In April, 1992, her thirteen-year-old son, Shai, was kidnapped by a Brooklyn rabbi and hidden away for years in the hasidic underground. The Brooklyn D.A. wouldn't touch it. He was running for reelection, he needed hasidic votes. No one paid attention to her, an Israeli immigrant mother of four. Until Rubenstein and Meyerson, two New Jersey lawyers, took on the system and demanded justice.

The search for Shai, led by the FBI and the NYPD, began in New Jersey, then to New York, Jerusalem, Paris, and Canada. *Two* legal battles. A *kidnapping trial* before a jury that made international headlines. And a *custody fight* with two family court judges at each other's throats.

13

When I left the Glenpointe Marriott, I was reeling. Hana Fhima's story of scandalous political corruption and ultra-orthodox religious kidnappings rocked me to the core. Because until Hana blew the whistle, kidnappings by hasidic groups were largely ignored. Kids vanished. Their parents never saw them again. Nobody did a thing about it. Hana convinced me that attention must be paid. I hope I have told the story well.

The events in the kidnapping are not in dispute.

Larry Meyerson sent me a heavy package of clippings from many newspapers including the *New York Times,* and the *New York Post.* The Israeli tabloids *Yediot Ahronot* and *Maariv* also tracked the story. Articles appeared in national magazines and arguments raged in the Jewish press. From the opening day of Rabbi Schlomo Helbrans's kidnapping trial, reporters jammed the Brooklyn courthouse to cover the events. Photographers vied for pictures and video cameras rolled. Hana herself gave count-less interviews. The trial record turned out about 2,500 pages.

So why write a book?

Because looking into Hana Fhima's tortured face on that winter morning, I felt enormously drawn to her. What astonished me was the depth of her emotions. Her tenacity. Her determina-tion. Her persistence. Hana Fhima was only a fly buzzing around the powerful. But she refused to go away.

"I want people should know what really happened," she told me in her flat Israeli accent, her eyes filling up. "I want it to be a book, people should read it."

For more than a year and a half we kept talking. On the phone, in her apartment, in courtrooms, in hallways, and in parking lots we talked. I am enormously grateful to Hana Fhima. I hope she is pleased with this book.

I am also deeply indebted to Steve Rubenstein and Larry Mey-erson, who represented her pro bono for four years with unfailing loyalty and professionalism. Like Hana, they never gave up. They demanded justice for their client and, like Woodward and Bernstein, defied a legal system that failed. They provided me with hours of interviews, insights, and information.

In preparation for writing, I examined press releases and official documents, did computer searches, and had conversations with many people whose lives intersected with Shai and Hana. Their observations richly informed this book.

However, some of them asked me not to acknowledge their help, they didn't want it known that they cooperated with me. Because I promised them anonymity, I cannot name them. They know who they are and I am grateful. Often a conversation with one person led me to someone else, and someone else. And so it went.

Almost without exception, everyone who spoke with me described Shai's disappearance as "tragic." Even Rabbi Aryeh Zaks, Hana's adversary who was granted custody of Shai by Judge Stanger, told me on the telephone: "It's a tragic story, tragic. But I know only what the boy told me over the years." Then he clammed up, despite my letter asking for an interview. So did his father-in-law, real estate tycoon Lieb Waldman, whose legal problems are documented in the Harrisburg, Pennsylvania, court records.

Many people, off and on the record, gave me help and wished me luck. For example, Judge Thaddeus Owens, who presided over the kidnapping trial in Brooklyn, spoke with me as did lawyers and district attorneys who cooperated beyond my expectation. Several provided me with court transcripts and official papers. Their enthusiasm for this book spurred me on.

To place the many convoluted events in order, I had to make choices. What to leave out and what to include. It is the writer's dilemma: a struggle that never completely satisfies. For the sake of clarity, but not at the risk of compromise, I reduced the cast of characters to about twenty-five, though others played their parts.

Along the way I had the assistance of researchers and librarians who made the difficult job easier. I am indebted to librarians at the Ruth Rockwood Memorial Library, the Fairleigh Dickinson University Library, and the Waldor Library of the Jewish Community Center (JCC) where, on a snowy Friday afternoon, Bracha Weisbarth translated documents for me from Hebrew to English until custodians threatened to lock us into the building.

Beyond the public records and interviews, I immersed myself in studies of cults, religious abductions, and law. I wanted to understand the subtext: what really happened? I talked with a number of therapists with a specialty in cults, deprogramming, and mind control and they helped me to understand how brainwashing works.

One question continued to plague me: Is there an international conspiracy in which small but highly dangerous religious cults kidnap secular boys and turn them into ultrareligious hasids? Did Rabbi Helbrans act on impulse perhaps, and only then did the hasidic community start covering it up? Perhaps we will never know the answers fully about how brainwashing works, but we do know how Rabbi Helbrans stole Shai's soul.

From 1992 to 1996, media articles poured out the details of Shai's kidnapping. Each time he reappeared and was secreted away again, Hana was hurled forward and yanked back in a roller coaster ride of despair and hope. There are police records, court records, and pounds of public records. These are real characters and real events. To the best of my knowledge I have represented them honestly, using quotations from public sources and articles in the press.

Other quotations in the book represent substantially what I believe might be spoken under circumstances reported by sources I believe reliable. I recreated for the reader what I believed to be likely given the true circumstances. Based on what I read and gleaned from the interviews, I created patches of dialogue which I thought were likely and I created scenes I was not privy to.

For example, when I interviewed Police Captain Bill Plackenmeyer in Brooklyn, he did not tell me the actual words Shai's father, Michael Reuven, used as a signal to the NYPD when they wired him. In chapter 17, "I have a headache," is my interpretation relying heavily on information from police officers who described to me the process of wiring someone in a stakeout.

Another example. In chapter 20, for the fight between Hana and her husband Jacky, I did extensive research on battered women, read many books and visited the secret location of a battered women's shelter. Conversations with professional social workers helped me construct the scene and the dialogue.

From the first day I met Hana, I felt that on some level her pain would always be with her. Later, several cult therapists shed light on the guilt and remorse a parent feels. Why did it happen to me? What did I do wrong? Hana struggled with these emotions over those years.

Regrettably, the person I was not able to interview was Rabbi Schlomo Helbrans. Though I wrote to him and visited Woodbourne Correctional Facility twice while he was an inmate, his attorneys would not allow him to speak with me.

In my effort to tell the story richly, I made use of published information by competent reporters from New Jersey, New York, and Pennsylvania who shared their impressions with me. Steve Lieberman, Jack Sherzer, and Pete Shellem were open and helpful. What I tried to do was create a reality which transcended journalism. My hope was to expose the many layers and reveal a deeper truth.

Some people told me that *not* knowing if your child is dead or alive is worse than facing your child's death. Therefore, I wrote certain sections to illuminate the terror inside Hana's heart, inventing conversations and thoughts, liberties many biographers take to make their subject come alive. It is my hope this book will convey, in addition to Hana's pain, how dangerous is the power of cults. And how some courts and judges fail to dispense justice in religious kidnappings.

Of course, every phenomenon remains a puzzle because we never have all the pieces. Many nights I lay awake debating a point, ruminating and arguing with myself and playing the devil's advocate. Like many authors, my perspectives and life experiences are folded into this book.

To Hana goes the lion's share of my admiration. Her steadfast courage and unwavering love for Shai are on every page. During one of her darkest hours, I told her as we sat at her kitchen table, "One day Shai will read this book and see how hard you worked to find him and how much you love him."

I am grateful to two friends who are attorneys: Lee Brenner who listened and commented; and Richard Kapner, who read the entire manuscript, made copious notes, and took my phone calls at weird hours. Thanks also go to my Scribblers buddies, Marjorie Keyeshian, Joan Morrison, and Carole Rogers, for their unfailing support as they critiqued chapter after chapter. To Peeps, my father, whose piano music sings in my head and helps me appreciate the loveliness of words. To my children for listening attentively and forgiving my inattention. And to my husband who has been there before and is always there for me.

Elaine Grudin Denholtz

# PART I

Brooklyn, 1992

# 1. SHAI

The winter of 1992 has hit New Jersey with ferocious force. In Ramsey, a town of about fourteen thousand, families awake with one question on their minds. Is it going to be a day of digging out? Moms groan when the phone call comes in that school will be on late opening schedule or, worse, closed. Snow days have to be made up at the end of June, taking slices off summer vacation.

By early February everyone is fed up and worn out by temperatures in the twenties, gloomy overcast skies and bitter winds. They ache to hear a birdsong at dawn or see a perky crocus in the snow.

Eric Smith Middle School is a typical suburban structure, a sprawling flat-roofed ranch favored by voters who want their children to have lawns and trees. There are four public schools and a high school, plus Don Bosco, a private high school. Parents care about their children's education and take pride in their community. They turn up for town meetings. When Ramsey police officers do an evening program for parents about DARE, how to detect and discourage student drug use, cars pour into Eric Smith parking lot. Most people read the *Bergen Record* and catch up on local news with the *Ramsey Reporter*, their weekly paper.

Say Bergen County to most people in New Jersey, and they immediately think *rich*. Not far off the mark because the per capita income for this northeast county rivals wealthy Essex County, New Jersey. Psychiatrists, stockbrokers, and media people maintain handsome homes in Bergen County because it is an easy commute to their offices in Manhattan and provides the sophisticated pleasures of New York City, the city that never sleeps.

Ramsey, however, is not rich by Bergen County standards.

21

Covering five and a half square miles, home owners, mostly white, are pretty middle class and a few households even receive public aid. Rental units go for something around $900 per month.

At 3:10, the seventh graders at Eric Smith burst out of the front doors like bullets shot from a cannon. Even the cool kids brace against the slap of bitter cold. The *Ramsey Reporter* has published the Groundhog Day prediction of February second forecasting six more weeks of blustery winds and bone chilling days. Everyone feels like hostages to the arctic winter.

The boy hears David calling him. "Shai, Shai, wait up!"

But no way will he turn around and face into the icy wind. Instead he hunches his shoulders and slows down, letting the other kids pass him. He glances up at the granite sky and mumbles *Shit* into his parka, noting dark clouds gathering. Winter sucks. New Jersey sucks. And Mr. Silba sucks. Second period, the asshole hands back his math quiz with a C minus. He hates Silba. Hates Wednesdays. Sometimes he even hates his mother. Nag, nag, nag.

*Come straight home, Shai, it's Wednesday, don't be late to the rabbi.* Like he needs a bar mitzvah lesson. Ramsey is not Jerusalem. Only two Jewish kids in homeroom, him and David. Christmas decorations are still up in the library, the school, and the stores.

His sneakers hit the frozen lawn as David's shout lands on his shoulder. "Shai. 7-Eleven. Pizza?" They fall into step. "I dunno." A casual flick of his head. David was the only kid who smiled at him the first day he walked into fifth grade with his terrible Israeli accent. David had Nintendo, a CD player, a computer, a color printer, a scanner, and a ten-speed Schwinn. It seems to him that kids in Ramsey have everything.

"C'mon," David's elbow gives him a poke, "Cindy'll be there."

"Like I care," he lies, remembering that on Friday, when he shoved in behind her at the checkout line and said *hi*, she tossed her hair, long and silky, golden blonde like Madonna. God! When she goes up to the board, with those sweet bumps in her sweater, he could die. Girls. He knows they like him. "I got Hebrew."

"So?" A challenge.

He shivers and pushes his backpack into a better position. He walks faster. "I got a bar mitzvah lesson," he smirks.

"So ya get there late. Big deal."

"Yeah, pizza sounds good."

"Wanna go to the mall Saturday?" David is shorter than him, his steps not as bold. A freckled kid with a mouthful of shiny braces, he is glad another Jewish boy is in his class. Even if Shai is Israeli and living in an apartment for abused families. "I got twenty bucks. You?"

"Saturday I get my birthday money."

They slap each other a gleeful high five.

"How much?"

The boy shrugs. "I dunno yet." Shai Fhima is a skinny kid with ears too big for his head, white teeth too big for his mouth, and a sweet open face he'll grow into. A face teachers like. Except Silba who hates him. He is still smarting from the C minus because he studied for that quiz.

Thinking about Saturday makes him feel better. Thirteen is gonna be cool. He knows it's gonna be a lot better than last year when Jacky beat up his mom and they had to go to a battered women's shelter. Now they are rid of Jacky, safe, and the social workers are talking a lot to his mother and she seems to like them. He tries hard to figure it out. Why did she marry the jerk and have three more kids? Who is dumber? Jacky or her?

Sometimes he really hates her. Sometimes he wants to run away. Yeah, just get on a bus and scare her to death. Like she'd care a lot, sure. Always Osheri needs new glasses. Or Eliran has an earache. Or the baby needs new shoes—Shiran gets anything she wants. Him? He has to do whatever she says because Jacky lost their money and beat her up and put her in a terrible mood.

But sometimes he loves his mother. Loves her so much, he

could cry. Loves his two brothers and his baby sister like crazy. Loves them all. Loves how his mom says: "Shai honey, you're my Number One, I depend on you. Here, go down and bring us back something sweet." She winks at him and hands him a five dollar bill. "Go. You'll surprise us."

Oreos? M&M's? Sweet means chocolate. He rolls his big brown eyes and stuffs the bill into his jeans pocket. At the shelter, they tell him he has his mother's eyes. He likes that. She is pretty in a shy quiet way and maybe she does love him best.

He knows she counts on him to help her with the kids. He knows if Jacky lays another hand on her, he'll kill him. He knows his mother is ashamed of the mistakes she made, like marrying Jacky. And even though Jacky says he's sorry and buys them presents on the weekend, he's still an asshole because you never know when he'll blow up. But considering what went on, they are doing okay. His grades this marking period are definitely going up which will make his mother smile.

Sometimes the boy feels a surge of love so strong he almost hugs himself. To be the man in the family feels good, they need him. On his essay for Social Studies he wrote: *I love my mother so much I would die for her*. He means it. He got a B plus and he didn't even bring the book home.

An icy gust whips against his back, whirling white flurries down the school driveway and leaving paint strokes across the yellow buses lined up. No sunny Israeli sky overhead. Afternoons dark by four-thirty. He is freezing.

"What time Saturday? I gotta go to shul til eleven-thirty," he tells David.

"Cool. Come to my house. My mother'll drive us to the mall."

He loves the mall. It's always bright and warm. Cute girls hanging out. Video stores. Radio Shack. The newest tapes and CDs. Computer stuff you can mess with. And salty pretzels in the food court at the top of the escalator. Saturday he'll buy whatever he wants.

The two boys cut across the street to 7-Eleven, their heads lower into a biting blast that nearly takes off Shai's Nets cap, but he slaps it back hard over his mop of brown hair and they duck quickly into the heated store.

A mob scene. But no Cindy.

David grabs two cans of coke out of the refrigerator. "I feel like salami. You?"

"Pepperoni. I'll get in line."

He's going to be late. But Rabbi Weinberg is a cool guy, he won't go ballistic. He'll tell his mother he had to run back for his math book. Let her yell all the way to shul.

Defiance rumbles through him.

Then he spots Cindy and his knees turn to water.

# 2. HANA

Hana Fhima is a petite woman, five feet tall, with flawless olive skin and a slim figure. Just past thirty, wearing jeans and a black sweatshirt, with not a trace of makeup, she could pass for a college student. Her straight brown hair hangs down her back, her shiny bangs trimmed by her own scissors.

She stands at the sink, rinses her coffee mug and turns it upside down in the drainer. With one hand on her hip, she sighs. Should she call Israel? The three boys are in school and Shiran is on the rug, belly down, watching cartoons and sucking her thumb. It would be a good time to phone. Friday morning almost ten would be afternoon in Jerusalem and Ema would be home cooking her shabbos chicken.

She awakened before dawn feeling jittery. Calling her mother is still on her mind from last night. She feels guilty about putting it off. They speak every few weeks. But when the trouble with Jacky started, it got harder to tell. It shamed her that she made so many mistakes. Decisions that seemed right turned out wrong.

When she and Michael got divorced, she left Shai with Ema. It was Ema who raised him when she married Jacky and the other three kids came along. By then she knew the real Jacky, a hothead, a wild man with a terrible temper. Shai didn't have to see that. So Ema kept him, what could she do?

When they decided to sell the apartment and come to America, it seemed like a good idea. Jacky had big plans. He'd use the money for a business and they'd start over. America was every immigrant's dream. In America, anything was possible. But leave Shai behind? No, she couldn't do that. So, without a word to Michael, she took Shai with her.

Whenever she phones, it is Shai her mother asks about first.

26

She is crazy about him, she misses him terribly. Does he like school? Is he happy in Ramsey? Tell her news of her darling Shai and Hana can hear the smile.

About Jacky, the shame cuts deeper. A man who hits his wife in front of his own children—this is not Jewish, Ema says. Poor Hanale. No luck. With Michael, it was another story. Hana was only seventeen when she fell in love with the handsome soldier. A sweet boy, charming. And Shai—well, it happens. But Jacky? Ema hates to hear about it, what he did to her daughter, how a Jewish family has to go for safety to a shelter apartment. Ema longs for a piece of good news.

Which is why Hana puts off phoning her. What can she say? Even when she tries to lighten it, her mother knows and in a few days a check arrives, a little something for the children is what Ema writes. Though she needs the money, it bothers Hana. She has pride, and the checks from Israel have *poor Hana* written all over them. What can she say this morning when she calls? What good news can she tell her mother?

About Shai, Hana feels an enormous burden of guilt. Look what she put him through. A stepfather, a new family, a new country. She took him from Ema in Israel to Jacky in America, from New York to New Jersey, and now to an apartment in Ramsey for abused women. Plenty—she has put Shai through plenty.

So for his birthday, his *bar mitzvah* birthday, she has to give him more than ten dollars. She knows he is saving for a Sony Walkman and it means a lot to him. So she slides her purse off the counter and checks her wallet. Ten dollars is not enough, what can ten dollars buy today? Make it twenty, give him an extra ten. She pulls out two crisp bills—her hidden emergency money—and folds them into her jeans pocket. She feels better.

Like other abused women, Hana Fhima seems fragile and confused, a victim mentality. Perhaps because she is tiny and shy, her voice soft and low, her appearance modest. However, she is stronger than she looks and her eyes, sad and downcast, give no hint of stamina or endurance. Too many defeats have made it difficult for her to smile easily. So mostly, she listens. It is this quality of wide-eyed girlish attention that makes people want to help her. Though she only got past high school and never read Tennessee Williams, Hana knows instinctively how to rely on the kindness of strangers. She is intuitively savvy, a card she plays close to her chest.

She reaches for the kitchen phone. She knows what to tell Ema it will be good news. Enough about how Jacky lost every cent they put into the Tile and Marble Store. In America, you want customers, you talk nice, you don't insult people. Not Jacky. What they say bad about Israelis is Jacky. Out for the last dime, afraid to look like a *freier* and come out on the wrong side of the deal, he drove everyone away. Forget Jacky. Talk about Shai. Tell how he's making bar mitzvah in May, chanting already from his *haftorah*. Tell about Shai, make Ema smile.

She reaches for the kitchen phone and punches in the numbers for overseas.

"Shalom, Ema, it's me. How are you, how's Aba?" They lunge into an eager chat. Speaking Hebrew, she tells her mother how sweet the baby is, how the boys do good in school. "And Shai is thirteen tomorrow!"

"I know, I know. Oh, how I miss that sweet face."

"I'm baking a birthday cake. Chocolate, you know how he loves chocolate." She pauses. "He's already studying *haftorah*, In May will be his bar mitzvah."

"In May?" Her mother's voice turns to ice. "May? No, no. February."

Hana can feel her jaw tighten. Ema and Aba are orthodox. "We got a wonderful rabbi," she coos, "a very nice shul. Beth Haverim. It's reform, it's different here and . . ."

"No, no, Hanale. Listen. It's wrong, you don't do it May."

"But we're not religious, May is better because . . ."

"No, no." A firm interruption. "By me, May is no bar mitzvah. You'll call Tante in Boro Park. *Understand?* Do it right. For your firstborn son, you don't make short cuts."

"But . . ."

"Call Tante Rivka, I got here the number, she'll find you a rabbi. February, Hanale. This is the right way."

"Tante Rivka?" Her head is starting to throb.

# 3. BORO PARK, BROOKLYN

In Brooklyn, the Williamsburg section known as Boro Park is a world apart, something right out of *Fiddler on the Roof*. It is a neighborhood turned back two hundred years, where devoutly religious families conduct their lives much like Eastern European Jews did centuries ago.

Row houses and two flats dot the area, their yeshivas located on the first floor of the houses they occupy. In this tight knit community crime, drugs, and theft are almost unknown. Like insular cults, they monitor their own. The cops of Boro Park rarely have to be called in.

On Friday afternoon, with the shops closed in preparation for shabbat, bearded men walk on the streets with purposeful strides. They wear the traditional hasidic attire, the long black coat, black fedora or broad rimmed fur hat, their sidecurls bobbing. Only a few women are out, their heads down, their eyes modestly averted. Swaths of cloth cover their hair, avoiding the sin of displaying anything sexual to distract men.

As she drives to Tante's apartment with her four children, Hana takes in the sights. She is familiar with the extreme orthodox. She had seen them in Israel where men and women are sharply separated, forbidden to sit together or pray together in their shuls. Only males, men and boys, are permitted to enter yeshivas and many devote their entire lives to the study of the Torah.

Girls are excluded from yeshivas. They are raised to accept a different destiny. They are educated separately and marriages, preferably at an early age, are arranged by their fathers or through a *shadken*, a matchmaker. Once a girl is married, she settles into a life of making babies: eight, nine, ten, because the ultraorthodox believe fervently in obeying God's law to go forth and multiply. Married women dress with extreme modesty and all females follow a code that requires strict rules for bathing, hygiene, sexual intimacy, social contacts, and matters of such precise detail as the thickness of their stockings. Women are required to cover their arms and legs; bare skin is forbidden even in an August heatwave.

The hasidim flourish in Boro Park, living peacefully among their own. Some married women have a small side business, a store to run, merchandise to sell. But their husbands and families remain their primary and foremost concern. The laws are spelled out, allowing little room for interpretation.

Each ultraorthodox sect has its own fervid followers who give unquestioned loyalty to their revered rebbe. He alone dispenses decisions, his word is final. He might be a *zaddik*, a man so pious he has God's ear and speaks directly to God in a special anointed relationship. Although different sects fight among themselves, they are joined in their battle against common enemies. These consist of sinners, who flout God's laws and do the work of the devil; Jewish secularists, who refuse to keep kosher or observe the sabbath; and gentiles, who are perceived as enemies out to destroy them. These cursed people are a threat to their survival and an effrontery to God.

In Israel, it is not uncommon for the ultraorthodox children in Meah Shearim to hurl stones at cars driven on the shabbat, a flagrant insult to God's commandments. On one occasion, Hana herself had dodged their stones.

But entering Boro Park on this Friday afternoon, *ere shabbos,* she gets no stones, only dirty looks. No cars are moving, everyone is on foot. As she pulls up to the address scribbled on the paper, she reminds her children that Tante's family, a husband and teenage son, is orthodox and strictly kosher. "Do what she says, eat what she gives you."

The Boro Park apartment is so overheated that by eight-thirty, Hana is worn out. She has helped Tante wash the dinner dishes and clean up, but odors of garlic and boiled carp still hang in the air. Her bangs are damp against her forehead and the back of her neck feels sticky. Shai looks equally uncomfortable and they have the whole evening ahead.

She tiptoes into the darkened living room to check on the three little ones asleep on the sofa bed. With hardly a place to set her foot down, she steps around tables, chairs, sofas, bureaus, and floor lamps. They sleep pressed against each other, a small light left on for Shiran. Next to the sofabed, a cot is set up for Shai, and on the other sofa Tante has piled a pillow, a sheet and a blanket for her. She nudges her suitcase a few inches to make a little room. What a difference it is in Boro Park. A million miles from Ramsey.

The shabbat meal has been conducted in the orthodox manner with candle-lighting ceremony, hand washing, saying Kiddush on the wine and Hamotzi on the bread, with blessings on the children and prayers to God. Tante has outdone herself, she has prepared a feast. Matzoh ball soup, homemade gefilte fish, and platters heaped with kasha and fried onions, four vegetables, schmaltz smeared thickly on challeh, and boiled chicken so soft it falls off the fork. Hana has eaten with gusto and has extended dutiful compliments for each dish.

But once the meal is over and Tante's husband and son leave the room, she sees that Shai, fidgeting on his chair, is bored. Nothing for him to do. No TV, no videos, no music.

So when Tante asks sweetly if Shai wants to go along with her husband and son to a talk by the local rabbi, Hana turns to Shai. "You want to go?

He hesitates, weighing the options.

"Go, kindele," Tante urges. "Go, it's a nice walk, only a few blocks to Lev Tahor."

"Okay."

Left alone, Hana and her aunt settle down to women's talk.

"Hana, listen to me," the soft round little woman leans

earnestly across the table. She has a task to perform. "Make the boy a proper bar mitzvah. Do it February like your mother says. I'll find you a yeshiva."

"In May," Hana replies politely. "I want to get on my feet."

"No, no, not May." The woman's smile fades. It is no secret to her, the whole story about Jacky, the second husband, how poor Hana had to run to a shelter with four kids. "Look, what's to hide, we're family." She folds her hands and purses her lips. Such a pity. Young and pretty, dark eyes big as plums. But no mazel, no luck. "February," she insists. "Do it here in Boro Park."

They argue a little, the pros and cons, until Hana, feeling beleaguered, switches the subject to their cousins in Israel.

At the sound of footsteps, Tante jumps up. "They're back." She hangs up their coats and shushes them past the sleeping children into the kitchen.

"Sit, I'll make tea." She pulls out kitchen chairs and starts fussing over teacups and saucers.

"You liked the rabbi, Shai?" she asks, producing a platter of mandelbread. "Sit, sit. It was a good talk Rabbi Helbrans made?" She directs the question to Shai. Such a handsome boy you could fall in love with him.

Hana takes in her son, waits for his answer.

What she sees is a strangely detached and silent Shai. His eyes are squinting like someone trying to adjust to the light, or someone emerging from a darkened movie trying to return to reality. It crosses her mind that he must have stood out in his hightops and baseball cap, a little boy among those bearded hasids all in black.

"Shai?" she prods. It made a big impression on him?

Silence. His body is folded into himself, his hands in his lap, unaware of the kitchen table, of them, like a rag doll placed into a position.

Alerted, nervous, Hana looks harder. She detects something. He seems caught in the grip of a deep concentration. What is the matter? What is wrong? "It was a good talk?" she repeats the aunt's question.

Silence.

"Shai? Shai? What happened?"

He twitches. He is staring over their heads, unblinking, focusing on something they can't see. "Rabbi Helbrans . . . he was sitting at a long table . . . he was giving a lesson . . ." His words are slurred and dreamy, halting and disjointed, his voice is not his own.

"So?" Hana huddles closer.

He stares straight ahead, making no eye contact. "He stopped . . . in the middle of his talk . . . he looked at me . . . he said . . . he said. . . ."

"What?" She knows something is wrong, very wrong.

"He said . . . *I see a light shining in your face. Come. Sit by me, my son.*"

"Oy, oy!" gasps the aunt as she slaps a hand to her chest. "Such an honor." Her face glows and her husband and son nod vigorously, their eyes glued to the boy.

*Shai sees the rabbi gazing at him. Watching him. Rabbi Helbrans has magic powers.*

Hana's heart starts to pound. He seems mesmerized. "What Shai? What?" she demands. *What's wrong with him?*

"Rabbi Helbrans . . ." he turns to her. "He talks to God."

"What?" An overwhelming dread clutches her.

*"He saw . . . a light . . ."*

"A light? What light?"

*"A light . . . was shining . . . in my face."*

"A light? What light?"

Shai doesn't answer. He turns his face away and his gaze moves steadily upward.

The next morning the rabbi calls.

# 4. RABBI HELBRANS

Rabbi Helbrans chats with Tante, then asks to speak to Hana. "It's the rabbi." Tante hands her the phone and stands by.

"You'll come to tea at noon?" asks the voice.

"You mean today, rabbi?" The invitation baffles her, but she can see Tante nodding vigorously, so she agrees. "Yes, rabbi, noon, thank you."

Tante sends up a keening *geshrai*. She offers to lend Hana her best scarf to cover her hair, but Hana declines.

When Hana arrives at Lev Tahor, Mrs. Helbrans greets her and explains that the rabbi is busy downstairs in the yeshiva, so she will speak to her first. She is a dark and somber woman, swathed in long, loose-fitting clothing that conceals her shape, but Hana has the sense of a large-boned woman, a sturdy type.

In the living room, they take seats opposite each other, a small table between them. Mrs. Helbrans pours tea and offers a plate of cookies. Though close to the same age, the two women are keenly aware that they are worlds apart. To make conversation, Mrs. Helbrans tells Hana she has two small boys. "A handful."

Hana nods and holds up three fingers. "I got three, I know. My Shiran is easier, girls are easier." Silence.

Mrs. Helbrans moves quickly past the amenities. Her hostess smile vanishes and her mouth hardens. "Mrs. Fhima." She clutches her own hands in her lap and offers Hana a penetrating gaze. Her shoulders rise like a soldier about to go into battle. "My husband, he talked already to your aunt. How you don't live with your husband. How you got four children to raise. Alone." Her head wags sympathetically.

"It's true," Hana admits, trying to conceal her annoyance that

the rabbi and Tante have discussed her. "It's not so bad. The
shelter gave us a nice apartment."

Mrs. Helbrans clears her throat. She folds her hands prayer-
fully and begins to rock a little, back and forth. "Mrs. Fhima." She
pauses and her eyes say pay attention. *"Give me your son to raise.
Give me Shai."*

"What?" Hana stiffens.

"He will be . . . a great *zaddik*."

"A zaddik? My Shai?" Did she hear it right?

"The boy is special. Special. He will be a holy man between
God and us. You understand?" Her hands are pleading, begging.

Hana's throat dries up, she can't speak. All she wants to do is
get out. But Mrs. Helbrans's eyes do not allow it.

"Shai will talk to God, *your Shai*. But you," she adds, "you'll
still be his mother."

Hana has scarcely rebounded from this pronouncement
when Rabbi Helbrans arrives. He is a heavy man with a scruffy
dark beard, a black yarmulke, and scholarly eyeglasses that perch
on the end of his nose. At first glance, he could be forty or fifty,
but on closer inspection, he is probably much younger, thirties.
His portly figure and full beard add years.

"Come, Mrs. Fhima," he smiles pleasantly looking over his
glasses and gestures for her to follow.

They enter a long study. A curtain is strung down the center
of the room separating the two sides. He takes a chair on one side
and she, understanding that they will talk with the curtain
between them, takes a chair on the other side. It is the way of Satmars and hasids: women are forbidden to sit with men or pray
with men. She folds her hands in her lap and waits. Who is this
rabbi and what is his crazy wife talking about?

"Mrs. Fhima," he begins. His voice is soft and gentle. In the
silence of the room, there is only his voice. Sonorous and hypnotic. His voice pours into the room with gaseous sweetened
authority. "Pick up the book next to you on the table."

She obeys.

"Open to page 206. Read out loud."

She reads the Hebrew words. What is the meaning of them? Some kind of ghost story, something about a forest. She keeps reading.

"Stop." He holds up a hand. "I'll explain you." The hand drops and the voice pulls her in. "Do you understand?"

"No."

"What it means . . . it means . . . after you die . . . you will go to hell. Hell. The ghosts will be there, the devils will be there, you will be in hell." His voice chants. It starts. It stops. It repeats and dances around her. It snags her like a fish hook and trawls her through the dark waters. Deep waters. Deeper and deeper. She feels herself pulled under. "Read," the voice commands. "Read."

She obeys. She dips her head into the Hebrew words. "In hell are the sinners." It is hard to follow, but she has no will to resist. He says read; she reads.

"Stop."

She stops.

"Understand?"

"No."

The voice explains the words, casting a spell over her. She must do whatever it says.

*Start. Stop. Listen.* The voice commands.

She obeys.

*Start. Stop. Listen.* The voice chants.

She obeys.

The voice sedates her. She feels light headed. A kite aloft in a pastel sky. The voice tugs her gently and lets her go, turns her this way and that way. Tethered to the voice, she passes into another world beyond the earth. Higher. Purer. Lulled into a trance, her bones liquefy. Her flesh softens. And a warmth, like the drizzle of morphine, flows through her.

She reads.

She stops.

She listens to the voice.

She reads.

She stops.

She listens to the calm, commanding voice.

Leans into the music. Sways. Feels the beats.

"Read more."

She obeys. Her tongue thickens, her mind is drugged.

"Stop."

She obeys.

"The devils send the spirits of sinners to cut wood. Sinners get no rest. In hell you get no rest."

She can't think. Can't move.

"Now close the book."

She closes the book.

"Put it down on the table."

She obeys. She understands the reading part is over. The voice has taken her to another level. But now it returns her.

She awakens feeling refreshed. She is back in the room with the curtain. Rabbi Helbrans is sitting on the other side, a soft smile on his lips.

"Tell me please," he asks her in a straightforward, conversational tone, "you are a Jewish mother?"

"Yes." The curtain between them doesn't flutter. In the silence Hana can hear his labored breathing, the steady exhale old men and fat men make. *Hng. Hng. Hng.*

"You believe in God, Mrs. Fhima?"

"Yes, yes."

"Then you cannot send your children to public school."

Her head is clearing. She folds her arms and pinches her own flesh. Respectfully, *very* respectfully, she replies, "Rabbi, I don't see what's wrong my children should go to public school."

"It's not good for Jewish children to go to school with Italian kids and Spanish kids and black kids and all the other Christian kids."

She doesn't reply.

"This is a terrible sin. If you live in sin, you'll go to hell." His voice gathers an edge. "You'll cut wood in the forest, you'll cut wood for the fires that burn in hell. The ghosts will be there."

Hana shivers. What is she doing here? She glances at the door, sees it is slightly ajar, and she thinks about standing up, just picking herself up and leaving. But she can't move off the chair. She needs the rabbi to release her.

"I want to help you, Mrs. Fhima."

"Thank you."

*Hng. Hng. Hng.* "I will prepare Shai for bar mitzvah. You'll leave the boy here with me. We'll study together every day, every day, six in the morning to eleven at night. Thursday I'll make him a bar mitzvah."

Leave Shai with the rabbi a few days? A bar mitzvah on Thursday? She tries to think it out. Today is Sunday. She counts out Monday, Tuesday, Wednesday, Thursday. Four days and done. No school this week in Ramsey, so nothing to miss. She glances at her watch, it sobers her. Five o'clock? Impossible. For five hours she didn't eat, didn't go to the bathroom, didn't move.

His voice draws her back. Pleasant. Engaging. Congenial. "Let Shai stay with me, Mrs. Fhima. I'll prepare him. Thursday your son will be bar mitzvahed. My wife, Malka, will make for your family a wonderful celebration meal. You'll be very happy you did this." *Hng. Hng. Hng.* "You agree?"

Agree? A February bar mitzvah, not May. In four days, done. What will Shai say? She has to ask him.

"I can help you, Mrs. Fhima. We'll find you a nice apartment. You'll live rent free, you'll move here. A lot of Israeli boys are here, they study together. In the shelter," he scoffed, "what do you have? They only help you because they want to turn you to be Christian. With us, you live Jewish. You'll put your life back together. You'll be with your husband and children normal in a nice apartment."

The offer is tempting.

Hana is tired. Expelled from the sedation of the hypnotic voice, no longer adrift in a pastel sky, she rubs her eyes and lands with a thud. Earthbound, she returns.

The bar mitzvah meal Thursday is held upstairs in the living quarters. Malka Helbrans wears a wide smile. She has outdone herself with a festive spread and clearly this pleases her.

Across the room crowded with hasids, Hana beams proudly at Shai. He has read from the Torah perfect, perfect. And now, it is done, over. A bar mitzvah in February. She did it right.

Only Jacky is out of sorts. Combative as a Bantam cock and normally on a short fuse, he stands feet apart, on guard and mistrustful. From the moment he meets the rabbi, he takes an instant dislike. All he wants to do is grab the four kids and get the hell out. They give him the creeps, these pious ones with their self righteous grins and fat bellies. He is a small and compact man. Wedged against them, he feels jumpy.

He leans into Hana's ear. "Look, look at him." He gestures to Shai who is talking to Mordecai Weiss, the nineteen-year-old who has tutored him whenever the rabbi was busy. "Who the hell gave them the right to shave the back of his head? Look, Hana, they made him sidecurls. Sidecurls. He looks like a goddamn hasid, he looks like one of them."

He grabs her elbow. "C'mon." His fingers clamp tighter and he pulls her along. He has fire in his eyes. Nothing is lost on him. The new black suit they bought Shai. How Weiss sticks to Shai like a goddamn bodyguard with that stupid smile like he knows something they don't know. How Weiss is all over them, congratulating them too heartily and too often, three times. What is he sucking up for?

"Please, please Jacky, a little longer, a few minutes." She resists his strong-arm maneuvers.

Just then, Jacky's eyes fall on Osheri, his oldest. A young hasid is walking away from him looking pleased as a pickpocket and Osheri's eyes behind his glasses drop to his feet. Bristling, Jacky cuts a path to his son. "What'd he say to you?" he demands, "what'd he say?" Nine won't lie.

"He said *thanks for giving us your brother, thank you for giving Shai to us.* What does he mean?" The boy looks up at his father, confused and embarrassed.

"Shit." Jacky spins around and makes a beeline to Shai. He draws him aside. He'll get to the bottom of it. He begins nicely.

"What happened? You look different, you look changed." It's an opener. Shai can be touchy. At that age they want a little privacy, they want independence. Like when the kid got mad because they wouldn't let him go on the bus to the ballgame. He searches the boy's face.

"Nothing," Shai says. But his eyes look scared and he turns away.

So it amazes Jacky when Hana phones a few days later.

"You what? You let him go back to the yeshiva? To those nuts? They're meshuganas. Crackpots. You don't know about the satmars and the hasids? They hate Israel, it's not even a country to them until the Messiah comes and . . ."

"It's okay, Jacky." She pulls out the voice she uses to appease him. "I'll explain you. Listen." The social workers at the shelter are teaching her new skills: communication techniques. "What happened, Shai wanted to go back, what's so terrible?" She doesn't mention how many times the rabbi phoned her and pressured her and talked to Shai. "Listen. The rabbi's going to find us an apartment in Brooklyn. Free, Jacky. He wants to help us."

"Sure, sure," he jeers. Free? A free apartment? It stops him cold. He could use a break from the bad luck. His voice softens. He lets her talk.

"The rabbi told him if he studies to be religious, we'll all go to heaven. Shai says the rabbi talks to God and God wants him to do it. It is a test. He *wants* to study with him, Jacky, that's what he says. He wants it. What's so terrible?"

"To be a fucking hasid?" he mutters. But Hana can tell he is losing steam. The free apartment is dangling in front of his eyes. "Okay, okay. But I don't trust them. You know what the police had with them in Israel? You know how it goes with them? They run things their way and the police stay out of their private wars because . . ."

"Eh!" Hana brushes it off. "Newspaper headlines."

"Two boys, brothers," he persists, he has a story to tell. "Goldman, I think. The hasids convinced the kids to become religious. Secular parents, like us. Professors at the university. You know what happened? They brainwashed the kids and the parents never had contact with them again."

"Come on," she chides him. "We'll have an apartment, we'll be living near him a few blocks away." She knows those stories, how the religious right picks out kids with problems. Trouble with the police. Skipped the army. Broken homes. Always teenage boys. But not here, here is a different story. "This is America, Jacky. We're in America."

"You sure you want to move to Brooklyn?" Let it be on her head.

# 5. THE YESHIVA

In two weeks, Hana changes her mind.

She calls Lev Tahor, but they won't let her visit Shai. Imagine —you can't go see your own son. And each time she phones, they give a different story. Shai is studying, he can't come to the phone. Or he's praying. Or he went out to buy milk. She leaves messages but he doesn't call her back. She feels cut off. At thirteen he is still a little boy and two weeks is a long time away. Denied any access to him, she becomes suspicious. Why can't she talk to him or see him? Why doesn't he call her back? What's going on?

Maybe Jacky was right. It was a mistake to take him out of public school. The hell with their free apartment. I don't want to become ultrareligious like them. I miss Shai, the kids miss him. Whatever made me think leaving him there was okay? A mistake. Big mistake. All she wants is to get her boy back.

She talks to Elaine and Lil about her change of heart. "What I want is to bring Shai back. What should I do? Tell me. Should I go there and take him back?"

Elaine Meyerson is one smart lady. So is Lil Corcorhan. Trained social workers, professionals, they understand how she feels and they don't judge her. They listen, they let her talk it out. That's what the shelter is all about. First safety. But also learning to look at the reality of your situation. Figuring it out for yourself, then acting on it. Taking control of your life. "It's up to you," Elaine encourages her. "What do *you* want to do?"

She pauses. "I don't know, I'm not sure. I made a lot of mistakes. I'm afraid to make another one."

She decides to phone Rabbi Weinberg at Beth Haverim. Only

a few weeks ago he was preparing Shai for a May bar mitzvah. He likes Shai and he understands teenage boys.

She lays out the facts for him.

"He said he wanted to be religious, rabbi, so I let him stay with them in Brooklyn. But now I want to take him home, I want him back here with us. I don't want him to be ultra religious and I don't want to move to Brooklyn. This I know."

He hesitates. It's a delicate situation. Milton Weinberg is a mild mannered man, his skin pale and pink, his hair snowy white and his manner kindly. What can he say?

Poor Shai, a nice kid. Intelligent. But hard for an Israeli boy to be plunked down in Ramsey, a world of suburban gentiles. An abusive stepfather sends them to a shelter. And now more *tzuris*. He falls in with this ultraorthodox sect. They have an answer for everything, which is very attractive to a troubled kid. What can he say to Hana? He scratches his chin, pondering. What can he do to help them? And if she brings the boy back, then what?

He has an idea. The Glucksterns.

"All right. If that's what you decide, okay. When Shai comes home, I'll introduce him to a nice orthodox family. The Glucksterns. They live nearby and they have two boys, one about Shai's age. I'm sure they'll be glad to show him a more orthodox Judaism. They'll include him, he'll enjoy it."

Hana brightens. He sounds upbeat and cheerful, no wonder the kids like him. Such a generous man, this reform rabbi.

"A good idea. Thank you very much, rabbi. I'll talk to him when he comes home." She hangs up and mindlessly gathers up the wads of tissues she's been tearing off and rolling into balls. She feels better already.

While her courage is high, she phones the yeshiva.

"I changed my mind about moving to Brooklyn," she tells Rabbi Helbrans, her voice quavering. "I don't want to be religious. I'm coming to take Shai home. He should be waiting outside ready." Quickly, before he can reply, she adds, "Three o'clock," and hangs up.

✡    ✡    ✡

Inside the tan brick building on Dahill Avenue everything is quiet. Only a few people are out on the streets when she parks at the curb. But Shai is not there waiting for her, so she leaves Tante in the car and goes inside to get him.

Tante sits there alone, her arms crossed, her expression pinched. Reluctantly, she has agreed to drive with Hana to take Shai back. Such a mistake. But what can she do? Hana is the mother. She waits uneasily, watching the front door.

"So?" she asks when Hana slips behind the wheel. "He's not ready?"

"He's coming, I told him we're waiting." But when the yeshiva door opens, it's not Shai. It is Mrs. Helbrans, screeching like a black crow, her fists flaying in the air, cursing and shouting at them as she heads full steam for the car.

"Aren't you ashamed?" she screams at Hana and bangs on the car window where Tante is cringing. "We make your boy a bar mitzvah. We teach him to be religious. And you, you . . ." Anger takes her breath away. "You'll go to hell for this!" Her finger stabs the air.

Hana sees Shai emerging, coming toward her. She opens her door and gets out to shield him. But there's someone right behind him, another hasid, a large man with thick glasses. "Leave him alone, he belongs to us." He blocks her way.

As she reaches Shai, he grabs her arm and twists it behind her, holding her back. "Run, Yishi," he yells. "Go back inside. Go!"

"No, no, Shai!" She's pinned to the spot, pain shooting into her shoulder and across her back. "Let me go."

Mrs. Helbrans, screeching in Hebrew, is cursing her with a face purple with wrath. "I have a right to take him, he belongs to me. If you won't make him religious, he belongs to me. We'll pray bad for you. Bad things will happen to you!" She gives Shai a shove. "Run, Yishi, run inside. I'm your mother." To Hana, "Die! Die!"

"Call the police! Call 911!" Hana screams to her aunt. But Tante is frozen with fear. She has rolled herself into a ball and slid down in the seat. Hana, wrenching and twisting to get away, can barely see her.

"Don't hit my mother," Shai screams, "leave my mother alone." His toothpick arms strike feebly on the man's back.

Mrs. Helbrans grabs him. "Stop, Yishi." But he pulls free of her and jumps on the man's shoulders with the full weight of his hundred and five pounds.

And then they are drowned in a sea of hasids. Black coats stream out of the yeshiva door, shouting. The rabbi screaming. Mrs. Helbrans screaming. Someone pulls Shai off the man's back and Shai is lost in the mob. Out of sight.

"Shai, Shai," Hana yanks herself free, where is he?

Mrs. Helbrans's fists fly at her face. "Devil. Devil. Go to hell!" She blocks her way.

With a force she didn't know she had, Hana shoves her aside. *Run. Run. Find a phone. Call 911.*

Blinded by tears and breathless, she screams the address to 911. "Help me! Please! Please! They got my boy! Lev Tahor on Dahill!"

She races back to the yeshiva. Flings open the front door.

She can hear him crying upstairs. Male voices are shouting at him. She runs up the steps. Breaks through the knot of hasids surrounding him on the bed. A crumpled little heap. Sobbing, covering his ears, a small terrorized animal, ambushed by men shouting, "Don't go with her, Yishi. Don't go with her. She's the devil. She's not your mother."

Two police officers appear at her side. Taking her elbow. Freeing Shai. Rescuing them. Moving them down the stairs to safety.

Only out on the street and gasping, does Hana realize what happened. "Shai, Shai," she holds him tight. "Oh, God. I got you back. Oh, God, oh, God."

✡   ✡   ✡

Back in the apartment, with the four children asleep in their beds, she puts her head down on the kitchen table. Soft sobs release the pain. Thank God, Shai is back. My children are safe in their beds. She weeps softly into her arms and lets the tears flow.

When she lifts her head, she has to check again. She needs to make sure. She goes from bed to bed, one at a time, gazing at her children, her beautiful children with their smooth olive skin and innocent dreams. Yes, they are safe. Shai is home.

Osheri snores a little—his tonsils maybe will have to come out. Eliran's head snuggles against his Ninja Turtle. Shiran's thumb is jammed in her mouth.

And Shai? One of his curly sidelocks is pressed against his soft baby cheek. He's asleep. He's safe. It's over.

Monday he'll go back to Eric Smith Middle School. Back to seventh grade. Shai is safe. Shai is home.

# 6. PHONE CALLS

"**W**hat do you mean, they keep calling you?" Jacky's voice on the phone is edged with irritation. What's Hana afraid of? "Shai's home—what can they do to him?"

Actually, he's gotta hand it to her. Once Hana makes up her mind, get out of her way. She's one determined woman. Look how she drove from Ramsey to the yeshiva in Boro Park and got Shai back. He can just picture her with her long hair brushed smooth and shiny, her huge brown eyes giving off sparks, warning others not to mess with her. And the Tante that smells like fish is sitting outside in the Honda. It amuses him, the whole event is wild. How two little women went against the whole fucking yeshiva of men. How Hana called 911 and got the cops on them. She's one helluva fighter, you have to give her credit.

"Helbrans is calling Shai," she reports.

"Stop worrying," he tells her. "He's back in school, he's thirteen. He's a kid, he'll forget all about it."

"I don't know." She curls the telephone wire around her finger, her voice is edged with concern. "He's not the same child, Jacky. One minute he's running to David to play computers. And the next minute when Mordecai phones . . ."

"Mordecai is phoning Shai? That putz." His anger rises. "What for? That little snot-nose with the stupid grin, what does he want from Shai?"

"He tells him don't watch television. Don't go to public school. Lay tefillin. Study Torah. Don't eat from your mother, eat only kosher."

"Shit."

"Three times he called already. He says he misses him, he

wants him to come back. He wants Shai to study with him. And when Shai hangs up, he's a different kid."

"How?"

*"I see scare in his eyes. Scare."*

"What does he say?" Jacky wants the facts. Women get too emotional.

"Nothing. He just walks away when he hangs up, very quiet. Goes away by himself."

She's overreacting. "Give it a little time. He's a kid. He'll be okay. He'll get over it."

In the morning when Shai sits down at the table for his Frosted Flakes, Hana sees he has cut off his sidelocks. She gives him a wide smile of approval. Jacky was right. He just needed a little time. He was torn, a little confused from the pressures they put on him with the phone calls. But he's okay now. He's done with the sidecurls, a good sign. Very good.

She puts down his glass of orange juice and takes the chair facing him. "So?" It is a question. They are alone, the little ones aren't up yet. She invites him to say something.

"Don't tell the rabbi, Mom. Say you cut them off while I was sleeping. Okay? Okay?" he asks nervously. He wants her to agree to his story. "Sure. I cut it." She'll gladly take the blame, he shouldn't feel guilty. "You look good."

He bows his head, a little embarrassed. He wants to tell her something maybe he shouldn't be saying, but he has to. "Mom? Be careful. The rabbi cursed you. He spoke to God about hell and the World to Come and, and . . . you. I mean how our immortal souls will be . . ." he chokes up.

She reaches across the table and lays her hand lightly on his arm. "What? Tell me," she gently urges. A little boy of thirteen should not be so worried about the World to Come. He should not have dark circles under his eyes. Last night she heard him cry out in his sleep. What is he scared of? "What did the rabbi tell you?"

He looks away, then his eyes return to her.

"He said . . . God is testing me. It was the same for him when he was a boy in Israel. He wanted to be religious, but his parents wouldn't let him. He says I have to be strong like him and fight back. Because God wants me to be religious. God wants to save our immortal souls. God told him we would all go to heaven, *all of us,* if we're religious like him."

Hana sighs. It's hard to talk about this, she wants to say it right. "Shai, listen. Me? I don't want to be religious like the rabbi. Do you want to be religious?" She invites him to talk about it. "Tell me, I want to know."

He doesn't answer. He shrugs. "Sometimes I do." Abruptly, he pushes his chair back and stands up. He can't talk about it anymore.

"Wait." She stands up and stops him. She has seen this before: the scare in his eyes. One minute he's a noisy fun loving kid with his baseball cap on backward, racing another boy on rollerblades. The next minute, he falls silent, worried about his immortal soul. Something is weighing heavy on his mind.

It's the phone calls, she concludes. Each time Mordecai calls, Shai gets moody. The same with the rabbi, he called twice in four days. When the phone rings, Shai grabs it, all the talking comes from their side, Shai only says *Yes. Yes.* Then he goes away and shuts the bedroom door.

"Shai, listen," she says as she stands facing him. She tilts his chin up. He is only a couple inches shorter. "I see scare in your eyes. Scare. What's wrong?"

"Leave me alone, I'm not hungry." He bolts out of the apartment. The door slams.

# 7. MORDECAI WEISS

The parking lot at the mall is so full Hana has to go around twice to find a spot. Shoppers are pouring out of their cars, you can feel spring in the air. Today the March wind is gentler and the late winter sun seems a little warmer.

Hana wants to be happy like them. Americans smile at you. It's nice. You smile back.

She strolls through the mall with Shiran and Eliran in hand. She can feel the energy of the crowd. Osheri is playing at a friend's house and Shai is at David's. An easy afternoon. She looks at the shop windows. Shorts and sleeveless shirts in sunny yellows and bright corals, even a few bathing suits. Shiran's earache is gone, she took her last Amoxil pill this morning, so everyone is healthy, thank God. With four kids, always someone got something. But not today.

Hana inhales the brightness and with it comes a sense of optimism. Spring. Pesach. A new season.

She treats the kids to ice cream cones at Baskin-Robbins and picks up two packages of socks for Osheri and Shai. For herself— well, money is tight. But it's okay, she had a good time trying on earrings from the Macy's clearance.

Back home, she lets them watch television while she prepares dinner. With the living room window open to the street, she can hear the thud of basketballs; every kid on the block is trying to be Michael Jordan. Nice kids. New Jersey kids. Any minute Shai will come in dirty and tired and hungry.

She takes extra onions out of the refrigerator for him, he likes the kasha that way. And when he smiles, the whole world lights up. That's how it is with your first born. He's special. She loves

51

them all. But Shai, from all she put him through, she has to make Shai smile.

Last week when he ran away to go back to the yeshiva and she called the police and they brought him back from the train in Hoboken, things felt bad again. Terrible. All weekend, Jacky was ready to kill Shai. In front of the kids, he mouthed off at Hana. "Shut up, goddamn it, shut up, Hana." But he didn't lift a hand to her, he only screamed.

Jacky's sick of Shai-this and Shai-that, always Shai. But then he cools off and sometimes he's very good with Shai. He encourages the boy in school and tells him he's proud how he got a B + on his math test and the teacher wrote very good on the top of the page.

So why did Shai run away? The phone calls. The pressure. Rabbi Helbrans calling. Mordecai calling. Ten times a day, it drives her crazy.

She bends over and picks up the threadbare blanket Shiran dropped on the linoleum. It's her binky, a nice American word. It's a rag already, in the washer it would fall apart. But Shiran sleeps with it, sucks her thumb, and strokes it to fall asleep. Hana folds it neatly and places it on the kitchen chair.

This week things are better.

Maybe because she agreed to let Shai spend shabbos with Mordecai. Jacky was furious, but she let him go anyway.

Sometimes you have to give a little, let a boy his age get his way, let him feel independent. Jacky's problem is that he always has to be in control—she understands that now, how he has to have power over her. That's what the fights are about: power and control. She's trying to break that cycle, trying very hard. Look how she stood up to him and let Shai go to Brooklyn anyhow.

Really, what's so terrible? Mordecai came, very polite, very nice, and picked him up. He drove him to Brooklyn and they spent shabbos together. Then Mordecai and another hasid drove him home.

"What's so bad if he wants it?" she argued with Jacky. "Shai wants to go." Well, maybe she gave in because the phone calls wore her out. Phone calls, phone calls.

"Bring the boy back, Mrs. Fhima," Helbrans kept at her. "He wants to be religious. Let's make peace, you and me." She didn't tell Jacky that part.

When she hears the front door slam, she knows Shai's home.

"I made for you kasha and onions," she calls out merrily.

But he's already roughhousing with his brothers and she can hear Shiran screaming with delight. She adores him and he shows off for his little sister.

In early April, Mordecai asks if he can take Shai overnight.

"Mrs. Fhima," he implores her. "I guarantee you I wouldn't let Shai go near Rabbi Helbrans. I'll take him to my yeshiva where I go in Williamsburg. We'll study together and I'll drive him home Sunday. Please. Trust me." He is very convincing.

"You want to spend overnight with Mordecai?" she asks Shai.

"Yeah. Cool."

It doesn't make sense. Only last week, he went berserk over going to see a Nets game. Lil was trying to get tickets to take some of the kids and Shai was delirious.

"The Nets game, Mom, the Meadowlands Arena." His dream come true. "Maybe, we'll get lucky, we'll sit so close I'll see them sweat." He threw his head back and pinched his nose.

"You want to see them sweat?" She swatted him with the *Bergen Record*.

"Lil says we'll try to get an autograph."

The Nets, the Nets, he talked about it incessantly. What he was going to wear, a certain T-shirt to bring him luck. A kid crazy about sports.

And now the same boy wants to go to Brooklyn the day after the Nets game to lay teffilin and daven? The boy who hangs out at 7-Eleven to meet girls and eats *treyf* pizza with pepperoni wants to go overnight with Mordecai to study Torah? One day he's cheering the Nets, the next he's praying for his immortal soul.

Well, to make peace, you bend a little.

Hana has to admit Mordecai Weiss has been true to his word. Twice already Shai spent shabbos with him and twice he brought him home on time. Always polite. With that stupid grin on his face.

It's more than she can understand. As soon as Mordecai leaves, Shai gets back into his hightops and sweats and goes straight to watch television.

And now, after he ate every drop of kasha with extra onions, he opens his books across his bed to do his report on the Mayan Indians. He wants another B+.

Who can figure?

On shabbos, a frumah yeshiva boy. The rest of the week, school and sports. A typical American teenager.

# 8. MALKA HELBRANS

"What's so awful?" she tells Jacky. She's spending the weekend in his apartment with the kids. Shai is in Brooklyn with Mordecai for the overnight. "He wanted this, Jacky," she tells him. "He didn't want the Gluckstern family from Rabbi Weinberg. Let him do it his way."

"He's only thirteen." Jacky is annoyed with her. "You don't know who the hasidim are? Enemies of Israel. Cults. You let him go with dangerous people, Hana." He throws up his hands in disgust. "You let them get away with it."

"With what? Get away with what?"

"They're brainwashing him. That's what they do. They're saving his soul, to them it's a big fuckin' mitzvah. Don't you get it?" he smirks. She doesn't see the implications.

It's Sunday, April 5.

Yesterday when Mordecai picked Shai up, his smile was full of assurance. "Everything will be fine. Don't worry, Mrs. Fhima. I'll be responsible for him, I'll be with him all the time." The plan is Hana will meet them in front of the shul.

"Eight o'clock, Sunday night," she agreed.

She leaves Jacky's apartment in plenty of time. Not a bad drive to the address, she wrote it down.

But when she gets there, no one is there. Not Mordecai. Not Shai. Nobody. It's the right place? I made a mistake? She takes out the paper and checks it. Yes, the right place. She checks her watch. Waiting, her heart beats a little faster.

She gets out of the car, stands on the street looking up and down, pacing in front of the building. It's ten after eight, fifteen after. Why aren't they here? She hears Jacky's words: *You let him go with dangerous people.*

She finds a public phone and calls Mordecai. A sinking feeling when he answers hello.

"Where's Shai? I'm in front of the shul."

"Shai? I put him on the bus," his voice has a loopy grin. "I told him where to get off, I gave him instructions."

"Instructions?" she screams at him. "Where is he?"

"I don't know where he is, I put him on the bus."

*Oh God. Where is he?* Her head pounds hammer blows into her shoulders. Helbrans—is he with Helbrans in the yeshiva? Her mouth turns to cotton and sweat is running down between her breasts.

*Go there. No, don't go alone. Call Jacky. Jacky will go with you. Don't panic.*

Malka Helbrans plants herself firmly in the doorway of Lev Tahor, blocking their way. Defiantly, she looks past Jacky and shrieks at Hana, "Go away from here."

"Where is he?" Hana screams back. "You got my son inside, I want my son." She is crying and shaking.

"Where is he?" Jacky demands. "We want our son."

"The rabbi took him. Go away."

"We want Shai. You better get him. Go get him, get Shai," he demands with a menacing stance.

"Go to hell."

"You're crazy, get out of my way." He could shove her aside and lunge past her.

"The rabbi took him. You're not going to see him again." Eyes ablaze, she returns his fire. "He's my boy now, not yours." She slams the door in their faces.

If she could spit on them, she would. All of them. Feh! Who can say who is worse? The Jews, they don't follow God's commandments. Or the goyim, they eat pigs and pray to statues. Let them all burn in hell. Shai, they'll never get. He's hers now.

✡   ✡   ✡

They return later that night with two NYPD policemen.

At the front door, the officers step forward to take over.

Normally they steer clear of religious fights. This is Boro Park, hasidic turf, their ballgame. But the records of another dispute at this address came up on the computer. Police intervention removed the same boy from the same premise. It's a sensitive situation, they sure as hell don't want to get in the middle of it. The word is out. Leave them alone. But as police officers, they are obliged to respond.

One look at Hana tells them to keep a lid on this one. The mother is shaking. Deal with the stepfather—men are more rational.

"Ma'am?" The shorter officer guides Hana back a few steps.

"Please wait here. We'll go inside and get the boy, just stay put." He motions to Jacky. "Mr. Fhima, come with us, please."

A bearded hasid opens the door. "The rabbi and his wife are not home," he announces, his voice loud and rehearsed. "Go away. Go away."

This brings an avalanche of men thundering down the stairs, screaming in Hebrew at them, their arms waving. They are not the least intimidated by the police—they're goyim—they have no jurisdiction here. Look, that one wears an earring. "Go away. Leave us alone."

The two officers push their way inside, Jacky close behind them. They discover quickly that the boy is not there.

The 66th Precinct is a noisy station house even at this late hour. Hana and Jacky are ushered past a cacophony of static radio dispatches and ringing phones, then taken into a back room. Quieter. Desks piled high. Discarded coffee cups. Computers. File cabinets.

"Sit down." The officer behind the desk points to two plastic chairs facing him. "We'll file the report here."

Tasting fear on her tongue, Hana nods and obeys. Shai is gone and this policeman is her lifeline to get him back. She'll do anything he says. He's gonna find Shai for her, it's the law. She bites the inside of her cheeks, a little trick not to cry.

Jacky sits down and crosses his arms. Let Hana answer the questions.

"We'll need a full description, ma'am." He's a beefy cop, pleasant and polite. But it's Sunday night and it's been a long one. He reaches over for a report sheet. "Height? Weight? Age?"

"Five feet. Hundred five pounds. Thirteen."

"Color of eyes? Hair? Wearing what when last seen?" He doesn't want to look up at the poor thing, he hates filling out Missing Persons. "We need a full description, ma'am."

"His hair is light brown, his eyes are brown. He was wearing . . ." she wants to be clear, "a black T-shirt, black jeans, and a red and blue baseball cap."

He writes it down. "Last seen?"

Jacky takes over. "Yesterday. Mordecai Weiss, he took him from my apartment." He's gonna tell it straight. "They kidnapped him, they're fuckin' kidnappers. They do it in Israel, they kidnap boys and make them religious." He wants the cop to write down the whole story. "Rabbi Helbrans's wife, she said to us, she admitted *the rabbi took him. You're not going to see him again.*" He turns to Hana, blaming her. "What did I tell you?" But her face is so stricken, he backs off and returns to the cop.

"Was he removed against his will, sir?" The stepfather is hot as a pistol, keep it down.

"No," Hana jumps in. "I'll explain you." She tells how Mordecai called her and promised not to go near Rabbi Helbrans. How they were supposed to meet eight o'clock. "At this address." She hands him the paper.

"Uh huh." He takes it all down. Better be a thorough report. "Date of birth?"

"February 8, 1979." Her voice is splintered. She hesitates. "Maybe . . . they'll change his clothes."

"To what, ma'am?"

"To hasid."

He nods. Every cop in Boro Park knows what that means. But

for the record he lets her describe it—the black hat and black suit, the shawl with the fringes hanging off of it.

"We'll run off a Missing Person bulletin." He reads it all back for accuracy, then adds, "May be dressed in garb of Hasidic Jew." He looks up. "Any distinguishing features?"

Hana tilts her head sadly. "He's only a little boy." She wants to tell about his beautiful smile, his perfect white teeth too big for his face, how his eyes light up.

"We'll run the hotline number. Like those, up there." He swivels his chair and points to the Missing Person posters plastered all over the wall. A hotline number in bold letters runs across the bottom. "Just sit tight, ma'am, we'll get right on it."

He likes her clean face, those innocent big brown eyes, all bloodshot and red now. Something tender about her, the kind of woman a man wants to protect. The long silky hair she keeps shoving behind her ears. The way she bites her lower lip.

He takes the measure of the husband. Scrappy. Lean and mean. "You are the boy's stepfather, correct?'

"Yeah. And those bastards aren't gonna get away with it. We want our boy back. This is a kidnapping. Understand?"

"We'll do our best, sir." The husband is used to giving orders. Does he punch the wife out? Betcha.

Suddenly, Hana flies off her chair and leans across his desk, her body taut, straining. "Please. Please. Find my boy." Panic overcomes her. A shortness of breath. "They got him . . . the hasids . . . go to Rabbi Helbrans, go to the yeshiva . . . they're hiding him. They know where he is." Her hands are splayed across his desk.

Normally Hana's movements are graceful in their economy, a containment of wastefulness. Now they are jerky, her head is bobbing, her shoulders twitching. She is out of sync with herself, a robot operating on a faulty battery, too low to sustain her.

The officer watches the husband stand up. To his credit, he puts a comforting arm around her. "Get a hold on yourself," he says. A tough guy trying to be a decent husband.

He finishes up his report after they leave. Runs a check on the rabbi. Schlomo Helbrans. No priors, but that's no surprise. Keep a soft lid on them. They can pick their nose and eat dirt. As long as they don't make big time trouble, Hynes kisses their ass. Shit, every fur hat is worth two votes, the wives do whatever the husband says. The men sit on their ass and pray all day. The women make babies. Holy, very holy. You mess with them, you mess with God.

His shoulders scrunch over the M.P. report. Gotta fill in every goddamn blank. Date Prepared? *April 6, 1992.* Be out Monday, tomorrow. *Re: UF61 # 3957, Case 418.* "And who's gonna get this baby?" he mutters to himself. *Assigned to: DETECTIVE DEFILICE. SHIELD# 2720.* Last item on the form: *No. 92/041.* The posters will be limited to department circulation. Done.

He pushes his chair back and rubs his eyes. A cold beer would be nice. Fuckin' paperwork'll put you in the grave. All he needs now is a recent photo of the kid. Which she'll give them tomorrow.

Start with the rabbi. Schlomo Helbrans. Lev Tahor on Dahill. Shee-it. He hates going into Jew turf.

Maybe they'll get lucky. The kid'll turn up and save everyone a shitload of trouble. If not, they got a possible kidnapping on their hands. Joe Hynes ain't gonna like this. A D.A. running for reelection? No way he's gonna pull in a rabbi. The hasids can swing it for him. The word is you tiptoe around them. Collar a fuckin' rabbi on kidnapping? Sure. Sure.

By the time he checks out of the 66th, he's dragging around a doozy of a headache.

But pulling out of the lot, he smiles. He can see the mother straining over his desk, begging him to find her kid. Nice tits. Cute little thing. Under different circumstances, who knows? Women go crazy for a uniform. He's had his share. Pussy perks, they call it.

Not this one. The husband'll bust her face wide open, she gets out of line.

# 9. LARRY MEYERSON AND STEVE RUBENSTEIN

I t hits the papers.

From the mighty *New York Times* to the New Jersey *Record*, every reporter worth their notepad jumps on it. Fantastic copy. Sidebars galore. The *New York Post* runs the headline B'KLYN RABBI ACCUSED OF ABDUCTING HIS STUDENT, and papers as disparate as the *Jewish Standard* and *Newsday* latch on to it. One helluva story.

Hana, with her pretty face and sad limpid eyes, captures them. Distraught, she agrees to pose for pictures with Jacky and the three younger children. To get the word out, she talks to the media. She talks and talks and talks. She cannot stop talking. It becomes her crusade.

To each reporter who phones, she recites the same story. Describes the events. Fills in the details. How she herself was mesmerized by Rabbi Helbrans when he gave her a book to read in the yeshiva with the curtain separating them. How Shai changed because he was brainwashed. How phone calls from Mordecai Weiss and Rabbi Helbrans turned him against her. How scared he was. How he cut off his sidecurls and asked her to say she did it while he was asleep.

She is lovely, this terrified, trembling mother. When she says she is convinced her boy has been kidnapped so he can be brought up by the ultrareligious Satmars, the press eats it up. Satmars? Hasidim? Exotic stuff. Not since Patti Hearst fell for her captor have they had a kidnapping this juicy involving an extremist group. This one has more. Not just a kidnapping, it's loaded with political and religious ramifications, maybe even a plot linking the religious right in Israel to yeshivas that hide the kids in Brooklyn.

A *Newsday* reporter who telephones Rabbi Helbrans's yeshiva is told he cannot be reached until after Passover. "It's crazy," shouts the irate hasid who answers the phone. He is shocked at the charges filed against the rabbi. "The boy is not kidnapped. There is no kidnapping in this," he insists.

"No kidnapping? They lie, they lie," Hana cries to Elaine Meyerson. "What should I do? Tell me, Elaine. Please. I don't know anymore what's right." Long sobs wrench her body. "What can I do? Tell me."

Larry Meyerson is at his desk when the call comes in.

"Your wife on line two," his secretary announces. He's just back from court, tired and hungry. Elaine rarely calls him. Something wrong with the kids? His eyes fly to their framed photographs prominently displayed: his handsome ten-year-old son, David, his little daughter, Rachel, two great kids.

"Hi, what's up?"

"Larry." Her voice is a fierce whisper. "Listen to me. One of my clients needs help. Hana Fhima. Her kid was kidnapped by a rabbi in New York. You gotta help me."

Larry sighs, relieved that the kids are okay, then focuses on the urgency in his wife's voice. She never lays a shelter problem on him and he never brings his firm's work home to her. They don't get involved that way. And they respect the confidentiality of their clients. This must be special. "What?"

"You gotta help me, you gotta help this woman. No one else will help her. She has no place to turn and if you don't help her no one will." She barely stops for a breath. "There's a police officer in Ramsey that seems to be helping a little, Kevin Kelly. But it took place in New York even though she lives in Ramsey. You gotta do something."

"Okay, okay. Lemme make a few calls."

"Kevin Kelly in Ramsey. Also a Captain Plackenmeyer in Brooklyn, the 66th precinct."

"Okay, I'll talk to them."

Lawrence N. Meyerson, partner in the law firm of *Rubenstein, Rudolph, Meyerson, Blake, and Strull,* is in his mid-forties, trim and fit, blessed with a nice head of well-cut graying brown hair, a salt and pepper beard, and a lifestyle that befits a young successful attorney. He's also funny and easy going, proud of his family, and a man who loves the practice of law. His Oakland firm has expanded and his redecorated office in the large wing of a prestigious professional building sends ribbons of sunshine across his new carpeting and handsome desk.

Though the firm's ad in the yellow pages lists personal injury, municipal court, medical malpractice, drunk driving, real estate, divorce, wills and estates, corporate and business, to Larry none of it is mundane. Sure, the system moves too slowly for his impatient streak, but he has respect for the law, he honors the law, and he's proud to be an attorney. He truly loves that moment each morning when he twirls his swivel around and sits down to attack his day.

Best of all there's Steve Rubenstein, senior partner of the firm, only a few yards down the hall, with his wife Susan who's an aspiring artist and two terrific daughters Beth and Katie, who are a little older than his kids. The friendship reaches beyond law partners, though their personalities are quite different.

Larry, the effusive one, goes bonkers over a judge whose conduct sullies the law and his wrath spills out a stream of curses. For Steve, equally uncompromising and principled, there are no words. He doesn't swear, just shakes his head in disgust. He is a man of rationality, thoughtful and reasonable. Together, they complement each other. In fact, one will often drop into the other's office to schmoose, argue, bitch, or get the other's point of view. It is Larry's nature to make the joke, Steve's to laugh appreciatively.

Both men are smart, very smart. Both are baseball fans, they never miss opening day at Yankee Stadium. Never. Though Steve is a little older and a little shorter, his head of thick curly black hair is barely hinting at gray and he prefers a dark bushy South American mustache to Larry's graying beard. What Steve carries is the unmistakable authority of decency. You don't cut corners, you don't cross the line, you don't back down.

They have a lot in common. Both are men of substance. Both are urbane, lovers of popular culture, from movies to mystery novels, from Broadway theatre to television sports. Both have done their share of pro bono work. You have to give back.

Larry picks up the phone to make the two calls for Elaine. Though he likes to joke that if he doesn't make it as a lawyer, he can always go to Atlantic City or Vegas and work the casinos like his father, anything that has to do with the law intrigues him. So okay, he'll do the Hana Fhima thing. Kelly first. Then Plackenmeyer.

Hana decides to move into Jacky's apartment in Manhattan.

Better to stay in touch with the Brooklyn police and talk to reporters. All her energies are now fixed on recovering Shai. She telephones people, she calls Jewish organizations, she forms a local Shai Fhima Committee. She gives her number to the press. They agree to publish it. Anyone with information is asked to call the 66th Precinct. The press mobilizes around her. She is a fountain of dramatic, emotional quotes and offers them great chunks of copy.

"Even if I'm not religious, when your child is thirteen," she explains to a friendly reporter, "you must give him a bar mitzvah."

Is there a Jew in New York that doesn't understand? Is there a Jew in America, from Miami to Beverly Hills, that isn't following her story and shaking their head?

Brooklyn Detective Captain William Plackenmeyer, in charge of the investigation, reaches for the ringing phone. He's already told the press what Hana Fhima, the mother, has told him. It's all public record and his answers are guarded and moderate. A seasoned law enforcement officer, he doesn't want to inflame the situation.

He has sandy hair and a graying mustache and he wears his dark glasses at the end of his nose, his tie loosened. Hell, he knows who he is: a middle-aged public servant in a cinderblock office in the basement of the station house. His arena is the Brooklyn splattered streets of abandoned refrigerators, junked cars rotting in alleys, and garbage overflowing the sidewalks. His single window offers a view of rubble and graffiti. To take his mind off the visual vomit, he keeps music blasting from the radio on his file cabinet and a pack of cigs close at hand.

Meyerson? He imagines the Jersey lawyer on the other end of the phone. A three-piece suit leaning over a polished teak desk fingering a fresh Danish on a china plate. But listening to Meyerson, he revises his estimate. Guy sounds like he's trying to help the mother find her kid. Bill Plackenmeyer has a nose that ferrets out phonies from real people. He also has one tough job. But what the hell. He takes pride in what crosses his desk and exits his eight-by-ten cubicle. Larry Meyerson from Oakland, New Jersey, sounds like the same kind of guy. He's not a reporter so he can be easier with him.

He tells him about the incident on Sunday night when his men went to the yeshiva to get the boy. "The rabbi's wife said my husband took your boy, you'll never see him again."

Larry jumps on it. "So this a kidnapping, right? A felony punishable by law?"

Plackenmeyer hesitates. He could feed him garbage. Tell him it might be a religious dispute or an internal tiff among the hasidim. But it sticks in his craw. What the hell, tell it straight. Because to see someone deprived of their child, well, he's a family man and it gets to him.

"I got the call, I saw it's a collar. I say who's the detective?" He takes a breath. "It's incredible that it happened," he comments, "that people do it and think they have a right." He fingers his pack of King Kools.

"So what happened that night?" asks Larry.

"That night my sergeant had night watch, one to eight A.M." He recounts the events. "I came on eight A.M. 'We got a unique situation,' he told me. 'Expect phone calls. Waddaya think?' "

Larry is scribbling notes, taking it down.

"I told him: 'You're dealing with a kidnapping.' "

"Really? You figured it for a kidnapping?" Elaine was right. Although the NYPD voice on the other end is gravelly, Larry detects sincerity. The police captain seems like a decent cop. Which ain't easy. Not in Brooklyn. Not in Hynes country.

"Not a word from Hynes?" "No." Waddaya expect? He'll sit tight.

By the end of the conversation, there is the sense that they will be speaking to each other again. Often. Before they wind it up, they are Bill and Larry.

In one emotional interview after another, Hana retells the story of Shai's disappearance. Bombarding the press with incident after incident, she builds her case. Newspaper pictures show her with eyes downcast, her children and Jacky at her side.

Is there a mother anywhere, reading the paper, who hasn't feared the kidnapper? The child molester? In urban cities and small towns, parents talk about her story and tremble. To lose a child, is there any greater pain?

Hana's appeal is visceral. People remember the Jones cult. Jews For Jesus. The Hare Krishnas. To have a child stolen away by fanatics, oh God. *Vay is mir*, Jews mutter. The secularists among them also resonate with the tragic story. They debate the issues. Who has the right to decide about a child's religious training? Who has a right to a child's soul?

Sergeant Tina Mohrmann, a police spokeswoman, tells a reporter, "The parents didn't approve of the rabbi and the rabbi didn't like the parents' influence on the boy."

After Kevin Kelly files the police report in Ramsey on Monday, some journalists speculate that the boy's disappearance appears to be linked to a power struggle between the parents and the rabbi. A power struggle? Is there a parent anywhere who hasn't choked when someone captures their child's allegiance? A hippie teacher? A smart-ass older kid? Bad influences are everywhere awaiting innocent children.

The battle for a boy's soul rages in newspapers across the country. In Europe and Israel.

Secular Jews are appalled at the power of the hasidim. The ultraorthodox have always been an embarrassment to them. Their weird way of dressing. Their refusal to meld into the American culture. They provide ammunition for the gentile world to focus on dirty Jewish linen. Isn't there enough anti-Semitism in the world? Do Jews have to give them more fodder to feed on?

Nevertheless, Hana continues relentlessly to tell her story. It seems to her that her only lifeline to Shai is to keep talking about his kidnapping. Explaining how the Rabbi tricked her, how Mordecai Weiss tricked her. How the ultraorthodox have power to control everything.

To one reporter who seems sympathetic, she says, "The rabbi told him: 'Your mother isn't religious and doesn't keep kosher.' He said Shai should fight his family. He stole my boy to make him religious."

To another reporter she says, "He told my son that someone who isn't religious he will go to hell."

She tells the story a hundred times. To a press hungry for new details, she supplies conversations, opinions, and quotes. Having repeated it so often, she has ironed out the inconsistencies. She knows where the drama unfolds, what grabs their attention and engages their sympathy. The media has polished her.

The battle now takes on intellectual and philosophical proportions. Religious Jews argue with secular Jews. Letters to the editor fan the flames. In coffee shops and at dinner parties, arguments break out. Some Jews merely shake their heads and walk away. Jews fighting Jews makes them uncomfortable, they want it to go away. Other Jews take heated positions that open old wounds and create new ones. Lawyers argue with other lawyers, some are fearful of the outcome. Will the religious right get away with it? Will the power of the extremists prove impenetrable? Will the laws against kidnapping be upheld?

Hana watches. Waits. Naively, she hopes that media attention will bring Shai back. Once the rabbi is placed under arrest, she reasons, he will tell where Shai is. But how long will it take? Thirteen is so young. Is he all right, is he safe?

Thank God, Bill Plackenmeyer takes her seriously.

In the Brooklyn police station, she feels the police captain's strength. He's gonna go out of his way to help her.

"I'm assigning detectives to speak with the rabbi. Maybe they'll persuade him to return the boy."

Her eyes brim with tears. "Thank you."

Larry Meyerson is on her side, too. From the day Elaine called him, he started phoning her and acting like he's her lawyer. Advising her. Answering her questions. Explaining how the law works.

So she has two on her side now. Two.


Later, Larry would look back at the day he walked into Steve's office and spilled out the story. He will remember the generosity of the man. Hell, senior partners of law firms don't give away billable hours.

He sits cross-legged, soberly explaining who Hana Fhima is and why he wants to help her. "It's a kidnapping, Steve. She has no one to help her. Her kid's gone and I'd like to help her. Do the work out of this office. Pro bono. Understand?"

It takes Steve less than a nanosecond to agree. His head nods vigorously. "Of course. Do it, Lar."

Larry lays it all out. "It's gonna mean hours outa the day. Phone calls. Court appearances. Motions to file. Hours stolen from the firm. Not one billable hour, she hasn't got a dime."

"Do it." Steve has made his decision.

"It's not even a high profile case. No sex crime. No celebrity. No murder." Larry's infectious laugh rolls out. "No bucks."

"It's okay." Steve can feel the raw emotion. A kid stolen by a rabbi. A mother with no place to turn. "Do it. You gotta do it."

Rabbi Schlomo Helbrans is arrested on Thursday, April 9. Dragged off in shackles.

But in a stunning reversal, District Attorney Joe Hynes drops the kidnapping charges the very next day. Canceled. Voided. Rescinded.

Charged one day with second-degree kidnapping and endangering the welfare of a child, the next day the rabbi goes free. Before his handcuffs warm up, he is back at Lev Tahor on Friday for the lighting of the Sabbath candles.

The media go wild. It's outrageous.

In Brooklyn, the power of the hasidim is greater than the power of the law. Hynes, up for election, called off the police to save votes. A flagrant abuse of power. How dare the D.A. let this crime go unpunished? How dare he bend to the power of the ultraorthodox?

The press reports that *the rabbi told the police he knows where the boy is, but won't reveal the location.*

The police say they have no reason to believe the teenager has been harmed.

What's really at stake here? What's the truth?

Pushed to the brink, Hynes issues a statement to the press.

"There was insufficient evidence to support the arrest that had been made. My office declined to commence a prosecution and directed the police department to discontinue its investigation."

✡   ✡   ✡

"What? What?" Hana chokes with anger. She is devastated. "How can this happen? Not in America. Not here."

On Saturday, April 11, the *Daily News* carries a photograph of Helbrans, smiling, his white tallis flapping as he walks away vindicated. A free man.

"Oh my God," she moans to Jacky. "Look." She slides the newspaper across the kitchen table and lays her head down on her arms.

Jacky picks up the paper. "Fucking bastard."

Only yesterday in *Newsday*, Officer Andrew McInnis, a police spokesman, told reporters, "The boy's parents who are not orthodox, enrolled him for religious education. But they did not approve of Helbrans's influence and Helbrans tried to keep him from going home. Then they enrolled him in a different school. The suspicion emerges that another person secretly diverted the boy to Helbrans's school and when he didn't return home, the parents called the police."

"A suspicion?" Jacky shrieks. He knew it all along. Fucking Mordecai was the accomplice. Well, didn't he warn Hana? Didn't he predict they were dangerous? But did she listen to him? No. Hana is gullible. It drives him crazy how she was taken in by Mordecai's politeness and promises. And what did he do? Took Shai straight back to Helbrans.

But now, watching Hana weep, Jacky feels sorry for her. Eh— what can you do with a *narishkeit*, a fool, she has no sense.

Yesterday Helbrans was in shackles.

Today, the bastard is a free man.

Helbrans and Weiss. Kidnappers. Free. Walking the streets. Looking for more boys to steal.

# 10. CAPTAIN PLACKENMEYER

Captain William Plackenmeyer of Brooklyn's 11th Detective Division is the overall supervisor of the Shai Fhima case. With bulldog tenacity, he's tracking down every lead, even the long shots.

One came from a rabbi that Mordecai Weiss studied with. He gave an address in Monroe, New York, suggesting they look for the boy there. Then he added with satisfaction: "Mordecai should be off the hook now." But it turned out to be nothing, only the address of a Helbrans follower Michael Apter. Shai was not there.

There were other leads. More dead ends. Like the two letters that seemed to be in Shai's handwriting. At first glance it seemed promising. At least they knew the boy was alive. Sent by Federal Express, they arrived at Helbrans's yeshiva. One addressed to Hana. The other to Helbrans.

In the first letter, Shai writes to his mother that he is happier in his new life and he'll return home only if she becomes religious. In the second letter, Shai thanks the rabbi for his help and writes that he is living with a hasidic family in Brooklyn and hopes to return to Lev Tahor. He says he doesn't understand why the police are giving the rabbi so much trouble and he doesn't want to go back home.

He is in constant contact with Larry and working on bringing FBI and federal authorities into the investigation. The letters will be useful. What to make of them? Were they written by coercion? Meant to influence the mother to become religious? Or just a flagrant piece of public relations to support Helbrans?

Reporters press the police captain. To their demands for comments, he simply points out the obvious. "In a dispute about child rearing, there are other options than kidnapping and the law provides for them." He stands tall, this disheveled Columbo, and speaks with authority. "That's why we have family courts. For God's sake, this family's not perfect. But is that an excuse for kidnapping? As an excuse, there is none. Period." He is emphatic.

To his officers on the case, his message is less restrained.

"Okay, listen up." Hard jawed, he orders a roomful of New York's finest, standing at attention, to go out there and bring him leads. "I want leads. Leads. This is your number one priority. Numero Uno." His finger stabs the air. "Got me?" His eyes are steely. *Don't fuck with me.*

They nod and file out. Yesireee. The captain means business. He's bringing in the FBI.

Alone at his desk, he strokes his mustache. It's perfectly clear to him that this case shakes the very system of American justice. Every eye is on Brooklyn. A police captain could make himself a national reputation. But Bill Plackenmeyer doesn't have to give himself any pep talks, he knows what he has to do.

There's the young mother, Hana Fhima, such an appealing little thing. She speaks with a shyness that he finds touching, her eyes begging for help. He wants to do right by her and fight the good fight. For the mother's sake, he wants to find the kid and return him to her. Let the courts do their thing, he's gonna do his. And if, along the way, he wins himself a few pats on the back, well, that's his job.

He hunches over the reports like a chess board, figuring out his moves. What's gonna work, what's gonna fail? Hell, this is America. Kidnapping is a felony. Religion has nothing to do with it. Whatever religion a family follows, it's their own business. If someone doesn't approve of the religion you teach your children, does it give him the right to take your children away? You spend your whole life in police work, you gotta believe in the system. So okay, this is Brooklyn and the orthodox Jews hold the trump cards. But kidnapping? You don't sweep *that* under the rug because the kidnapper's a rabbi.

Okay. Concentrate. Waddaya got?

First move: try leaning on Helbrans. Get him to tell them where the boy is, take it from there. What else, what else? He keeps stroking his scruffy mustache, it helps him think. Gotta be logical and precise. Waddaya got to go on? The letters. The leads. All dead ends. What's left?

Hey, he brightens, how about Rabbi Bernard Freilich. He's been useful before. It's not unusual in sensitive situations to call in a police liaison. Someone well connected to the community, a voice that's respected, speaks Hebrew, and is one of them. Rabbi Freilich, yeah, they've relied on him before in community outbursts. One of their own; they'll listen to him.

He reaches for the phone. Could the rabbi stop by the station house? His convenience, of course.

Around three-thirty, the rabbi and the police captain face each other across Plackenmeyer's messy desk. The rabbi smiles at him. Two patient men about to play the game. Plackenmeyer knows better than to lead with suggestions. Just lay out the problem.

"Rabbi, it looks like we need a little help here," he begins. "A boy is missing. The mother is suffering. How can we find the boy?" He never raises his voice, he is respectful. He avoids the word kidnapping, rattles no swords. "Rabbi?" He leans forward across his desk. "What do you think?" he asks his bearded visitor. It is a charming performance. State the problem. Then shut up and let the rabbi shuffle the deck.

"Hmmm." Rabbi Freilich's wise eyes squint and he purses his lips. He wants to cooperate. It's delicate, very delicate. In Boro Park one hand washes the other. You want a favor for tomorrow? Today you give a favor. Brooklyn is America and America is goyem; you have to live with them, make peace. "What we'll do," he strokes his beard thoughtfully. "I'll put out the word that whoever has the boy, he should please let the family know at least he's safe."

"Thank you, Rabbi." It's a start.

"I'll put out the word they should let the police know he's safe. They should call the police."

"Thank you, Rabbi. Much appreciated."

Days go by. Does it make a dent in the investigation? Not this time. Not a phone call comes in. Not a note arrives. No messages. No one steps forward. Silence.

Okay, rethink it. Try another move, study the board.

The hasids are a closed circle. Tighter than a steel link fence and not a weak twist in the chain. Whatever secrets they hold, no one will snitch, no one will speak. Secretive as any cult. They tell only what they want you to know. What the hell did he expect? Second grade this ain't. Inform the police? Tell where the boy is? Never. Say he's safe? No way. Even if a dozen families are in the net, hiding the kid and passing him back and forth, not one of them will breathe a word.

This failure only doubles Plackenmeyer's resolve. He is a man inspired to fix what's broken. To repair and put things right. With biblical zeal, he rededicates himself to finding Shai Fhima.

Hana is receiving threatening phone calls. They track her down at Jacky's apartment. Jews attack her, they are furious.

"Listen. You better stop or we're gonna make plenty trouble. You think you got trouble now? Watch."

"How can you do this to us?" a raspy woman's voice spits out contempt.

"Us? Who's us?" she shoots back. "Me. Me, I lost my boy."

"It's terrible," the voice concedes. "But you're hurting us. What's the matter with you, you gotta make Jews look bad?"

"My son was kidnapped," she screams back and slams the phone down.

While she's slicing an eggplant for dinner, another woman phones. "What're you doing this for?" she hisses. "*Past nicht*. It's between you and the rabbi. You got to advertise? We don't got enough hate from the anti-Semites?"

Their anger saps her strength. Where is the support she counted on? She goes down a list of Jewish organizations asking them to take up her cause, even the Lubavitchers; no one will help.

"We are sympathetic. But this is a police matter," one rabbi replies. Rivalries among ultraorthodox sects are immediately erased in the face of a common enemy. In this case, Hana is perceived as the enemy. Defend her? Go to the aid of a secular Jew against a rabbi? Punish one of their own? God forbid. A polite voice cuts her off. "I'm sorry, we can't get involved."

One organization after another turns her down.

"I'm so sorry. My heart goes out to you," one woman admits reluctantly. "But we have orthodox Jews, we can't afford to offend them." She takes a breath. "I'm so sorry," the kind voice apologizes again.

Some nights she crawls into bed weary of it all, tired of the sound of her own voice explaining and defending her position over and over. The real is becoming so polished it is hardening into a reflection of what it is. She's looking in a glass window. What's real?

She is bleeding, but she can't walk away. Somewhere out there Shai is without his family. Brainwashed. His soul stolen away from him.

The other children, they cry out in the night. They have nightmares. Osheri, the oldest, is afraid he will be next.

"Will they steal me when I turn thirteen?" he asks. "Will they come after me?"

He and his brother Eliran stare at her awaiting the answer.

"No, no, they're not going to steal you, don't worry."

The boys turn and walk away, but they seem unconvinced.

Shiran is wetting her bed. "When is Shai coming back?" she asks at odd moments. "Tomorrow?"

Now, amazingly, phone calls are coming from parents in Israel. It begins with a trickle of hesitant inquiries.

"You are Hana Fhima? The mother of Shai, your boy was kidnapped?" The woman is from the settlement of Netzarim. "My boy the same, he was taken from us two years ago," she weeps.

A mother calls from Jerusalem. The same story: a rabbi took her son.

A father from Haifa. A mother from Tel Aviv.

"I read an article about your son, how he disappeared. The same happened to us," a distraught woman babbles in Hebrew.

"What happened?" she asks. Maybe she'll hear something that will help. She listens for clues.

"My son became ultraorthodox. He went with Rabbi Helbrans to Brooklyn. We never saw him again."

"With Rabbi Helbrans?" Oh my God.

"He went away with Helbrans," she repeats. "Disappeared. Vanished."

"When? When?" Hana's throat catches.

"Four years ago. He was in his late teens. We're still looking, hoping. . . ." The voice breaks down, "We don't know nothing . . . nothing."

A father calls from Kfar Darom, a town ten miles southwest of Gaza City. He tells her about his boy. "He left without a word. Without permission. Without our knowledge." He is trying not to lose control. "It was four years ago. Before Helbrans moved to Brooklyn. He's twenty-one now."

"And you don't know nothing? Where he is?"

"No."

"Oh my God." In the background Hana can hear the mother crying and repeatedly asking her husband to hang up. "Don't be afraid," she tells him. "Don't hang up. Me, you can talk to."

"We have other children," he explains. "We live in fear."

Each phone call reveals a slightly different account. But every one ends the same: a boy vanishes from his parents' home.

Aghast, Hana reports each call to Larry and to Bill Plackenmeyer. Each call is a slice out of her heart.

"How do they go on living, the parents?" she asks Jacky. "How it's possible I don't know from these stories. We lived in Israel. Helbrans was for years doing this."

Jacky shrugs. He's tired, irritated. The world is full of shit.

Israeli parents phone her with details. Helbrans, they say, grew up in a nonreligious home and he became religious about the same age as Shai. His first name was Erez and his wife's first name was Leah. But they changed their names to Schlomo for King Solomon and to Malka which translates to Queen.

"Of course," she snaps back. "He wants to make himself big, a big rabbi. A king with a queen."

They describe the seduction of their child. How their young unsophisticated boy was taken in. How Helbrans operates. The Israeli newspaper *Yediot Ahronot* has reported it.

What happened to Shai, she sees now, is not an isolated case. Her son is not the first boy stolen away by the ultraorthodox. Helbrans has a history. Israeli by birth, transplanted to Brooklyn, he hid them in yeshivas.

"So why the Israeli police don't do something?" she asks the caller.

"Do? What can they do? They tell you keep quiet, don't make no fuss. You'll get your boy back if you don't make us trouble."

"The same what I heard here."

"The same in America?" Disbelief. "In Brooklyn they tell you the same?"

"The same." She hangs up, plunged into despair.

What's the solution? Shut up and wait? Or keep talking to the media? Checking with Larry. Begging Captain Plackenmeyer.

To the uncurious eye, Hana Fhima appears a shy and retiring person. Petite and soft voiced, she is a person of little authority. Conventional wisdom supports the view that the victim of a battering husband must have a terrible self-image. Who else would put up with a man who beats her except a woman of low self-esteem? You have to be a doormat. You could leave him. It's your own fault.

But Elaine Meyerson, the Director of Shelter Our Sisters (SOS), has come to know Hana in a different way. She has arranged for Hana's apartment, oversees her well being, and she sees that Hana is learning new truths about herself. It is a long and arduous process. Elaine and Lil have come to know the emerging Hana. The feisty, determined, steel-willed Hana.

Not fight for her son? Sit around and wait? Never.

"Hynes, he dropped the kidnapping charges. But me, I gotta get back my boy," she tells them. "What kind of mother would stop?"

She assesses her chances to find Shai. Who are her allies? Who can she count on? Jacky? He and Shai get along, but he's not the boy's father. It's complicated.

There's Larry Meyerson on the phone every day. And Bill Plackenmeyer's a good man. But won't he lose interest? Other cases will come in, he'll have to pay attention.

Unless comes a miracle, I'm alone.

# PART II

## Israel

# 11. MICHAEL REUVEN

Michael Reuven can feel the sun through his trousers warming his thighs. He stretches his legs out and holds his coffee cup aloft, inhaling the aroma. A mid-morning coffee at his favorite outdoor cafe. The newspaper spread out. A spring day. These are the small pleasures of life in 1992. Lilit and the two boys give him pleasure, too. And his job with the lawyers—well it's not a lot of money, but it's a living.

Life could be worse. In a couple days it will be May and Jerusalem nights will warm up.

Despite an uneasy peace with the Arabs, there is hope in the air. True, the border settlements are at risk and the problem of terrorism exists on every bus, on every street with the Hamas. But this is the first time he sees people holding a little optimism. Maybe, God willing, after so many years of bloodbaths, there will be peace.

He pours extra cream into his coffee and stirs, glad to be alone. Talking politics depresses him. You have ten Jews, you have sixteen opinions. Everyone's right.

Leisurely, he turns the page and looks up. A pretty girl in her army uniform is waiting on the corner for the bus, probably on leave and going home. She smiles at him and he smiles back, watches her slim legs board the bus. Nice. He remembers how it was when he was in the army, going home on leave.

He looks down again to read the paper. He stiffens.

*What's that?* He bends over it.

Shai's picture. *Shai? Shai?*

Under the picture, the caption: "Kidnapped by Brooklyn Rabbi."

*My son. My boy.*

His heart thumps so hard in his chest, his fist flies up to still it. Shai Fhima, it says. And the anger rises. *He is not FHIMA, he is mine, my son, he is Reuven.*

He is sucked into the words that spill out across the page. He tries to make sense of it, the facts that tumble over each other.

*Hana Fhima reports her son missing. . . . The rabbi, Schlomo Helbrans, is a former Israeli. . . . The NYPD continues searching. . . . Captain William Plackenmeyer is calling in the FBI. . . . D.A. Joe Hynes booked the rabbi and released him the next day. . . . The hasidic Jews in Brooklyn control the votes. . . . The boy was going for bar mitzvah lessons at a Boro Park yeshiva. . . . The mother called the police to take him back to New Jersey. . . .*

The details swim in his head, he is a man trained to look at details. The facts are pounding his temples, locking his jaws, stirring up old wounds. He and Hana. They were kids when Shai was born. The divorce. How she sent Shai to her mother and even after she married Jacky and had three more kids, his grandmother raised him. *Khana!* Shit! She took Shai away to the United States and didn't even give me any warning. Just took my son and moved with Jacky to the other side of the world. Just like her.

But this is *my* son, *my* boy.

*Kidnapped?*

Fury and rage congeal in his chest, hardening into rocks, hurling blows at him, pummeling him so fast his breath can't suck in enough air. He pounds the table top—two sharp blows—unaware of the glances of onlookers.

Whoever kidnapped him, this rabbi, he has to find him. I'm the father, I have to get my son back.

*Helbrans. Helbrans.* A Helbrans family still lives in Israel? The rabbi's parents maybe? Trained to ferret out facts for lawyers, he has his ways, he knows how to obtain information—it's his job. You begin with the obvious: the phone book. Or should he call first Hana? No. The hell with her. The hell with Hana Fhima.

He grabs the paper off the table and in his haste, spills the coffee all over himself. His trousers are stained, his thighs are wet where the sun had toasted him.

He throws down some bills and rushes off.

"What you have to do," one of the lawyers he works for tells him across his desk, "is track down his parents here in Israel. Call them first, Michael. Find out what you can. That's your specialty, right?" Zalman likes Michael, he's reliable, hard-working and he's good at what he does. Thorough about the details. A good-looking man. A head of dark hair. Young. Energetic. A certain charm that warms people up.

"You think so? The parents?" Zalman is one smart lawyer, a decent man not much older than he is, though white-haired.

"If it was my son, Michael . . ." the lawyer shrugs and trails off. What can you say? He starts again, drums his fingers on the desk top. "The hasidic sects, the Satmars, they've been at it for years. It's not news, kidnapping kids. To them it's not a crime."

He looks at Michael's stricken face. He has phone calls to return and a contract to clean up before lunch. But he's a father, too; he knows how he'd feel if anyone touched a hair on his son's head. To lose a boy from kidnapping—nothing could be worse. "Take the day off, Michael, it's okay. Do whatever you have to."

Michael rises. "I'll go in the back. I want to read it again, then I'll call them."

"Sure, call from here." He knows Michael won't let go of this. He watches him move toward a vacant desk.

Michael sits down and studies the newspaper. He takes out his pen and makes notes.

The rabbi, it says, denies all charges. Claims Shai only wanted to escape a terrible home and the child wanted a religious life. The police are stonewalled. Detectives tell about the endless dead ends, the secretiveness of the hasidic community. How they trust no one. Detective Sergeant Joseph Piraino is quoted: "If you're not part of them, forget it. It's a closed community. They're concerned about crime in their community, but a lot of them don't consider this a crime."

Exactly what Zalman told him. *To them it's not a crime.*

So he better be careful when he phones Helbrans's parents. They'll defend their son and try to cut him off. It's okay, he handles this type all the time. Does a lot of investigative work on the telephone.

To his surprise, the parents of Schlomo Helbrans unfold their own story of woe. "We lost our son, too," the mother says. "We know what you're going through."

"It was same for us," the father tells him.

"The same? What happened?"

"My son left Israel for good in 1990." He takes a breath as if wondering if he should share his story.

"In 1990?" Michael waits a moment, then prods him. "Why did he go?"

"It was just after Saddam Hussein invaded Kuwait. He had here a small yeshiva. Maybe the Persian Gulf war convinced him to go. He was afraid of another Holocaust. Or maybe it was the pressure from the government." He pauses. It's hard to say this about your own son. "He was an extreme anti-Zionist. The police wanted him out."

"How did it start? How did he become so religious?" Shai was never religious, never interested at all. Even with an orthodox grandmother, he was a regular kid. How do they make these kids so religious, how do they change them?

"He became orthodox on a weekend retreat. He was a boy, a teenager like your son. They went camping. And then. . . ." A deep sadness soaks his voice. "After that he was never the same. He complained we weren't religious enough, we should keep kosher, this and that. We're going to burn in hell. He was scared."

"Scared of what?"

"They instill in him phobias and fears about salvation, about his soul and the afterlife. They teach obedience to authority and to the rebbe. It's mind control. Like the cults."

"The cults?" Michael's heart beats faster.

"They recruit young boys and make them ultraorthodox."

"Who are they?" Michael wants to identify them, wants names, leads, where to look.

"They're not one of the Satmar sects." The father's voice is pained. "The police have been investigating them for years, how they operate, what they do."

"Tell me. Please." Pin it down.

He clears his throat. "They believe Jews should not live in Israel until the Messiah comes. They won't fight in the army." He pauses.

"I know, I was in the army," he says to keep it rolling.

"The newspapers call them Satmars, but they're really hasidim. Some organization they got." He sighs, a man who has uncovered his wounds and picked on the scabs many times. "They don't consider it a crime to steal a boy and make him religious. To them, it's a mitzvah."

"To them it's a mitzvah?" Astonishing. He feels more at ease with the man, he's talking to another father and, just like him, he lost a son.

"What they do, they take boys who have trouble, maybe divorced parents, they look for this type. Lost young people. Not religious. They pick them out in Israel and bring them into a yeshiva. They give them good food and lots of attention. And they feed them Judaism, their brand. Ultraorthodox Judaism. It comforts the boys, gives them answers. It makes them feel important. They get new clothes and everyone focused eyes on them. Then they steal them away to Brooklyn. Some yeshivas are based in Jerusalem. But their counterpart is in Brooklyn. I'm not sure exactly," he trails off, defeated. There is more, but why make the young father feel worse?

Plenty stories he could tell this Michael Reuven, plenty. How the commandos and the Moral Patrol in Meah Shearim operate. Thugs, that's what they are, thugs in yeshiva garb.

They work the streets in groups. In the name of purifying the morals of the community, they could put you in the hospital. Go to the police? Never. They don't allow secularists to be involved in their lives. They create their own laws, their own courts, and they guard their own streets.

Disciplining yeshiva boys or girls who don't follow the rules is their work. *Mishmeret hatzinius*, the modesty protectors. And the police don't do anything against them.

They're vigilantes, menacing, threatening, on the lookout to stamp out evil. They don't like what they see? A boy holds a girl's hand? They give a warning. His arm is twisted back, a punch is delivered to the gut. After that comes a beating, broken bones. All in the name of God. Their mission is to sanctify, to cleanse. Their particular rebbe is the last word. They are fanatics. Zealots. Their ultraorthodox laws cover every conceivable act of human behavior. What part of the face to kiss your wife. The only position for sex. Rules, rules, rules.

You think you're going to find your missing boy? Take him back? Not much chance.

He holds his tongue. Why make the desperate father feel hopeless? In America, in Brooklyn, maybe things are different. He said already too much.

"I'm sorry I can't help you. I wish you luck."

"Mr. Helbrans?" Time to speak up. "You'll please give me your son's telephone number in Brooklyn?"

Michael holds his breath. Grabs a clean sheet of paper. Writes it down in large bold numbers. Then reads it back for accuracy.

"Thank you."

# 12. MICHAEL'S PLAN

Awild man, he spills it out to Lilit who is at the stove stirring soup when he stomps into the apartment.

"Look, look!" he calls, waving the newspaper at her. "Come here, look."

She twists around. "What's wrong?" Too early to be done with work.

He spreads the pages out on the kitchen table. "It's Shai." His finger stabs the headline. "He was kidnapped, *kidnapped*. A rabbi did it." In white heat, he runs down his call to Rabbi Helbrans's parents, interrupting himself, reading sentences from the article, pounding the table, his fury building with each pronouncement.

"Oh my God, oh my God." Lilit wrings her hands.

"He won't get away with it, I'll get him, I'll go after him, I got his number." His hand grabs the phone off the countertop. "Ssssh. I'm calling Brooklyn. Be quiet."

"Wait." Lilit wipes her palms on her apron and lays a calming hand on his wrist. Michael is too hotheaded, right away he has to call Brooklyn. This minute? So impulsive, no restraint. "Michael, Michael, slow down, you have to be sensible. What will you say? This is delicate. Let's think it through."

Lilit can always sense danger, she sees the shadow before the figure arrives. She has this sense. About Shai, Michael is very touchy, this is his sore spot. He hasn't seen him for three years and he's furious how Hana snatched him away.

"What time is it there?" she asks, trying to distract him, though she knows she cannot stop him. Michael is stubborn, you can't budge him. She'd like to read the whole article through and get the facts firsthand. He was kidnapped? A rabbi did it? Oh my God.

She remembers reports in the press about teenagers either lured or abducted to American or Canadian yeshivas. The parents claim it started out here in Israel. A rebbe from the ultraorthodox picks out a secular boy, writes him letters, then follows up with long heart-to-heart conversations. They brainwash the kids to leave their parents and then take them to join their yeshiva. One teenager was spirited away to Brooklyn, she remembers, under false passports. Very organized. Very slick.

But it's not what happened with Shai. With Shai is a different story. Hana took him to New Jersey with Jacky and the other three children. No false passports. He went to live with his mother.

But now that she thinks of it, she remembers another Israeli boy who was . . . "Michael, Michael. Wait, wait." She tugs at his sleeve.

He cuts her off and bangs the phone down on the kitchen table. "I'll get him back, I'll get him back." He holds a finger to his lips, warning her to be silent.

"But Michael . . ."

"Shhh."

He sits down, ready to do battle.

"Eh." She acquiesces. Michael is headstrong. About Shai he has always felt . . . what? Guilty?

Rabbi Helbrans's voice comes to him from Brooklyn so clearly, he could be only on Dizengoff Street. A pleasant voice. Not what he expected.

The rabbi listens. Doesn't interrupt.

Michael sneers, he's sizing me up. Trained to pick up what voices say and don't say, he is careful not to reveal a shred of anger, he's only a father with a missing boy. "Can you help me find my son, rabbi?" His voice is controlled, while his mind is calculating, pumped up, on adrenaline alert.

"Michael Reuven." The rabbi repeats his name. "You are Shai Fhima's father?" He wants a confirmation.

"Yes. His biological father. I'm calling you from Jerusalem."

Rabbi Helbrans senses opportunity and his chest expands. Shai's *real* father is calling him? Exactly what he needs, he is delighted. "Yes, yes, maybe I can help," he replies with enormous interest.

Immediately, Michael is suspicious. The rabbi's voice has turned syrupy. What does he want?

"Tell me, Michael. You are Israeli citizen?"

"Yes, yes. You can help me?" he pleads.

"Yes. I can help you."

Ha. In the paper it said he doesn't know where Shai is, he's not involved. He told the police, *"The first two weeks he disappeared I was working all day to find him. But if he's happy and in a good place, what's the trouble?"*

"Rabbi? Is my boy safe? You know where he is?"

He doesn't answer. Only *hng, hng, hng,* exhaling into the silence.

"You know where my son is?" Michael asks again, pressing him.

"Michael. Listen." *Hng. Hng.* "You'll come to Brooklyn, I'll arrange you. You'll see him, you'll see Shai."

"You'll let me see him, you'll take me to him?" The back of his neck burns with excitement. Whatever the price, whatever it will cost, will be worth it.

He waits. He is not a man compelled to fill in the silence. A savvy investigator, he is trained to let silence hang in the air, forcing the other person to speak. He detects cunning lurking in the rabbi's *hng, hng.* He'll ferret it out.

"One thing." The rabbi speaks. "You have custody? The papers from Shai—you have Israeli custody papers?"

Michael's eyes narrow. An offer is coming. What does the good rabbi have in mind? Careful. Tread lightly.

He looks up at Lilit, sees fear in her watchful eyes. Her body is hunched and tense, her hands clasped in her lap. He holds a finger to his lips to warn her again to be silent. "Yes. Yes, I do," he lies.

"Then I can help you," the rabbi promises. "If you'll bring me custody papers, I can arrange you . . ." he stops. Should he say this on the telephone? Suppose it's an Israeli trick from the police? No, no, not this time. This is a father in despair, he's sure of it. The *real* father of Shai, not Fhima. Jacky Fhima is the stepfather and with Hana, together they are the enemy. Not this man. This Reuven is the link. A father who wants his son. Ah, G—has smiled on me. G—, in his infinite wisdom, has sent to me Michael Reuven.

"Michael. Listen to me. You'll bring me custody papers. You'll backdate them for me. Your son wants to be religious. We are going to raise him in the yeshiva. You understand? Your son is happy with us, his soul is at peace." He pauses to measure the response on the other end.

"He's happy, you say he's happy?" A fishing remark, not consent, meant only to draw him out.

"Such a good boy, a scholar, he could be for us a zaddik." *Hng, hng.* Now the bait. "We'll make for you an annual visit, we'll pay your travel expenses, you can come to see him." The barest pause. When no comment is forthcoming, he announces the deal. "For these papers, we'll pay $50,000."

Michael holds his breath. *What?* His eyes widen. The rabbi will pay $50,000 for custody papers? But he doesn't have custody papers. Custody of Shai was awarded to Hana and Jacky.

A small smile spreads to his eyes. His heart sings. So what? It won't stop him. He knows instantly that he's going to Brooklyn to get Shai back. *Ben Zona!* Son of a bitch rabbi.

"Thank you, rabbi," he gushes. Quick. Close the deal. "I'll have for you the custody papers. I'll be to you tomorrow. The next plane from Ben Gurion, I'll be on it."

"You'll bring me the papers?" Confirm it.

"Yes, yes." Hearty agreement.

"Good, Michael. Tomorrow at Kennedy Airport, you will see your son. We'll meet your plane."

"You'll have Shai there?" He can hardly believe it. "He'll be waiting at the airport?"

"You'll have for me the papers, yes. Shalom." He hangs up.

Shaking, almost in tears, Michael stands up. So does Lilit.

They face each other and embrace. He is dizzy, delirious.

When he lets go of her, he backs away and stands tall. Time to speak seriously, to outline the plan. "He's bringing Shai to the airport, Lilit. He offered me $50,000."

"Fifty thousand dollars?" she screeches. Her hand slaps her forehead.

He nods. He swallows hard.

"For what? For what? Custody papers?" She has heard that part. Michael will sell Shai for $50,000? No, never. She knows her husband. He has a plan, he has figured it all out in his mind. "Tell me."

He smiles. It will be easy to outwit that putz rabbi.

"He wants Israeli custody papers. Backdated. I have to bring them to Kennedy airport." He speaks in a flat tone, he is repeating the instructions for his own benefit. "He'll bring me Shai."

"But you don't have papers, Michael. You don't have custody," she reminds him.

"Don't worry. Tomorrow, I'll have papers." He punches a fist into his palm.

"You will? How?"

"I'll have something. Don't worry. I'll fly tomorrow to New York. I'll see Shai and get him back here to us."

"What? How?" She wants him to spell it out. It means she'll be left alone with the boys. How long it will take? What will come from this? What will be with this kidnapping? Could be dangerous. "Oh my God."

"Don't worry." Michael grins. He has confidence in himself. The stakes are high, but he can do it. The army taught him well.

"Michael, listen . . ."

"Don't worry. I'll take care of it," he snaps back.

# 13. THE TRIP TO JFK

El Al security at Ben Gurion Airport is always tight.

Luggage must be checked in four hours before take-off. Sometimes even the night before. It all depends on what's happening: the immediate situation. A political incident, an act of terrorism, a bomb threat, almost anything can empty the airport and delay departures for hours. Vigilance, eyes everywhere, body searches— this is the necessary way to operate. Life is full of risks, all you can do is reduce them. An Israeli shrug is the national tic.

Tonight, everything is normal.

Flights leave and arrive smoothly and on time. Passengers embark and depart to destinations all over the world. Israeli Jews. Palestinian Arabs. Israeli Arabs. Moslems. Christians. American and European tourists. They all mingle, joined briefly as they travel, dependent on Ben Gurion's security.

Michael looks around. With Passover week done, he sees groups of American Jews on United Jewish Appeal tours returning home. Easy to spot in their expensive sweatsuits and Nikes. They are upbeat and joyful, in a celebratory mood, laughing, exchanging photos and addresses. For many, this is not their first visit. Some have family, others have friends and warm ties to the land of their people. They love Israel and are the heart of the tourist business. So Israel loves them, too.

For Israelis, Passover means everything crawls to a halt and many people skip work. For American Jews, Moslems, and Christians, it means something else. A travel season, time to visit the mosques for religious reasons or see the historical sites on holiday. At museums and points of interest, busloads of tourists are poured out and scooped up. En route, Israeli guides do their spiel, complete with borscht belt jokes thrown in to liven up the biblical descriptions. Makes for better tips.

Michael has delayed the day of his departure to arrange for custody papers. Not hard to do. If you know where to go and who can fix it, you can get any kind of paper. He is pleased with what he has. It looks quite authentic and it is backdated exactly the way the rabbi asked.

Pacing the airport, he pats the inside pocket of his zipper jacket, it feels good against his heart. In ten, twelve hours, it will deliver Shai. He has phoned Rabbi Helbrans with the flight number and time of arrival. Tomorrow, May 2.

He looks around. A knot of businessmen with portfolios are chatting near the El Al counter. European kids in jeans and backpacks are collecting in groups. Parents are tending infants. A knot of Israelis in hasidic garb are praying silently and rocking back and forth. Teenagers are noshing falafel. An international mix. Tonight, Ben Gurion is a hub of activity.

It is late evening when the plane rises off the runway and Tel Aviv fades from view. Above the lights of the airport, Michael hears the roar of the jet taking off. On time. Good. No body searches, no delays. Undercover agents are surely seated on the plane, indistinguishable among the passengers.

As the flight reaches cruising speed and the seat belt sign is turned off, people relax. A few stand up to find friends seated at other locations and schmoose with them. A few pull out paperbacks to read, others tilt their head back to nap.

Michael is traveling light. He has checked in his one bag and has one carry-on piece, his nylon duffel. He's stashed his raincoat in the overhead compartment and wears a white open-neck shirt and no tie—typical Israeli informality. His *new* shirt, he wants to look good for Shai.

He will miss Lilit and the children. He will miss Jerusalem, beautiful Jerusalem, with its skyline of domes and stark white mountains. How drastically the landscape is changing. Some Israelis are disturbed by the new development.

Ugly orange cranes are slicing lines across the holy city, carving out shopping malls and apartment complexes from the golden stones. There is rampant land speculation and terrible traffic. Michael has read the arguments and watched the television debates. Opposition between architects and preservationists has heated up, and some fear the destruction of the city's soul.

Not Michael. For him Jerusalem's powerful spiritual appeal will never fade. The biblical landscape—with shepherds' flocks grazing and groves of olive trees dotting the landscape—those will not be erased. No. No matter what modern buildings go up, the city's holy sites will be meticulously preserved and respect given to the world's Christian, Jewish, and Moslem religions. But you have to make room for the newcomers.

Michael's view is realistic. He is a pragmatist. The army taught him that you do the best with what you have. In the face of fire, you must be practical. Alert to change. These are survival skills.

True, in Ein Keren, the little pastoral village that was the birthplace of John the Baptist, there is talk of a hotel for tourists. And a high-rise might be going up downtown in the nineteenth-century area that's adjacent to the holy sites of the walled Old City. Another political fight. Always, the secularists, for modern adjustments, against the ultrareligious, devoted to preserving the old world. Some even want to see rapid transit come to Jerusalem although it will pollute the pure mountain air.

The ongoing arguments about pollution bring a smile to his lips. Hell, Israelis, with their cigarettes dangling, already pollute restaurants and shops. Worse than Europeans, they can't give up their cigarettes. He's a pack-a-day man himself.

He leans his head back and closes his eyes. Will be a long night. The expense of the trip. Time lost from work. But what can he do? It's for Shai, to find Shai.

Was it a kidnapping or a conversion? With a boy thirteen, what can you say? So young is easily swayed.

It's Hana's fault. The paper said she let him go to the yeshiva, she sent him. The rabbi claims he was only rescuing him from a terrible home. What was so terrible? Hana has her faults, but the children she loves dearly. Of this he is certain. Was it Jacky? He will ask the rabbi and get the facts. He will ask Shai. His son will tell him the truth.

He taps his jacket pocket again. The papers, like a talisman, make him feel good. He knew exactly who to go to for them. Investigators have their contacts. A combination of Israeli savvy and trade secrets.

Lulled by the sweet buzz of the plane's engine, awake but day-dreaming, he pictures himself reunited with Shai. Runs through scenarios. Will he be much taller? Of course, he was only ten then. Will they go directly to the yeshiva? How can he outmaneuver the rabbi? It will be a game of cunning and he is prepared for it like a dance that you know all the steps. The moves, the slides, the turns—he doesn't have to rehearse. Once the music begins, he will know what to do. The moment he sees Shai it will all become clear.

The plane is crowded.

An American couple seated next to him are tourists returning with a B'nai Brith group. The husband has the window seat, the wife is in the center seat, and Michael has the aisle. She smiles pleasantly and dons a head set. He can hear her switching music channels. The man reads a paperback, but Michael can't see the title. They settle in.

Michael plays back his telephone conversation with the rabbi. He imagines a bearded man his own age, thirties, in hasidic clothes, a description that could fit a dozen men on the plane. So how will he recognize Helbrans? Look for Shai. Shai will be with him, just look for Shai. He will see me and come running, shouting *Aba, Aba,* leaping into my arms. Such an affectionate boy, so loving. His mouth turns up in sweet anticipation.

Aloft a few hours, with the dinner trays collected and the tray tables returned to locked position, he tilts his head back. But he cannot sleep. He reruns their reunion, imagining how Shai will look as a teenager. Has he really become a hasid? Hard to believe. The boy showed no signs when he lived with his orthodox grandparents. This alone is suspicious. What about Hana? What is her life with Jacky? What will Shai say about living in New Jersey? Will he be to him a hero or a villain? Boys his age are unpredictable.

Anxiety pokes him, keeping him awake.

He remembers an old photo of Shai in his wallet. With the seat belt off, he is free to wriggle it out of his pants pocket. He holds it up close, studying it. Look, he and Hana were so young. They are standing together cuddled close, his arm around her shoulder. Shai is maybe two and she's holding him proudly in her arms. Look at him, such a bright-eyed little boy. Smiling, always smiling. But that was long ago, eleven years. Before Jacky. Before Lilit. Before life got complicated.

Suddenly, he shakes off his reveries. Enough dreamy meditations. He slides the photo back and puts his wallet away.

Concentrate. Calculate what you must do. Examine the options. How to play the rabbi? Pass to him the papers first thing. Take the cash—he should only deliver it. Then call right away the police. Papers. Money. Police. In that order.

It won't be easy.

With hours of airtime ahead, he starts to figure it out.

Don't underestimate the rabbi. He will be cunning, not easily duped. It is a mistake people make: they think religious people are unsophisticated and naive. Not at all. The hasidim have money, they're used to wielding power. Be careful, go slowly. Don't give him right away the custody paper. It has the seal, it looks authentic. It will pass. On this he is confident. But be careful.

Seated in the plane's tail section, it is a bumpy ride, and now fatigue sweeps over him. Apprehension has drained him, the scenarios he's played out have taxed him. He closes his eyes. In moments, he's asleep.

He sleeps fitfully, his head bobbing, his neck stiff.

He waves off a flight attendant's offer of another tray.

He awakens in the dark, feeling the weight of the hours yet to drag by.

He nods off again.

Another tray appears. Breakfast? He rouses himself.

It's morning. People are stirring, some are already lined up in the aisle, waiting to use the lavatories. Daylight has slipped in under the drawn window shades and the lights are back on.

Soon. Very soon they will land.

Now the captain's announcement: "We will shortly be beginning our descent for landing in New York's Kennedy Airport. Please fasten your seat belts. The weather in New York is mild and pleasant. A sunny sixty-four." A pause. "Once you leave the airport, *the dangerous part of your trip is about to take place.* Drive carefully." A joke.

People chuckle. A few applaud. See? Even pilots do their shtick. A little fun to relieve touchdown.

The American couple next to him hold hands for the descent.

He runs his fingers through his hair. How does he look? Will the rabbi be easy to find? Will Shai be happy to see him? Will the custody papers pass? Will he really hand him fifty thousand dollars? God, he could use a cigarette. But the no smoking sign is already on.

He can feel his stomach turn over and knot.

It's all about to happen. The captain was right. *The dangerous part of the trip is about to take place.*

At the El Al baggage carousel, Michael waits for his suitcase to roll out, looking around for Shai. Ridiculous, he can't be here. On this side, is Immigration. Passports. Customs. Lines to go through before you are allowed to pass into the main airport. But his eyes refuse to behave, they are hungry to see his boy.

At last, his papers approved and his heart pounding, his hands grip the two bags. He steps boldly through the double swinging doors marked EXIT.

Expelled into the vast belly of the airport, he searches the welcoming crowd pressed against the ropes restraining them, looking for their arriving relatives and friends. Names are shouted. Someone shoots through the flapping doors and cries of joy greet him. Families rush into each other's arms.

So where are they?

He keeps walking. Slow, even steps. Craning. Searching.

No one approaches him. He sees no hasidic rabbi with a boy. *Keep walking around. Keep looking.*

Nervous, he makes a larger circle. Taps his jacket pocket, yes, it's there.

*No, don't sit down. Be visible.* He pulls himself up taller, easier to pick him out in the crowd. He paces. He stops. He looks around.

Paces again. Stops. Looks around.

They'll be here. Late from traffic. Be calm.

He begins another circle.

A soft *Michael?* from behind spins him around.

Three hasids, young men not much past twenty, converge around him.

"You are Michael Reuven?" the tallest one asks pleasantly. He is wearing thick glasses.

"Yes, yes." Can't be Rabbi Helbrans, too young. "Where is Shai?" His eyes dart past them, searching, scanning. Is the rabbi hiding on the side? Waiting someplace with Shai? Watching for their signal?

"Come with us. We'll take you to the yeshiva." He motions for him to follow them. "You'll come with us in the car."

"But where's Shai? Where's the rabbi?"

Bitter disappointment has delivered a punch to his gut. His throat aches. The rabbi *promised.*

He stands firm, steadying himself. He makes no move to follow them. "I want to know. Where is Rabbi Helbrans? Where is Shai?" He has to control himself though his heart cries: *Liar. Fucking liar. Where's my son?*

"You'll come with us," the tall hasid repeats. "The rabbi, he is waiting for you." He smiles congenially and leads the way.

# PART III

## Brooklyn

# 14. THE MEETING

In the living room of Lev Tahor, Rabbi Helbrans welcomes him warmly. But Shai is not with him.

"Where is my son, rabbi?" Michael asks, controlling his rancor.

"Sit down, Michael, you'll p-p-please sit down." He motions for him to take a chair. Clearly a conversation must take place first, this will be the procedure.

*Okay, okay, let the rabbi call it.* Nothing to be gained by confrontation, play it out his way.

He takes the chair facing the sofa where the rabbi has ensconced himself. But he can't help it, he asks again. "So where is Shai?" It's a polite inquiry, not an accusation. "I expected . . ."

The rabbi smiles and holds up two restraining palms. "We'll talk a little, Michael. First we'll talk."

Michael studies the man.

Not a threatening figure, this overweight doughy man with the unkempt beard and heavy eyeglasses perched on his nose. More like a dark rumpled Santa Claus. Early thirties? He could pass for forty, fifty, maybe. Slow moving and plodding, a heavy *hng, hng* as he breathes.

The rabbi is smiling benignly at him now as if this is only a pleasant visit from a congenial neighbor, nothing more.

It doesn't fool Michael. He has experienced such easy going manipulations before, and he's still aching with the disappointment of not seeing Shai at the airport. Don't let your guard down, he warns himself.

"Your son, he is in g-g-good hands. Believe me, he's happy. A fine boy you got, Michael."

"So where is he, rabbi?" Polite. Respectful. *I came half way around the world for him, where the fuck is he?* To show he is at ease with the rabbi, he rests one ankle on the other knee, a relaxed position. Do it his way, whatever he says.

The rabbi does not reply. Instead he takes another tack. He has information to impart. "Your son, he was living in a terrible home, a terrible home life, understand?"

"How is that?" Michael asks, a willing listener. He wants to talk? Let him.

"The mother and stepfather beat him. He wanted to escape."

"No, no." Michael cries, registering disbelief. "Terrible," he adds to show he is on the rabbi's side. *Could it be true?* Shai's safety is all that concerns him, what put him on the plane from Jerusalem. Did Hana and Jacky harm him? He read the rabbi's version in the papers. How he was only rescuing him. Could it be true?

"The husband Jacky beats the mother. Shai, too." He pauses to let it sink in. "This from a Jewish home. Comes the police, she calls them, the p-p-police."

The rabbi has a stutter. Michael pretends not to notice.

"They take her to what you call battered woman shelter. Such a shame. From a Jewish family four children go to live with goyem. What they try, Michael, is to turn them Christian, this is why they help her." His eyes darken, squinting at the evil. "Terrible, terrible. The mother, she don't live with her husband no more. The stepfather moves to New York. A janitor for a building."

He pauses to measure the effect of his tale on Michael. An emotional type, he's shaking.

Is it true? Is it possible that Hana would harm her own child? Jacky he can understand, the man's a hothead. But Hana?

"Hard to believe it." Sweating, he expresses honest doubt. He is bewildered and confused. "Tell me, rabbi, you know Jacky hurt my boy?" He'll break his fucking face in half. "They beat him? Jacky hit him?"

"He told me, the boy said it, every day how they beat him."

Fury pulsates through him. Shame, too. What father lets another man hurt his own flesh and blood? He lowers his eyes and his fists ball up. "I don't know from this, rabbi, I don't know."

His anger, directed first at the rabbi who failed to deliver Shai at the airport, is now skewered to Hana. A worse situation than he thought. Hana is weak and Jacky sucked her into it.

"Michael." The intensity in the rabbi's eyes drills holes into him.

"What?"

"It's worse, there's more."

"More?" His crossed leg is twitching so he places both feet firmly on the floor. "What?"

"She don't let your son be religious. She makes him eat treyf, he wants kosher. She don't let him lay teffilin or make the daily prayers. Your son, he loves God, Michael. He wants to study Torah. She laughs at him, she laughs." He reaches forward and lays a thick hand on his arm. "A tragedy."

Michael is now consumed with fear. The hell with kosher. *They hurt him. Where is he? Is he okay?*

"He ran away from them. He tried to come to us on the train. She called the police. They took him back, they forced him to go back to live there." He repeats the story, shaking his head, a man who cannot understand goyisha police justice. "The mother is a d-d-devil. Her soul will burn in hell."

Michael can't hear anymore. His head hangs low, propped up by his palms for support.

The wallet snapshot flashes before his eyes. His bright-eyed son, two years old, his arm around Hana. How did she sink so low?

The rabbi sits back, content. He has the father entranced. "Look at me, Michael," he croons. His voice tugs him to attention.

Michael straightens up to receive the next blow. What could be worse how Shai ran away from them, how the police came from the beatings. Bastards! And all along he thought the rabbi was the villain. Hana and Jacky, he could tear them apart for what they did to Shai.

"It's true, it's true," the rabbi insists, shaking his head sadly. "So how we send him back to them? We took him in, he wanted to be with us, he wanted to be religious."

It's too much for Michael. He expected to dance around a disgusting rabbi who wanted to buy his son. To outfox him with a phony custody paper, to collect money, and blow the whistle. Now he's faced with a different situation. Maybe the rabbi really did rescue him.

Emotions well up in him. Fear. Shame.

What to believe? Who to trust?

He clears his throat. Hana and Jacky, he'll tear them apart.

Michael's sigh is long and painful. Conflicting emotions are pummeling him.

"We took good care of Shai. God gives us strength, Michael. God helps us to rescue him. And he's safe now. A good boy. He studies hard."

They sit in silence.

Suddenly, it comes to Michael that he must test the rabbi.

"I have for you the custody papers, rabbi. See?" He pulls it out and ceremoniously unfolds it. He hands it to him.

The rabbi's thumb runs lightly over the seal. "Thank you, Michael. But we find out how you don't have custody. The mother does." He makes a coy pout.

"No, no," Michael protests, jumping to his feet, thinking fast. Alert. On guard. "We have *joint* custody," he cries.

Rabbi Helbrans scratches his beard. "Joint custody? You and the mother together?"

"Absolutely," he insists. "In Israel, the court made us joint custody."

A slow smile. "Very good." He stands up. He hands the paper back to Michael. "This what you bring me is not—how you say?— valid. But you'll go to her and get from Hana custody. Yes?" The smile widens. "You can do this, Michael? You'll get from her custody and you'll bring me new papers." He seems satisfied, it has gone well. "We'll make from your son a zaddik, your son will talk to God."

"You'll raise him in the yeshiva?" Get it straight.

"We got plenty boys from Israel here." He fastens his gaze on Michael. "Plenty."

Michael feels the heat penetrating to his toes. He is awash with anger. Furious at Hana. At Jacky. At Helbrans. At the world. Only Shai is innocent. A boy who needs his father. He has to protect him.

"You'll do this for your son, Michael, your firstborn son. Go to her and bring me the p-p-papers. We will pay for this like I told you."

"No problem, rabbi."

"God bless you, Michael."

"And then I'll see Shai? I want to see Shai."

"You'll see him, you'll see him." He takes his elbow. Positions him so they are standing side by side. "Pray with me, Michael. Pray with me." He bows his head.

"*Bo-ruch A-toh A-do-noy, E-lo-hay-noo Me-lech Ho-o-lom . . . ,*" he begins. Rocking fervently, he chants in Hebrew a prayer for times of trouble.

"*Out of the depths of my sorrow, I cry unto thee, all wise Ruler of the destinies of man. Thou hast laid upon me a heavy burden and tried me with sorrow. Days of anguish and nights of weeping hast Thou meted out to me. Humbly I bow beneath Thy decree and try to accept Thy will.*

"Pray with me, Michael. Pray for your son," he wails. "God will hear you. Pray, Michael."

Sweating, overcome with emotion, his legs turned to pudding, Michael is nearly weeping. He stands beside the rabbi, his head bowed, praying fervently.

✡　✡　✡

In the taxi, a cool breeze slaps his face.

It comes to him now that Helbrans has turned him around. Has mesmerized him.

He left Lev Tahor without Shai. Without money. With only fierce determination. To go straight to Hana and Jacky.

# 15.  A NEW ARRANGEMENT

"Hana," Michael says tensely, trying to disguise his fury at her and Jacky. His chair is facing them, they are sitting on the sofa. "I come here to help you, I come to find Shai." *You beat him,* his heart screams at her, but his tongue is silent.

Jacky's apartment is clean and tidy. Their three children are asleep in another room and there is nothing out of the ordinary here, nothing at all to be seen. Newspapers, magazines, the usual scatter children leave behind, a sweatshirt, a hair ribbon. Child abusers? He examines their faces. What he observes is that a heavy sadness unites Hana and Jacky. A stepfather enraged by Shai's kidnapping. Not exactly how he figured. And Hana, poor Hana, she looks defeated.

Still a pretty woman, he has to admit. But trouble has pulled her mouth down and dimmed the brightness in her eyes.

"You talked to that fucking Helbrans?" Jacky jabs at him suspiciously. He is fishing. "You phoned him from Jerusalem, that's why you come here?" More to it than that is his implication. "C'mon. You left your job, your family, and you come just from a phone call?" A snicker of disbelief. *Putz. Schmuck.*

"What did he tell you?

Michael doesn't flinch. He lets the insult slide off him, a little trick. "You wouldn't do this for your child, Jacky?" A small smile.

"You think you'll come from Jerusalem and do right away what the New York police can't do?"

Michael ignores the taunt. "He promised to bring Shai to the airport. Like I told you on the phone, he promised me. But he didn't deliver him."

"He said he would bring you Shai in the the airport? This is what he said?"

Michael nods. "Yes, like that."

"He promised you'll see Shai right off the plane? This is why you came?" The interrogator snorts. "And you believe him?"

"I swear to you, this is what he promised." He leaves out the fifty thousand dollars. Not yet. He'll wait. See what's what.

Jacky's look is disdainful. "You got a promise from a kidnapper, a liar. That's what you got, Michael."

Hana has set out a bowl of fruit, Israeli style, a plate of sliced coffee cake, and mugs of tea. Her arms are folded tight against her chest. Palpable between her and Michael is a long-standing, festering anger. He will not forgive her for whisking Shai out of Israel. She will not forgive him for . . . what does it matter?

Seeing her now, so shaken, so squashed, like a bug struggling to survive, Michael's rancor melts a little.

Suddenly, she explodes at him. "Helbrans stole him . . . the hasids . . . Helbrans's wife . . . Helbrans and his wife . . ." she starts sobbing. It is too much to tell again and again. She dabs her eyes with a balled up tissue. Too much, too much.

"You know how they did it?" Jacky will lay out the facts. "That bastard, that Mordecai, he tricked Hana. She let Shai stay overnight with him. You read it in the paper?"

"A little, I know a little." Michael wants to hear *their* version.

"It was a plot. A conspiracy. They kidnap boys from Israel and make from them hasids. Take them away to yeshivas in Brooklyn." Jacky pauses. He regards Michael with unvarnished contempt. "C'mon, Michael, you know this. Why you come to us—why?" A rude and pointed accusation. "The truth, Michael. Don't bullshit me."

"He's my son, that's why. He's not your son, Jacky, he's mine." He looks sharply at him. He could tear them into pieces, but what would it gain? He came mistrustful. But now an inner voice asks: *Are they the enemy—Hana and Jacky? Or is the rabbi and that Mordecai guy the enemy?*

Jacky stares back.

"He's my son, too." Hana mutters into her open palms. "He's my son, too."

"Listen, Michael . . ." Jacky is impatient to get this over. "What did he tell you? What lies Helbrans fed you about us? How we beat Shai? He's fulla shit. How Shai wants to be religious? Another fucking lie. How they rescued Shai from us? More bullshit. You fell for it, that's why you're here."

Michael stands up, he sways from exhaustion. Only hours ago, he was praying and rocking with the rabbi, davening in the yeshiva, mesmerized by his chanting. Caught up in his thrall. Wailing to God, *Out of the depths of my sorrow, I call unto thee.*

Now he knows better. You were duped. Conned. Captivated. The rabbi outsmarted you. Think. Think. Shai was delivered to the airport? Your son fell into your arms crying Aba, Aba, I love you, take me to Israel?

A weighty remorse claims him. How did I fall for that crap? How did I let three hasids deliver me to the rabbi? Then I walk away without Shai. All the trouble I went through to get custody papers fixed. What a fool.

And now a new deal he makes for me. I should go to Hana and get her to sign off.

He looks at Hana. At Jacky. No chance. Walk out of the apartment with Hana's agreement she'll give her son away? Never. He came to trick them. Not so easy.

"Hana," he takes a conciliatory tone. "I'll explain you why I come to you." He is the voice of reason. "I can get Helbrans to turn Shai over to me. He trusts me, understand? He knows where Shai is."

"Of course he knows," Jacky spits back with a sour smile. But he's interested, he wants to hear more.

So does Hana. She leans forward. If the rabbi trusts Michael . . . if he tells Michael where Shai is . . . "Let him talk, Jacky."

"We have to give him a custody paper. See?" He stands up and pulls it out of his pocket. He is persuasive and friendly. "You'll

sign here, Hana. You'll give me custody. And I'll go back to Helbrans and work out the deal."

Jacky's laughter punctures the room like a pneumatic drill
on concrete. "Don't play games." He is insulted. Michael is a terrible actor. Look how his hand is shaking holding the paper, emotional like a woman. "Get the hell outa here." His arm flies out,
pointing to the door. "Out! Don't fuck with me."

"Wait, Jacky, wait, wait." Hana lays a restraining hand on
him, why he always has to be a hothead? If Michael walks out, any
thread to get Shai back through Helbrans is lost. "Don't go,
Michael, sit down. You came from Israel to find Shai. It's what we
want, too, right Jacky? So we gotta work together, not fight." Her
eyes fill up, asking Jacky to behave. Her pretty mouth, set in a
rueful slash, begs him to help her.

True there's bad history between her and Michael. The only
good that came out of their marriage was Shai. And now it
shames her that Michael sees her this way. In this apartment.

To your ex-husband, you want to show off how good you have
it, how nice you live. Not how you made again a mistake. Not how
America turned out all pain. Not how Jacky lost every cent and
the business failed. Not how the second marriage. . . . She sees in
Michael's eyes what he's thinking. How the apartment is dismal,
with a couch falling apart and cheap lamps. The superintendent
gets free a furnished apartment. She has fixed it up a little but it
don't do much good. Michael sees this.

She puts on a brave smile. "Don't be foolish, Jacky. We want,
all of us, the same thing. Sit down, Michael, stay, we gotta talk."
Standing up to Jacky delivers a little energy her way.

Jacky is weary, the end of a long day. Fixed a toilet clogged
with a shitty diaper in 2-D, shaved two doors for the new tenant
moving into 3-B, and snaked out that slob's kitchen sink in 4-A.
Running around since six in the morning, does he need this shit?
He turns away and gives her a look that says: Okay, Hana do what
you can with that fool.

Seeing Jacky compliant, Michael returns to his chair though Jacky will not make eye contact. *The hell with you, wifebeater. Hana and I are his parents.* He knows Jacky's type from the army. Has to show everyone how tough he is, a peacock aggression and always on the brink of exploding. The apartment—tidy yes, but it holds the chill of a man caught in an event he didn't make. He scowls back at Jacky—this is what Hana married?

He folds his hands—better not to fight. Let Hana talk.

He offers her a sympathetic look.

Once he loved her, he was happy with her and their life together was blissful. But that was long ago when they were kids, different people. Old memories will do nobody no good. He's exhausted. The anxiety of the plane trip and the disappointment at the airport have sapped him. The meeting with Helbrans, it took plenty out of him, too.

Enough. He can see it clearly now. Helbrans tricked him. Lied about Hana and Jacky. Set him against them. *They* are not the enemy, *Helbrans is.* Look at them. Broken-hearted. All they want is to get Shai back.

"Hana?" He asks for her attention. "We're on the same team together," he says in a soothing voice. "We have to join up, the three of us, against Helbrans."

Immediately, Jacky takes over. "Right. Right."

"Yes." Hana nods vigorously. A wave of hope lifts her chin. They'll be allies.

"The police don't do nothing," Jacky sneers. "Fucking Hynes don't do nothing. We gotta do it ourself."

"Wait, Jacky," Michael stops him. "I gotta tell you first the rest with Helbrans." He seems embarrassed, he's about to admit something he withheld. "I came here to trick you. It was his idea."

Jacky's face contorts with contempt.

Michael continues. "He said how you hit Shai, how you . . ."

"He's crazy," Hana explodes. "He ran away because they put

scare in his eyes, scare. If he don't be religious, his soul will . . ." she throws up her hands.

"What else, Michael?" Jacky knows there's more to Michael's story.

"I came with this." Michael hands the paper to Hana. "Custody papers I fixed in Israel."

"Pfft." Hana knows they're phony. "*I* got custody. Not you."

"Helbrans, he promises me on the phone I'll bring to him backdated papers from Israel, he'll pay $50,000 . . ."

"What?" Hana screams.

"Fifty thousand dollars?" Jacky shrieks, jolted and recharged. He smells opportunity.

"I thought I'll trick him. He'll bring me Shai . . . I'll take the money . . . I'll call the police . . . I'll . . ."

They nod, they understand, they follow his reasoning. They are Israelis, honed to be shrewd bargainers.

"Instead, he tricked me. He sold me a false bill of goods. He knew already how Hana had custody, not me. He played us off, one against the other. He figured he'll use me to go to you and . . ."

"You see? You see what he does?" Hana jumps in. She wants Michael planted firmly on her side. That he flew from Israel and left his family for Shai shows his sincerity. Never, never would he sell Shai to them. Michael knows how to lie. But on this, she believes every word of his encounter with Helbrans. And she feels sorry for his pain. A father's pain, is it worth less than a mother's? She regards his rumpled shirt and creased face. Whatever bad they had between them, Shai is still *their* child, their flesh and blood. Michael came to get Shai back, she trusts him on this. She sees it in his bloodshot eyes and hunched shoulders.

"Here's what we'll do." Jacky pulls out a notebook. "Read." He hands it to Michael and turns pages, showing him lists of names, addresses, dates, and phone numbers. One page is marked Plan A, another is marked Plan B. "Plenty work we did already. Plenty," he brags. "You'll call him back, Michael. Tell him you succeeded with Hana. Arrange another meeting."

He turns to his wife. "Hana. Tomorrow morning you'll go straight to the police. You'll go with Michael, he'll tell the whole story. The phone call from Jerusalem, the rabbi's offer, everything. Go right away to Captain Plackenmeyer." He shakes a menacing fist, "We'll get that sunofabitch."

Hana's saucer eyes warm up into a hint of a smile. A nervous giggle escapes.

"What?" Michael asks. "It's a joke? Tell me."

"The three of us. Look at us." She sees the comedy of it, the craziness, and she's laughing, hysterical, losing it like at a funeral when you can't hold it back. "Look at us," she's babbling. Jacky, the stepfather, is a stick of dynamite waiting to go off. Michael, the father, first he believes Helbrans, now he doesn't. And me, I'm crazy from it, crazy. "No joke, no joke," she assures Michael, sobering. "Why I'm laughing? Maybe I'm all cried out."

He nods, he understands. Relief. If you don't laugh, you cry. They are Israelis, they know.

"It's late, Michael, you'll sleep on the sofa?" she asks.

"Of course," Jacky snaps back. "Tomorrow, we'll see what's what." Despite his exhaustion, Michael feels exhilarated. Maybe even a little heroic. "See? I brought my own pillow." He tosses his nylon duffel on the sofa.

# 16. PLACKENMEYER'S PLAN

Even with his tie loosened and his shirt sleeves rolled back, Captain Plackenmeyer is not a man to be taken lightly. He has an authority men respect and women find sexy.

"He promised you $50,000?" he asks Michael, jotting it down without comment.

"Yes. Yes." Michael is emphatic.

He is scribbling notes as Michael and Hana tell the story. Also running a tape recorder, but he still likes to take notes. It's the early training from the academy, you never shake it off. If he was nervous, if he avoided eye contact, if he was fidgeting, you write it down so when you play it back, you remember every detail.

Hana watches the two men, her eyes darting from Michael back to the police captain. He doesn't say a lot, but she can feel his concentration. And when she chimes in to add a remark, he listens with equal attention. Women are not invisible pieces of dust to him; he takes them seriously.

The station house looks exactly as she remembers it. Noisy, messy, busy. Phones ringing, cops in uniform slouched over their desks staring into computers or yapping to each other, their styrofoam coffee cups abandoned everywhere, on desks, file cabinets, even used as paperweights. The noise level is enough to give you a headache. But in Captain Plackenmeyer's private office, like the principal's office in Eric Smith Middle School, it is quiet.

As soon as they arrived, he closed the door against the bedlam outside. "Come in, Mrs. Fhima," he said politely and pulled up two chairs, then took the one behind his desk.

"It's Shai's father," she said introducing Michael, her eyes shy and downcast. "He flies from Israel, he wants to help us."

Michael extended his hand, "Michael Reuven," then claimed a chair.

Today, the morning sun is brilliant in Brooklyn. May has brought a thickening of green to the trees and a ribbon of warm sunshine dances across Captain Plackenmeyer back wall, lighting him up like kleig bulbs and putting him in center stage.

"Would you like coffee?" he asks like a host at a party. "Just made a fresh pot."

"No thanks," they say in unison, their voices tight with tension, ready to pounce. Plenty to tell him. What happened with Helbrans at the airport. At the yeshiva. The bribe. The custody papers. Michael's story will bring immediate police action.

Hana clings to her faith in the system. America is law and order, criminals get punished. It's the constitution. America is every immigrant's dream of a better life. Though it started out bad for her, already it's changing and it can still happen good. Plackenmeyer will find Shai. Especially now they got the goods on Helbrans. What Americans call *a break*.

She runs her tongue across her bottom lip and pulls her chair up a bit closer to his desk.

"Captain Plackenmeyer," she begins, grasping her hands. "Michael got plenty to tell you, what happened yesterday with Helbrans." She is rosy, wearing pretty pink beads around her throat and a modest smile. Her long brown hair is silky with a glint of red, though her eyes still carry worry.

Michael unfolds the story. Clearly, in chronological order, he tells it from his first phone call to Helbrans's parents in Israel to his arrival at JFK airport. Not once does the police captain interrupt, though Michael talks nonstop. No questions? Michael's pauses elicit none, so he continues.

"I arrive JFK. No Shai. No Helbrans. I look. I walk around. I wait. Three hasids come up to me. They take me away in a car to his yeshiva."

The police captain writes, looks up, writes, looks up.

"Did you get their names?" His first question in almost five minutes.

"No. What happens is like this. Helbrans..." he pauses, ashamed he was such a fool, "in the yeshiva he tells me how Hana and Jacky are child abusers. And Shai, he only rescued him, they were beating him."

"Uh huh." He observes the father. He seems genuinely stricken, sincere, not like the big mouth stepfather, a loose canon if ever he saw one. He reminds himself that Israelis are blunt, they don't beat around the bush. Even the liaison, Rabbi Freidlich, gets right to it. It's their way. Which is okay with him, he hates pussyfooting. Saves time.

He pays attention to every comment and every inflection in Reuven's voice. A shrug, a grimace, everything is useful. You watch, you wait. It's like fishing: you wait for the tug on the line. Pull in too soon and you lose your catch.

"Now comes the important part." Michael adjusts his position and sits up taller. "I hand him the phony papers I fixed from Israel like he wanted. But he knows already how Hana got custody, not me. I say we got joint custody. He says I gotta go to Hana and make her sign off. Then he'll pay me."

The two of them stare at Captain Plackenmeyer, holding their breath. "Understand? Helbrans wants to buy Shai for $50,000." This is proof. The break they needed.

Silence.

The captain puts down his pen. He sighs. "Let me check my facts, sir." He flips his pad back a few pages and rereads his notes. "You flew from Tel Aviv to JKF on El Al." He looks up. "Just want to verify the time sequence." His eyes back on his notes. "After you made a telephone call to Helbrans's parents in Israel, you phoned Rabbi Helbrans in Brooklyn. This was two days ago. And based on that conversation, you flew here. Correct?"

"Yes."

"During your first telephone conversation with the rabbi from Israel, he made the offer to pay you $50,000 for backdated custody papers. Correct?"

"Yes."

"And he promised to deliver Shai to the airport when you turned over those papers to him. Correct?"

"Yes."

"At JFK, he didn't show up or produce your son. Instead three men met you and drove you to his home. Correct?"

"Yes."

"And in his home, his yeshiva, he still didn't produce the boy. That was yesterday. And again, he restated the offer. To pay you for custody papers assigned to him. Correct?" Each time he asks *correct?,* he looks Michael squarely in the eye.

"Yes."

The police captain folds his arms across his chest. Ya gotta pose the same questions to see if you get the same answers. Sometimes it trips them up. You get different answers or weird comments. Not this time. Reuven's answers are precise. "Tell me, sir, were there witnesses present?"

"No."

"No one else heard the rabbi make this offer to you?" His eyes scowl.

"No."

"No one can confirm these facts?"

"No. We were alone, sitting alone in the living room, the two of us alone." Michael's voice is becoming shaky, defensive. He glances at Hana, her rosy glow is fading. Is the evidence evaporating?

"Without a witness, it's your word against his. He'll deny it."

"Captain Plackenmeyer." Hana's face crumbles. "It's the truth, Michael don't lie. It's true, it's true."

"I'm sorry. The rabbi will deny it. Without a witness . . ." he turns up his palms.

"A witness? A witness we can't get," Michael protests. "He's too clever. Even if I go back, he'll . . ."

*But Michael knows a way.* And from the look on Plackenmeyer's face, *he* knows the way, too. But neither one speaks.

Only Hana is in the dark. She stares at Plackenmeyer, crest-fallen. At Michael. Back to Plackenmeyer. Her disappointment makes him look away. With men, he can be tough as nails. But it's the women, beat up and cut up, that get to him. Compassion is not exactly a prerequisite to be a police officer. But he never could get it out of his system. How women get the shit end.

Michael inhales. Exhales. He reaches over and touches Hana's shoulder. Maybe what he feels is all wrong, he has a new family now, a wife and two kids to take care of. But me and Hana, we are Shai's parents. Wherever Shai is, we're always his parents. We have an obligation to do right by him.

Michael knows the way. *Wear a wire.* Plackenmeyer knows it, too; why doesn't he say it?

"You don't want to bother with us?" Hana whines, laying it on the police captain. She is very good at *poor me*. She knows how to play victim. She can don it like a silk glove.

"Mrs. Fhima." He speaks as the overall head of the case. "As far as I'm concerned, it's not an alleged kidnapping. Your son has definitely been kidnapped. We've been working on it since he was reported missing on April 6 and we'll continue to do our best."

"So why you don't arrest him? Michael don't lie." She brushes a tear away.

"We need evidence." He pauses. "And we'll get it," he says with such conviction, Michael knows what's coming.

"Here's what I want you to do, Mr. Reuven."

"Michael. Call me Michael. Tell me."

He nods. "Michael. Go back to the rabbi. Only this time, *we'll wire you.*"

Michael grins. "Yes sir, Captain." If he could jump up, he would click his heels and salute.

"Call me Bill."

Michael nods. "What you want me to do, Bill?" He is eager for instructions.

"Okay. Here's what you do. Go back in there with a hidden tape. We'll be getting every word. Your job is to get him to make the offer again, to repeat what he said on the tape. Understand?"

"Oh, good, good." It is Hana chirping in, full of excitement. Her face is rosy again and she is fingering her pink beads like a rosary. Her eyes are shining. "Yes, Michael, you can do this," she cheers him on. "You'll do it good."

Joyfully, their heads swivel to Plackenmeyer.

"What he should do, Captain Plackenmeyer?" She wants to move it along, she wants Michael to listen to his instructions. *This is the break.*

He turns to Michael. "Call the rabbi back. Say you want to talk to him again. Be polite. Very polite. Suggest that you had a successful meeting with Hana—may I call you Hana?"

She nods. She blushes.

"We'll set it up, have you wired. We'll be outside, staked out nearby. Ask to see your son. Ask for proof, say you need proof he's there and he's safe before you hand over the papers. Restate the financial arrangement. Make sure he says he'll pay you the money. We need the offer on tape. Understand?"

"Yes. Perfect, I understand perfect."

"My officers will be waiting for a signal from you that Shai's inside."

Hana is half off her chair. "If Shai is inside, you'll get him out?" She wants to be clear on this. "You'll get him out from the rabbi?"

He nods. "If he's in there, we'll get him."

"Thank you, thank you," she gushes. Is it possible tomorrow or the next day I'll have Shai back? *Please God. Please.*

"So Bill? You want to rehearse me?" Michael jokes. He is raring to go. He's been wired before, he knows exactly how to proceed. This time, he'll do it right.

"Please," Hana jumps in. "You'll rehearse him, Bill, he'll know exactly how you want him. Please."

"Of course," Plackenmeyer agrees. "Can't afford to mess up."

Michael stands up. He's all fired up. If he could go back to the yeshiva this minute, he'd run all the way. "How you want me to signal?"

Bill Plackenmeyer feels their surge of energy. Good. He pushes his chair back and stands up. What he has to do next is map out the details. Preparation is everything. The father will get only one chance. Better not blow it.

He flips his notebook closed and presses stop, reminding himself to make a dupe of the tape. If the wire works, he could break the case wide open and return the boy to his mother. A helluva feather in his cap. A whole goddamn headful of feathers. If Michael can get it all on tape, we got one fucking airtight case.

"Let's take a break." He rakes his hair back with his fingers. Gotta make calls. Set it up. Reserve the stake out van. Rehearse the signal. Assign the police officers. No slip ups. "Okay?"

"You want we should wait outside?" Hana asks compliantly. "You want we should come back later?" Her eyes are brimming with hope. Finally comes a break.

The whole nightmare could be over tomorrow, the next day. Shai will be back home. The kids will be crazy to see him. *Please God. Please.*

# 17. THE STAKEOUT

"**H**ow are you, rabbi?" Michael inquires cordially, keenly aware that he's wired. Sure, he's done it before. But this is different. It's for Shai.

Though it weighs next to nothing, a couple of ounces, he can feel the transmitter in the small of his back and the athletic tape on his skin. He's glad the NYPD rejected using a pager clipped to his belt. True, people are used to seeing them, but the rabbi might get suspicious. The microphone, no bigger than a thumbtack, is hidden in his phony shirt button. Light. Invisible. But it's a heavy presence to be a party to a stakeout.

A dozen cops are outside waiting in a parked van, with Bill Plackenmeyer in command. The large utility vehicle carries a magnetic sign MAINTENANCE—for another stakeout they change the sign to CONSTRUCTION. Very clever, everything under control. Headphones on, tape recorder rolling. Waiting for his signal.

It's all up to him. He can feel his scalp tightening.

Mrs. Helbrans appears with a tray. She sets it down, tea and cookies, and disappears, a silent waitress. Men in conversation you don't interrupt.

With his pulses racing, Michael smiles pleasantly at the rabbi. On the outside, he plays out a host-guest scenario. On the inside, his mind is sharp, pumped with adrenaline and tethered to the two tasks he has to accomplish.

Bill has gone over each one. "*First*: you gotta get Helbrans to repeat the $50,000 offer. Make sure it's clear he's paying for the boy's custody. Get it on tape. *Second*: you gotta give us a signal if Shai's there. If he's in there, say *I'm getting a headache*. That's the signal, okay?"

"And you'll bust in and get him out?"

"We get your signal, we go right in." He is decisive.

*I'm getting a headache.* He practices those four words. Recited them over the sink shaving this morning. *I'm getting a headache.* And now he actually has one. A blazing headache. It is hammering against his temples and something like a fork is jabbing him in the chest.

Sitting in the living room chair, facing the beefy rabbi who has sunk into the sofa, he is on overdrive. Bill's instructions in his head. *Be friendly and agreeable. Make him think you're on his side.*

He begins.

"Let me tell you, rabbi, you were absolutely right about Hana, absolutely right."

"Yes?" Helbrans is pleased, his curiosity aroused. He adjusts his thick glasses. "So what happened, Michael?"

"The way they live, terrible, terrible." He shakes his head frowning with disapproval. "What you told me, every word what you said, I couldn't believe my eyes."

"You saw it? You saw like I said?" Satisfaction creeps across his mouth and he scratches his dark beard. "Poor Shai, poor Shai, such a good boy, he told us everything."

They are stroking each other. No one getting down to business, not yet. First, you schmoose.

"You were so right," Michael repeats, establishing they are on the same side.

This done, a cat and mouse game begins. Feeling, testing to see how much weight each will bear. How far to go? Which words are safe?

Michael has done this before; bugs, tapes, and cameras are not foreign to him. Also, you spend time in the army, you get wise. But never have the stakes been this high. He is playing a game for the life of his son. If he blows it with that sunovabitch kidnapper, he could lose Shai forever.

Contemplating the rabbi who sits only a few feet away, he

measures the duplicity of the man. Under his innocent rabbinic grin lies a clever criminal who thinks he is above the law. A slippery snake he has to handle delicately.

*Best case* scenario is he produces Shai, I give the signal, and an explosion of NYPD cops are all over him. *Worst case* scenario . . . no, no don't even contemplate failure. The loss, the shame. How could he face Hana? How could he live with himself? Years later, what could he tell his son?

He reaches for a cookie. The rabbi will try to out-con. But the game must go on.

"Rabbi, I made for you very special arrangements. It was difficult what you wanted. But I'm happy to tell you everything will work out good, very good."

"So tell me, Michael." He says Michael a lot. He is relaxed. Overfriendly. Like Mordecai Weiss, too congenial.

"What I found out is to get from Hana custody, this is not going to help us."

"No?" He sits up a little straighter, alert to danger. "She don't sign? It was Jacky, he told her no. What?" He wants more information.

"It will be fine. But we have to do different."

Helbrans squints through his thick glasses. "Different?"

"We want everything should be legal for us. Yes?" *We. Us.* Say it over and over, show we're working together against Hana. She is the enemy.

The rabbi ponders this, but makes no comment.

"Hana, she's no good. From her we'll get only trouble even if she signs."

"You think so, Michael?"

"You can't deal with this woman. She's a liar, I don't trust her."

"She's a d-d-devil. A wife, she don't live with her husband. A mother, she don't let her children be religious. They eat treyf. On shabbos, she sends them to a mall shopping."

"I saw this, it's true, every word you say. She's no good."

Michael repeats the tiresome observation, shaking his head in disgust.

"The husband, he beats the wife. The mother, she beats Shai every day, he told us."

"That's my point, rabbi. Exactly what you say. You can't trust her, she's a devil." Michael has the lead now.

"So? You got a plan, Michael?"

He draws himself up. "What we got to do is this, rabbi. I made already arrangements."

"W-w-what arrangements?" His fat fingers are rubbing his thigh.

"I'll take Shai back with me to an Israeli court . . ."

"An Israeli court?" he interrupts, his eyes grow suspicious. "No, no, no."

"Only from an Israeli court can we get proper custody papers. Shai, he was born in Israel, he is Israeli. They have complete jurisdiction over him, we can't do it here. This custody paper for you got to be perfect, rabbi. Then you can raise Shai here in the yeshiva like you want." His face hurts from smiling.

"You think so?" He sounds uncertain.

"Absolutely. I can do this for you. And as long as my boy is happy, I'm happy." How long this will go on? He's getting tired.

Silence.

They stare at each other. Each waits for the other to make the next move.

You can't trick me, the rabbi's eyes say, don't try. But his smile remains cordial. "So, Michael? How you want to do?"

It is his cue to restate the offer. "What I'll do," he says distinctly for the tape, "is what you told me. Exactly how you want to make it." He speaks up a little louder. "I'll deliver you Shai's custody papers from Israel and you'll give me $50,000. This is our agreement. Yes?" His heart thumps.

Thuh-thump. Thuh-thump.

The rabbi nods his consent.

Sweat rolls down his armpits. What good is a nod? How the hell can he get it on tape?

"Also . . ." he continues, "I'll come every year, I'll visit Shai. And you'll pay my expenses. This is also agreed. Yes?"

"Yes, yes, yes." A brief irritation. "But the custody—why it has to be from Israel?"

It goes back and forth, an expenditure of energy that exhausts Michael. But he got it on tape. The offer. The money part. Custody. The annual visit. Everything. *All on tape.*

He takes a breath. Half way there.

Now comes the second part. Is Shai here? Upstairs? Downstairs? Where are they hiding him? He girds himself. This part is the most delicate.

"Rabbi?" He leans forward, sadness in his posture.

"What, Michael?"

"I want to see my son. Can I see him now?"

The rabbi pulls himself up heavily out of the sofa and lumbers forward a few steps. "Don't worry, Michael. We take g-g-good care of Shai."

Michael stands up. "I know this, rabbi. You rescued him, thank God, but . . ." he bows his head, a forlorn father. "I don't see him so long . . . years, years. Let me see him now. Please."

Helbrans's bulk reminds him of the difficult task ahead. This fat man with the fat fingers is in his face. How to get Shai away from him? He imagines him with a bloody apron around his belly instead of the fringed tallis. He sees a butcher, not a rabbi. He could strangle him.

He begins to shake. Maybe he can't do it. Too hard.

How long can a secular Jew from the Israeli army keep pretending to hold hands with a hasid? His hands refuse to pick up a gun to defend Israel. Or work a plough to till a field. Just sits on his fat ass all day studying Torah. His wife and kids waiting on him hand and foot because he talks to God.

We are Jews, yes. Connected by history and destiny. The

Mosaic laws, the prophets and the Songs of David. But who is Helbrans to steal my son's soul? Who is he? I want Shai now, his heart cries. Seeing his hands shaking, he clasps them behind him.

*Stop. Stop. You gotta do it. They're outside waiting.*

Do like Bill said. Make a bridge.

You are the father. He is the kidnapper. Gotta hold hands.

He swallows his disgust. *For Shai's sake. For your son.* Steady yourself. Smile. "So tell me, rabbi, can I see my son now?"

"A good boy. He studies hard. He could be for us a zaddik."

"A zaddik? Really?" He pretends to be impressed.

"He wants to be religious. She sends him to public school for Christians." He shakes his head. "So he ran away from them."

"I know this, I know." He nods, clucking his tongue to show his horror. "And with you, he's happy? My boy is happy?"

It's getting harder to maintain this insipid conversation— where else can it go? The rabbi is dodging every punch.

*Just keep talking*, Bill told him in the station house. When *things get tough, just keep talking. The more we get on the tape, the better. Schmoose him*, advised the police captain, winking to show off his Brooklynese.

"With us, Shai made friends. When he studied for bar mitzvah, he liked the boys. We got here a lot of Israeli boys."

Michael clears his throat. Enough bullshit. He has to pee. He's tired. He can't keep it up.

"Rabbi." He speaks respectfully. "You promised you'll bring me Shai to the airport." His knees begin to buckle.

Silence. Stares.

"You promised on the phone how if I'll bring you custody papers backdated, you'll deliver me Shai." Still polite and avoiding accusation, but his voice is shaking with honest emotion. "Please. Let me see my son. I want to see my son." He is close to tears.

"Don't worry, Michael."

"I want to see him, years I don't see him. I want to see he's okay, he's. . . . Please, rabbi," he begs. His whole body is trembling. He's an emotional man, this is his trouble.

The rabbi has the upper hand. He makes a dismissive gesture with his head. "Don't worry, Michael, don't worry."

"Please. I want to see him." He feels dizzy, overheated; there is not enough air in the room to breathe.

"Michael." He lays a heavy hand on his arm. "First, we will pray. Come," he gestures. "Come with me, Michael, come downstairs to the yeshiva."

Shit! The fucker plays rough.

He follows him.

In a small room with no sunlight, the rabbi takes a tallis and yarmulke from a bench and holds them out to him. Michael puts them on. He steps up and stands beside the rabbi. And together they daven. They pray. They rock. They chant.

They go through a series of morning prayers in Hebrew.

*Hear, O Israel: The Lord our God, the Lord is One.*

*Praised be His name, whose glorious kingdom is for ever and ever.*

*Thou shalt love the Lord thy God, with all thy heart, with all thy soul, and with all thy might.*

In a religious frenzy that goes on and on and on, in an ecstasy of outpouring, in a flood of fervent prayers, Rabbi Helbrans directs Michael toward God's will. Captivated, drawn into the swell of it, the power of the chanting, like a great symphony orchestra, transports him to another world. He is locked into it, his mind is not in his body.

*I will lift up my voice unto God, and cry;*

*I will lift up my voice unto God, that He may give ear unto me.*

*In the day of my trouble I seek the Lord:*

*With my hand uplifted, mine eye streameth in the night without ceasing;*

*My soul refuseth to be comforted.*

*When I think thereon, O God, I must moan.*

There is no let-up.

✡   ✡   ✡

It is the tea that saves him. The pressure of a full bladder, the physical need to relieve himself that returns him to the room. He can't take it any more.

"Excuse me, rabbi," he says softly at a pause. "I need to use the bathroom."

The rabbi does not see this as disrespect, he understands.

He holds up a finger, warning Michael they must conclude properly.

Then together, the two ascend the steps.

Thump. Thump. Thump.

Outside in the van, something has gone wrong. The recorder is rolling, but all they're getting is static and *glub glub.*

"Shit, we lost him," snaps the officer monitoring the recording device.

"What?" Plackenmeyer scrambles over two cops crouched in the rear. "What happened?" he demands.

"No signal, we lost him."

Silence. Every officer leans in, listening, alert.

Plackenmeyer hunches over his shoulder, watches him fiddling with adjustments. "Keep trying."

He works on it. "Nope. Nothing."

"Keep trying."

Another shot at it. "Nothing." He turns to the captain. "Wanna go in?"

"KEEP TRYING."

All eyes fasten on him. He's responsible for Michael's safety. If they found the wire and ripped it off, if they harm him, it's his ass. But if he busts in and blows it . . .

Time is ticking away . . . Bust in? Or hold off?

*Glub. Glub.* A sputter of static. *A flushing sound.*

"A toilet!" an officer shouts, all smiles. "Got him back."

Plackenmeyer is grinning all over. Michael's taking a leak.

✡   ✡   ✡

Alone in the bathroom, the door closed, Michael relieves himself. Peeing, he drops his chin, aiming his mouth at his shirt button, flushing the toilet to muffle his voice.

"I can't take it no more," he cries to the invisible cops in the van. "I gotta get outa here . . . I don't see Shai . . . I don't know where he is . . . I don't know what to do . . . I can't take it."

Outfoxed, Michael weeps into his shirt button.

# 18.  JACKY

*A*nyone with information, call the police.
*Please call NYPD.*
*In New Jersey, call the Ramsey Police.*

The numbers are all out there in the press. Coverage by the *New York Times,* the *Record, New York Newsday,* the *New York Post,* the *Daily News,* the *Jewish Standard.*

Hana becomes a media figure. She gives interviews and poses for photographs. In America, publicity is the way to get action. She establishes a Shai Fhima Committee, urging people with any information to call yet another number. Or to call the 66th precinct at the number printed on the bottom of Shai's poster.

"Make our family whole," she pleads in one teary-eyed newspaper photo.

She poses with her children and the caption identifies them as *Osheri, Eliran, and Shiran.* She poses with Jacky, eyes downcast. What else can she do?

Because, *astonishingly,* the tape Michael made of Helbrans, the tape recorded in the van by the great and powerful NYPD . . . what happened from it? Nothing.

Larry is livid. Almost daily, he roars into Steve's office to vent his frustration.

"It's like banging your head against a brick wall. I'm on the phone every day to the D.A.'s office. I can't get a decent answer. If they call me back, it's like who the hell is this New Jersey attorney? Go away, kid, you're bothering me."

"And the tape?" Steve asks

Larry scowls. "The tape? The tape?" Every day he's arguing with the D.A.'s office. Talking to Plackenmeyer. To Rabbi Weinberg who's trying to galvanize the Jewish community. Screaming through the thin walls. Every day, making calls to the NYPD, the Ramsey Police, the U.S. Attorney's Office, Hynes's office. Reporting back to Hana and Michael. Trying to make anyone blink. "Hynes refuses to act." His brows knit. "What I can't figure out is . . ."

"What?"

"How to circumvent him? How to get the investigation under way . . ."

"You got the tape. That's your evidence."

"The tape? It's taking them forever to even transcribe it. It's clear to me the D.A.'s office wants to shove it under the rug. They don't give a damn if Shai is ever found, if Hana ever gets him back."

"Of course," Steve nods. "Different agendas. Hynes won't antagonize the hasidic community, he's running for attorney general. That's *his* agenda."

"Yeah, yeah, yeah." Larry ambles out of Steve's office, shaking his head in disgust. You work your ass off behind the scenes. You get the press involved. The FBI. The U.S. Attorney's office. Hana's even enlisting other lawyers willing to work for her pro bono. She's a high-profile client now and she evokes sympathy. For a lawyer with a taste for media attention, a kidnapping offers lots of good publicity.

"Why don't the D.A. arrest Helbrans?" she wails to Captain Plackenmeyer in his office. "Why it don't do no good? Michael, he got the tape, he made you the evidence. Why don't Hynes arrest him?"

In less gentle terms, Jacky echoes the same complaint. "What the fuck's going on? Hynes is kissing ass for votes."

Michael cries. Jacky curses. Hana moans.

But the tape, and everything Michael went through to get it, doesn't bring them a step closer.

Frustrated and demoralized, they are a sorry triumvirate. The police tape does nothing to force the D.A. to indict the rabbi. Shai is gone. The rabbi goes about his business. Even Captain Plackenmeyer seems stumped. Though he calls in the feds, nothing moves. It drags on and on.

"I'll stay till we find him," Michael tells Lilit on the phone. "We don't give up. We do something else."

"How long?" she asks.

"Till I get Shai back."

An uneasy silence.

"Me and Jacky, we'll find him. We got our ways."

"Michael," her voice grows throaty. "Be careful."

"Don't worry. It won't take long," he says.

"Okay, okay. Call me what's going on."

Michael and Jacky become an unlikely twosome. The husband and the ex-husband. The father and the stepfather. Can they do what the NYPD *can't* do? What the D.A. *won't* do? Can they join forces and *make* the D.A. run a real investigation? Force Hynes to indict Helbrans? To find Shai?

They have tried the normal channels. Gone to the proper authorities. They have waited on benches, filed papers, answered questions. Gone the legal route. Done everything strictly kosher and by the book. What good comes from this? *Nothing.*

They have gone to the media and pleaded with the public to come forward with information. They have provided telephone numbers. Someone, somewhere has to know something. Someone is hiding Shai. Does it do any good? *Nothing.*

Hana has nagged and begged and wept. Started a Shai Fhima Committee. Acted within the law. What good comes from this? *Nothing.*

"What can we do?" she implores Captain Plackenmeyer. "Over and over, the same garbage answer: insufficient evidence."

Jacky stares belligerently across the desk.

The police captain takes in the mother's frustration. It's pitiful, he'd like to help her. He has called in the FBI and has asked federal prosecutors to look into the case. "We're not giving up. We'll continue our search."

"What can you do?" Hana's wet puppy dog eyes fill up.

"It's not hopeless," he tells them. "We're doing our best."

Jacky glowers at him.

On the way out as they walk down the hall, he sums it up. "He's fulla shit."

Jacky and Michael take matters into their own hands. They hide behind dumpsters. They wait, slouched down, in parked cars, hoping to catch a glimpse of Shai. But the streets of Boro Park are closed tight against outsiders. You see only what they let you see. Not a clue emerges.

In despair one evening, Hana pushes her coffee mug aside and lays her head down on her arms on the kitchen table. "They don't do nothing," she sniffles. "I'll never see Shai again. Never." She cries louder, letting it all out, wailing, "I want my son back, I want Shai."

"Shut up." Jacky bolts off his chair. He grabs a fistful of hair and yanks her head back. He's sick of it. That mournful face she gives him morning and night. Always Shai, Shai, Shai.

"Don't . . . no, Jacky . . . please," she begs, tasting fear. He's gonna explode. Maybe he'll kill her. She knows that look, it carries him over the edge. The mad glint in his eyes flashing like a switchblade. Nothing to stop him. He's small and wiry, strong as steel.

"Shut up. Shut up." He jerks her head back further, out of control, his other self taking over.

She blinks. Signals *okay, okay, whatever you say.* Neck snapping with pain. Hands balled up. *Whatever you want, whatever you say. Don't hit me. Please.*

"Shut up. Shut up about Shai."

He jerks her head back harder, further, tighter, tearing her throat out. "Fuck the police. I'll do it my way. Shut up!"

Another fierce yank and miraculously he lets go.

Her head bobs forward, relief flooding through her. The wrenched neck and pounding ears tell her she's alive. It could be worse.

What's he gonna do about Shai? His methods won't be gentle. Some of his four years in the Israeli army he was in trouble—and not for parking tickets.

Stay out of his way. Don't talk about Shai. Not a word. Not a tear.

He glares at her rubbing the back of her neck, her throat.

She rises softly off her chair and slinks off.

He swings around. A warning finger in the air. "You! Shut your mouth. Me and Michael, we'll take care of it. Shut your mouth. Or I'll shut it for you."

Her back is to him. She is rinsing off her mug at the sink. She lets the warm water run over her wrists. Don't answer. Don't say a word.


In bed, she rolls away from him. He's done with her and that's okay.

Jacky. Michael. Two husbands. Four children.

With Michael was another story. Two kids, what did they know about life? She was seventeen when Shai was born. What does seventeen know? But thirty should be smarter.

She would divorce him, but she's afraid. Jacky is a violent man. You never know how far he'll go. She has to get away from him. Not yet. Not now.

Like the women she met in the shelter, she makes excuses for him. But inside her head, a plan is forming. She will divorce him at the right time. Not now. Now, she needs him. For the children. For the money. She couldn't make it alone. What she'll do, she'll use Jacky to find Shai. Jacky and Michael and Plackenmeyer. Till I get on my feet, I need them. They think I'm pathetic, maybe even stupid. Let them. I'm their poor stray cat. Like Shiran's cat posters tacked on the bedroom wall.

She turns on her side, away from Jacky.

His steady breathing tells her he's asleep. Good. When he's asleep, she's out of danger.

It's crazy. Sometimes she loves Jacky. Look how hard he's trying to find Shai.

Maybe it's my fault he gets mad at me. I cry too much, I get on his nerves.

So shut up like he says. SHUT UP.

Jacky and Michael together, maybe they'll find Shai.

Once I have him back, it will be another story.

Carefully, not to disturb Jacky, she tugs a small corner of the blanket across her shoulders.

God is watching. He sees everything.

God is taking care of Shai. He should be safe.

# 19. A SEVERED FINGER

I t is Wednesday night. May 14. A week of fruitless searching. Not a clue. Not a sign of Shai. Jacky and Michael have gone into hasidic neighborhoods every night. They hide, they stalk, they wait. Nothing.

Hana is preparing a roast chicken dinner and listening to the men arguing strategy. The kids are watching a cartoon channel and their giggles fill the air. She enjoys cooking, it is a kind of therapy to peel and chop and slice. But Jacky is complaining about his meals, this is too salty and that is too bland. To avoid a confrontation, she nods, buttoning her lip. Her job is to please him, he's working hard for Shai.

"They got him in Lev Tahor. Face it," Jacky snaps at Michael. "He's inside with the rabbi. Right under our nose." He's edgy, chafing at the bit. Enough waiting around shit.

"Maybe you're right." Michael is tired and dispirited. Lilit is asking when he is coming home.

"Tonight we go in there. We get him out."

Tonight? Break in? "He wasn't there when I made the tape." Let Jacky convince him.

"Because they took him away. But they brought him back, he's there. They moved him around, families were hiding him. But he's back there in the yeshiva."

"You think so?" Hana chirps in, drying her hands.

Jacky ignores her. "We go in tonight." He is gleeful, a manic counterpart to Michael's brooding.

It is 11:30. A dark night. No moonlight, no stars. People asleep in their beds. Unguarded. Defenseless.

Jacky, Michael, and two other men park on a street not far

from the yeshiva. Jacky has selected the stakeout location. A house occupied by some of Helbrans's students. He's seen them going in and out.

He turns off the ignition. Douses the lights. "We'll wait here. Who knows? Maybe they got him with the others, here inside. Either this house or the yeshiva."

Michael peers at the building. "They sleep here, the yeshiva boys? Like a dormitory?"

Jacky shrugs. "They could easy be hiding him inside. Twenty, thirty boys come and go. In and out. Who would notice another one dressed like them? Who pays attention?"

He's right, Michael thinks, his eyes glued to the front door. Only a small light comes from one window. No one moving. No shadows.

They wait. Will Shai come out or go in?

Midnight passes.

"Look," Jacky hisses.

A figure steps out of the front door. A young hasid. He approaches the car. Bends. Peers in. "What you want here?" he demands.

"Want do we want?" Jacky jeers back at him. He lowers his window and cocks his head out. "Who the hell are you?"

"What you want here? What you want?" He takes in the four men. "Get outa here."

They are face to face, inches apart. "Go to hell," Jacky taunts him.

Out of the darkness of the night, a flash of knife. A blade plunging through the open window, slashing at his throat. His hands fly up for a shield. The blade stabs and slices at his hands. Blood spurting out, running down his arm. Two fingers dangling. Pinky chopped off. Searing pain. A hunk of bloody flesh in his lap. His hand hacked into raw meat.

The press pounces on it.

Up to now, what did they have? A standoff situation. Court

orders. Papers filed. Statements. Issues to kick around. Political. Religious. Philosophical. A battle for a boy's soul. Too cerebral, where's the juice? A kidnapping story is fine to a point, then readers lose interest.

But now, the bloody attack against the stepfather heats the story up, whetting the public taste for spectacle. Attempted murder, a bloody knife, a severed finger—the tabloids love it.

From his hospital bed, Jacky conducts interviews. He is a star. "See?" He holds up a hand swathed in bandages. "Two of my fingers he cut off and they got reattached. But my pinky, even my wonderful doctors they couldn't save it, it's half gone." He shows them bandages over what must be the stump of a finger. "See? He tried to kill me."

The photographers snap and snap. A good looking man, a devoted stepfather. Went all out for his stepson.

Dismissed from the hospital, Jacky poses again in a crisp striped shirt and tie, the fingers of his right hand splayed for the cameras, his pinky ugly and deformed.

"The doctors, they can do nothing. See what he did?" His right hand mangled to a paw.

He tells the reporters he got laid off from his superintendent job. "How I can work with such a hand?" He shakes his head sadly. "Crazy people."

Accusations are traded by each side. It appears that Joseph Cohen, twenty-two—a bodyguard or a yeshiva student? it's not clear—is the man who stabbed Jacky.

But Rabbi Helbrans, asked to comment, replies that it was Jacky Fhima who tried to kill Joseph Cohen. The young man was attacked by Jacky and his men when he walked up to the car. They were planning to abduct him and Fhima was cut with his own knife.

The court accepts Jacky's version. Cohen will face first-degree assault, attempted murder, and other charges.

✡  ✡  ✡

In June, the U.S. Attorney in Brooklyn, Andrew J. Maloney, and the FBI begin a new concerted effort toward investigating Shai's disappearance.

"There is evidence that the child has been kidnapped and that individuals associated with the rabbi may know where he is," one official, close to the inquiry, tells a reporter.

Cohen's attack on Jacky has heated up the story of the mysterious disappearance of the bar mitzvah boy.

Hana and Jacky and Michael view this as a victory.

"We will continue to search for Shai," Hana tells reporters. "Me and my husband don't get scared. I won't stop looking for my son, *even if they try to kill me.*"

The hasidic community of Boro Park lays low. No one will talk. They shun publicity. Problems? They deal with them in private, their own way.

Asked if they are searching for the boy, they seem reluctant to respond. No one can get a clear picture.

"We basically are an insular community, not trying to reach out," explains Rabbi David Niederman to a persistent *New York Times* reporter. "If the boy were lost, that would be one thing. This is a more sophisticated incident. And generally I think this is the kind of thing we leave to the professional people, the police and other specialized agencies."

With different versions of the Cohen attack still out, Helbrans engages attorney George Meissner to defend Cohen.

"Cohen feels they were going to kidnap him so they could make a prisoner exchange," Meissner tells the press.

"A prisoner exchange?" Michael roars.

Despite the hasidic versions floating around, one thing has come out of the bloody attack on Jacky. An unwelcome spotlight has been cast on Brooklyn's insular hasidic community. Some papers describe Helbrans and his yeshiva as a small obscure group that left Israel because of continued pressure from the police. Some call Helbrans a loose cannon, a weirdo, an embarrassment to the Jews. Some worry that the anti-Semites will chew on it and spit out their own version.

"Helbrans is a kidnapper. I don't care what Cohen or Meissner lie. Even the Satmars don't want him." Jacky has spilled blood for Shai. He has earned the right to speak with authority.

"Maybe . . . maybe we need now a criminal lawyer. Someone famous." Hana offers the suggestion timidly. "What you think, Jacky?"

Eyebrows raised, the two men stop talking. Something to consider.

Larry has done the bulk of the work to move it from inertia. Plackenmeyer and the FBI are cooperating. Elaine and Lil and Rabbi Weinberg are providing documentation. And now two violent acts, the assault on Jacky and the kidnapping of Shai, are linked together and tied to Lev Tahor. U.S. prosecutors are investigating. Israeli police are cooperating. With all this backup, maybe a famous lawyer would step in.

New York divorce lawyer Raoul Felder, a man experienced with high profile cases, takes it on pro bono. He tells the press the Satmars are "zealots" and "dangerous people."

Hana is clearing the table in the apartment. "Maybe from bad with your hand, Jacky, will come good." She smiles at him, a rare and radiant smile. "Maybe Hynes will pay attention, we got a chance now." She feels hopeful.

"We'll see," he agrees, pleasantly. He has basked in the publicity of a stepfather's heroic attempt to rescue his stepson. He has been center stage. There is good will between them, an easing of tension. Even a tenderness. Feeling magnanimous, he flicks his head around and yells playfully to the kids. "Who wants Dairy Queen?"

A tumble of voices screech back, "Me. Me. Me." They come running, Shiran tumbling all over her daddy.

"Watch out. Your hand," Hana yells, laughing.

Jacky holds it aloft. His torch. His badge of courage.

# 20. HOMESICK AND DESPONDENT

"Time to go back to my family and my job," Michael tells Hana and Jacky.

Hana nods. His return releases a longing for Israel. For Ema and Aba. For her brother and sister, her family left behind. She remembers Shai trailing after her mother on his shaky toddler legs. She misses them all. Misses the sound of Hebrew names. Shmuel and Sharona. Yitzehak and Aya. The names taste sweet as figs on her tongue. American names shoot out like bullets. Jack and Kate. Tom and Kim.

She misses the soft breezes of Jerusalem. The eating on the run, the restaurants that open and close down in a blink because their owners have more business moxie than cooking skill. Like Jacky with the tile store.

She remembers that little hole in the wall place downtown on Bezalel Street near the Urfali Synagogue. The fun of lining up on the street for pita stuffed with falafel, arguing about which place is better: that little closet they called Falafel Schlomo on Meissaief Street in the Bucharan Quarter or the other one, where was it? And the juicy schwarma, the lamb roasted on a spit and stuffed into pita. In Jerusalem, you don't go hungry even at midnight. You go on Agrippas Street. Anything from skewered shashlick to their version of pizza.

Here in Ramsey—where do you go for a treat at midnight? 7-Eleven. What can you get? She glances at the box of Entenmann's coffee cake on her counter. Soft as a sponge.

Months drag on.

Neither Helbrans nor Weiss are charged with kidnapping. Hynes takes no action.

Hana sinks into depression.

Even if he's found, will he come back? A child brainwashed by a cult, you could lose him forever.

She can't sleep. Her pretty mouth is perpetually turned down. She and Jacky fight about everything and about nothing.

Only Captain Plackenmeyer remains hopeful. When they repaint the walls of the precinct squadroom and all the posters come down, he asks Sergeant Piraino to find an old copy of Shai's poster. "Stick it up there, go on, right there. We gotta keep this case from being shelved."

He reports this to Hana.

"What good it does? We don't go nowhere," she replies glumly.

Rabbi Helbrans sticks to his story: that he has an affection for his former bar mitzvah student and he had nothing to do with his disappearance. The last he heard was the letter from Fed Express in April.

"I hope he writes me many letters," he tells a national magazine. Though he speaks with a slight lisp in broken English and an occasional stutter creeps in, his round face seems harmless. With his horn-rimmed glasses that keep slipping down his nose, he seems an unlikely kidnapper.

Indeed, he claims to be shocked by the stories about him. *Kidnap?* "If somebody comes to us, of course we try to make him close to Judaism. We take him in, we give him food and shelter. But we are not crazy persons."

He rambles, he smiles, he adjusts his glasses. He dismisses reports of his comings and goings published in Israel's paper *Yediot Ahronot*. He hasn't seen *Yishi* since just after his bar mitzvah in February. He laughs softly. Me? I arranged a kidnapping? "The child only wanted to escape an unhealthy family situation. He wanted to lead a religious life. But his mother, she wouldn't let him."

"Lies," Hana tells the press. "Helbrans couldn't get my permission to keep Shai. So he just went ahead and took him." Dazed and demolished, fatigued by lack of sleep, she speaks in a monotone voice.

In interviews, Jacky stands beside her, his arm protectively around her, answering the questions. "We believe Shai is hidden somewhere in Brooklyn. Or maybe in another hasidic community. Even another city. Maybe Canada," he tells reporters.

As 1992 comes to an end, Hana is despondent. She is no closer to finding Shai than last April. She is drowning in their charges and countercharges. Endless stonewalling and vicious accusations.

Sergeant Piraino tries to explain a point to a persistent press. "Look. If you're not part of them, forget it. A lot of them don't consider this a crime."

*Not a crime?* Hana screams, at her wit's end. "Kidnapping is not a crime?"

To make matters worse, Raoul Felder is getting anonymous hate calls.

"Tell the mother," a man's voice threatens, "if she doesn't stop looking for the boy, *we'll kill him*." The phone clicks dead.

He reports this to the police and calls Hana.

"We have to take these calls seriously."

"They can't scare me," she snaps back.

"I don't want to believe they'll kill him."

"They won't do nothing to him." Silence. "What you want? I should stop looking for him?"

"Take them seriously, they're dangerous people."

"I won't stop looking for Shai, I won't stop. *Even if they kill me.*"

PART IV

1993

# 21. SABBATH IN THE SLAMMER

It is a bleak winter morning in February. Eight A.M. on a sunless Friday. In unmarked cars, a team of FBI agents, New York State police and Brooklyn detectives pull up to a small hasidic enclave in Monsey, Rockland County. Their sealed indictment charges Rabbi Schlomo Helbrans and Malka Helbrans with kidnapping. The two are arrested. Handcuffed. Taken away.

"Arrested? In Monsey?" Hana shrieks with joy at Larry's call. "Shai was there?" Her hand tightens around the phone. Almost a year since she saw him. She has torn ten months of agony off the calendar, page by page, month by month.

"No. But now we'll find him."

"Arrested," she babbles, "now we'll get Shai back." The nightmare is over. *Thank you, God.* Her hand slaps at her chest to quiet her heart. What she believed all along, it's true. America is fair, America means justice.

"Call Michael. He's gotta come back to testify, there'll be a grand jury investigation."

Her mind is racing. "I'll call, I'll call." The arrests hit her like a torrential summer storm after an endless drought. The relief is so powerful, she stands there shuddering. "Helbrans was in Monsey?"

"Yup." Larry's voice is sparkling. "They nabbed him in Monsey. The FBI, the state police, and the Brooklyn police."

She whirls around. "Jacky, Jacky, come quick. They arrested Helbrans."

He flies out of the bathroom, shaving cream on his face, razor in his hand. "What?"

She hands him the phone. "It's Larry."

"They arrested Helbrans?" He wants facts.

149

Oh God, dear God, her heart is doing somersaults and her breath is coming so fast she can't think.

Jacky is interrogating Larry. "Shai wasn't there?"

"No, no," she shakes her head to Jacky, answering his question. "But now they'll make Helbrans tell."

"Shhh," he snaps at her, he wants it from Larry.

She calls Bill Plackenmeyer, flooding him with praise.

He is guarded. "Well, I don't want to take too much credit, my men worked on their own time. Besides, we still haven't got the boy back." He's trying to shield her from disappointment.

"But now, we got a chance," she insists. She can feel the wheels of justice spinning. Helbrans has to tell now where Shai is. She feels alive again. The numbness is thawing. The frozen part of her heart is warming up.

SABBATH IN THE SLAMMER screams the *Daily News* with a blowup of Shai's innocent boyish face. Set next to it is the rabbi's dark bearded countenance. The effect is stunning. A sweet young boy caught in the snare of a religious nut? A cult kidnapping?

Reporters lunge for their old copy. Gotta go back. Check facts. Make phone calls. Get quotes. ROGUE RABBI NABBED IN KIDNAPPING OF TEEN shouts a new headline. "He will have to spend the sabbath locked up. He's got the key, if he produces the kid," says an unnamed police source.

Michael flies in from Ben Gurion. Effusively, he gives reporters his version. "This is not a fight between Jews and non-Jews. We are religious, but not orthodox. You would be as upset as we are if someone took your son and said, *That's not the way to raise him.* I don't know who took my son and gave them the right to do this." His dark handsome head hangs down mournfully. "He turned fourteen last Monday."

The triumvirate of Hana, Jacky, and Michael resumes, concentrating on the next step: finding Shai.

Larry adds his input. "It all came to a head because of Bill Plackenmeyer's insistent prodding. The guy leaned on the FBI and the federal prosecutors."

"What happens next?" Hana asks.

"A federal grand jury will convene. The hasidim will be called in to testify."

"How did they know Monsey?" Michael asks.

"The rabbi and his wife skipped out of Brooklyn, left the yeshiva. It set off a police search. Monsey's known for their ultra-orthodox. Yeshivas all over the place. It was the right place to look. He was there with his wife and kids living in an apartment." Larry's voice rises with excitement. "Listen to this. The indictment comes in on *state* rather than federal charges. Smart move. The prosecutors are demanding Helbrans be jailed. They're afraid of risking another flight. There's no turning back now." It's looking good.

The rabbi and his wife are hauled off to Rikers Island. It's their Sabbath, the holiest day of the week.

On Saturday, Helbrans's attorney obtains a court order for a bail hearing the next day. He wants them *out*. It's an outrage.

Sunday. Outside and inside the Brooklyn courthouse, hundreds of Helbrans supporters have gathered in a black sea of fedoras and long coats. Rumbling with the thunder of their indignation, some have been up all night canvassing Brooklyn's Jewish streets to raise cash for today's bail hearing. They are exhausted and furious. This you do to a rabbi? Put him in jail on shabbos?

Satmars and hasids, joined in their rage, are deeply insulted. Such effrontery, such boldness and hate. What else explains how police go and arrest such a good man. Their rebbe, noble and God fearing, should stand accused? Terrible, terrible, they mutter. God will strike them for this. Watch. Their wrath beats against the walls of the courthouse and flows into the streets.

Rabbi Helbrans, wringing his hands, his head bowed, and his wife Malka, her head wrapped in dark cloth, stand before acting state Supreme Court Justice Alan Liebowitz. Eyes downcast, they rock and sway, praying silently.

Hana, flanked by Michael and Jacky, huddle together on a bench. Three bundled twigs, they sit tense and tight jawed.

Helbrans's defense attorney George Meissner charges that the prosecutors deliberately arranged the arrests to punish the deeply religious couple on their sabbath. A kidnapping? "No kidnapping. It's strictly a runaway child situation," he declares to the judge. "The boy fled from an abusive home."

Abusive? Abusive? Michael has had enough of their shit. He jumps to his feet and screams at the judge, "That's not true. That's a lie. A lie."

The judge orders Michael Reuven to be ejected. No outbursts will be tolerated in his court.

He orders both suspects to surrender their passports. They are illegal aliens from Israel.

Hana sighs with relief.

Meissner claims that Malka Helbrans was harassed at Rikers Island, that she is nursing a new infant only three weeks old. Return this nursing mother to Rikers? Unthinkable.

The judge agrees. He releases her on her own recognizance to take care of her baby. But for the rabbi—another story. The judge sets bail at $250,000 to a roar from the hasids. It does no good. Helbrans, hands behind his back, is ordered back to Rikers Island.

Outside, Satmars and hasids are pushing and chanting: *Shame. Shame.* Shouting to reporters to hear their side. *A terrible wrong. Terrible.*

One Satmar, fist in the air, pushes forward and outshouts the others. "They were mistreated and humiliated. A rabbi and his wife kept in jail on the Sabbath. Terrible. Terrible."

Felder offers the press a different story. Calm and reasonable, he is a sharp contrast to the crazed hasids. "The arrests give the parents hope. They have faith in the system."

And where's Mordecai Weiss, the third defendant charged

with taking Shai to Brooklyn and not bringing him back? He does not appear. Is he on the lam?

A reporter in a phone interview is told, "He was not willing to accept that kind of battering from authorities. He wants the government to show some respect for the sabbath. He did not want to experience the same situation as the Helbranses." However, he adds that he'll probably surrender to the D.A. in the morning.

As Hana, Michael, and Jacky leave the courthouse, a mob of hasids shake their fists at them. "Shame on you. Shame on you."

Hana huddles into herself. Let them scream. Helbrans is arrested. She's closer to finding Shai. The hell with them.

It is Tuesday. Hana sits on the edge of the bed fully dressed in a navy skirt and white blouse open at the throat. Today is the arraignment. She has slept fitfully and now she steels herself, she must be strong to face that sea of hasids. Michael, too, he better hold his tongue, not get the judge mad.

"Let's go." Jacky is dressed and ready for them.

Tense, they leave the apartment. Maybe a miracle will happen today. Helbrans will tell the judge where Shai is, she'll go and take him home.

In the Brooklyn courthouse, she and Michael and Jacky sit with straight backs, eyes forward. As the indictment is unsealed, charging the three with kidnapping and conspiracy, the air thins.

All three enter innocent pleas.

Innocent? *They're kidnappers*, her heart screams.

Helbrans testifies that he doesn't know where the boy is. "He's a troubled child who is emotionally scarred for life."

Hana hangs her head. Emotionally scarred? By *you*, not me. An abusive home? Another lie. A Ramsey policeman, when asked if it was an abusive home, told a reporter, "From our information, he was just a normal kid who had his ups and downs with his family. Like every other teenager."

Weiss, who surrendered in the morning, is released on $100,000 bond, paid by the hasids.

As the session ends and all three walk off scot free, Hana cannot hold back another moment.

"Your honor, your honor," she cries out to get the judge's attention. "It's not right they go free," she calls unsuccessfully. "It's not right they just pay money and they go free."

But it's over. Whipped, all she can do is weep.

Not Michael. Seeing them released and walking out, his rage explodes. *"My son is dead. My son is dead."* He is overcome with grief. He has held his tongue. Restrained himself. Sat like a stone, jaws clenched, as the rabbi and his wife rocked back and forth before the bench, praying. The righteous ones with God on their side. But now, Weiss with his snide smile, his long sidecurls flopping against his unkempt beard, his black skull cap slipping back over his thinning hairline, is also walking away free. *"My son is dead. Nobody cares."*

Michael crumbles to the floor.

Immediately, pandemonium breaks loose. Did the father faint? Was he struck dead by a stroke?

Outside the Brooklyn courthouse, paramedics and cops push the crowd of street gawkers aside. "Get back. Outa the way," they bark as they carry his body strapped to a stretcher. His head is slumped over, his eyes closed, an oxygen mask snapped over his face. As photographers shove for position, Michael's limp body is pushed into a wailing ambulance. With the siren blasting, it races to the emergency entrance of Brooklyn Hospital Center.

Hana stands in the street frozen, her feet cemented to the sidewalk.

First Shai. Now Michael.

Where is God? Where is justice?

# 22.  A RALLY FOR JUSTICE

**M**ichael's dramatic collapse produces a field day for the tabloids. Though he is released—he had only fainted—newspapers now plunge into the world of the ultrareligious. What goes on behind their closed doors? Satanic rituals? Animal sacrifices?

On editorial pages, civil libertarians defend Helbrans and cry out for religious freedom and constitutional rights. Secular Jews, ashamed of the crazies in their midst, scream back that kidnapping is a crime, religion has nothing to do with it.

Brooklyn's hasidic community, shoved into the unwanted glare of media attention, rallies around Rabbi Helbrans. Look at his gentle face and forgiving eyes.

Across America, a nervous pulse beats in Jewish communities. From Scarsdale to Miami, the outcome will focus attention on how the world perceives Jews.

From many, there is an outpouring of sympathy for Hana and rage against religious extremists. How do they get away with kidnapping and brainwashing innocent kids? Just because a rabbi does it, you don't excuse it. Kidnapping is a crime. Is Helbrans operating alone? Or are other hasidic families in on it hiding the boy? Is it a conspiracy?

At Oneg Shabbats following Sabbath services, couples huddle over platters of ruggalah in their social halls, whispering what they won't say in front of the goyim.

"It makes my blood boil. A rabbi kidnaps a kid and makes up a cockamamie story how the kid is dying to be religious? Sure. Right. Just like my kid. He's dying to skip soccer practice so he can daven."

A crime is a crime, shout many newspapers. Why didn't

Hynes nab the rabbi last year? What took him so long? He had the tape of the rabbi offering the father money. Why didn't he move on it?

Hynes is in the hot seat. It's getting hotter every day.

Hana, sensing another chance, invites reporters into her apartment. She poses for pictures. She wants them to get her story straight. And indeed, they find her a sympathetic young woman. A mother who lost her son. An innocent in America. An immigrant who only wanted a better life.

She tells it over and over. The heartache. The botched dreams. She begins to parrot her own story. To polish it and highlight the dramatic events. In the glare of the spotlight, she warms to the showbiz atmosphere. She winces. She shrugs. She weeps. She is Israeli.

"I made mistakes, sure. But does anyone deserve this agony? My boy torn away from the family. We don't know if he's dead or alive." She wrings her hands. "It was Shai's birthday. Fourteen. I don't know where he is. I don't . . ." Her eyes fill.

The *Jewish Standard* reports the battle as a culture war. It describes Helbrans as a lone ranger, disavowed even by the Satmars. Rabbi Moses Teitelbaum states: "I'm making it clear to the whole world that Satmar has nothing to do with this case or this yeshiva or with this person or with the boy. It's absolutely unfair to drag in the Satmar community." They came to the courthouse because of the insensitivity of arresting the rabbi on the sabbath.

Others disavow Helbrans, claiming he's his own rebbe. "He has no credibility and no standing. He's an unknown and the ones who know him stay very far away."

Jewish professors, scholars, and authors debate the issues in the press and from podiums. Many speak out for the Mosaic law to honor your mother and father.

In the war for a child's soul, whose religious convictions should abide: parents or child? Rabbi Ephraim Buchwald, director of the National Jewish Outreach Program, wrestles the situation right to the ground. He advises the child who wants to become orthodox, that while still living with the parents, they should avoid nonkosher food, make the blessings, and avoid desecration of Shabbos. "Try to influence your parents until you are of legal majority."

Yosele Schuchmaker, an Israeli pharmaceutical executive, gives an exclusive interview to the *New York Post* from his home outside Tel Aviv. In 1959, he was kidnapped in a story that closely resembles Shai's. HASID FANATICS HELD ME CAPTIVE is the *Post* headline. When he was seven, his grandparents had him kidnapped from Israel because he wasn't getting an orthodox education. He lived three or four months in Brooklyn, transported at night in a van, talking only to his captives. They told him his parents were his enemies and God wanted him with them. To get past authorities, they dressed him as a girl and they even talked about plastic surgery. It took three years before he was freed.

"I am outraged that such a despicable act can occur again. I cannot find words to adequately express my revulsion at these criminals. They have no right to take this child's life away."

*Revulsion.* It seems to be building against the rabbi. And against Hynes for taking almost a year to find new evidence. What new evidence?

"Even if we found the kid tomorrow," says one law enforcement officer, "there was no new evidence."

"It's maddening," another admits. "There was enough to make the case from the beginning. All I can figure is the hasidim in Brooklyn are a political force."

"It was not handled normally," another says. "We lost our hammer. The delay cost us. Eleven months—we may have lost our chance to recover the child."

Hynes, stung by the heavy criticism, bristles at the suggestion he played politics with Shai's kidnapping. "My total commitment is to that kid."

All of this wraps Hana in a new kind of strength.

In March, she invites a reporter into her apartment for an in-depth story. The three kids are romping through the rooms, adorable. Osheri wears his Green Bay Packers cap and black Converse high-tops. Eliran is reading *Charlotte's Web* for his homework assignment. And Shiran, only four, is trying to bounce a basketball. An enchanting family struck by tragedy.

The story, "A Mother's Heartache," recounts Hana's ordeal from day one. The reporter sees something marvelous about Hana Fhima. "You can tell by looking at her children: smooth, soft olive skin framing big, brown, dancing eyes. Their faces carry a gentle light."

With her face cupped in her palms and her eyes downcast, she tells how "America has become my nightmare." She is charming. A young immigrant mother, who must wait for the phone call: *Shai is found and he's coming home.* The story ends with: ". . . their once splendid-mother is dim with pain."

Clearly, sympathy for Hana is overflowing.

Almost a year has gone by. Hana plans to commemorate the anniversary of Shai's disappearance by organizing a rally for justice in April. City Hall Park, across from the Brooklyn Bridge and the Municipal Building, will provide a nice backdrop.

Elaine and Lil are wizes at pulling out lists of Jewish organizations, congregations, and community leaders. On Shelter Our Sisters stationary, Elaine outlines the events that led to Shai's kidnapping and asks people to come forward to support the rally. She pulls every string, calls in every due-bill, working feverishly with Hana. Letters go out. Join us on April 1.

"Thoughtful Jews of all denominations utterly reject kidnapping," she writes in her letter. "Not only is it a felony, it is a sinful, egregious transgression of both the letter and spirit of Jewish law."

Bright yellow flyers are distributed asking in English and in

Hebrew: *Where is SHAI FHIMA?* Two photos side by side show Shai as a typical toothy kid in a baseball cap. And Shai as a hasid wearing a black brimmed hat and black suit. Bus transportation will run from New Jersey to City Hall Park.

Rabbi Weinberg has convinced over a dozen rabbis to add their name to the list of sponsors.

Under a slate gray sky at noon at City Hall Park, a hundred and fifty people gather to support Hana. The public outcry against Shai's abduction has brought a heterogeneous crowd to the park on this Thursday. Journalists, television crews, and photographers stand by to report the speeches and exploit the event.

One by one, speakers come to the podium to decry the foot-dragging by prosecutors. To ask why this crime goes unpunished. To demand action.

Even Osheri makes his contribution. On unlined white paper, the little boy writes a message, each word printed by hand in bold caps.

"I want to speak for my whole family and for Shai's friends that we miss Shai and we want him brought back home.

"Shai once told us a story about Rabbi Helbrans that when the rabbi was small he tried to run away because his father hit him a lot. So then the rabbi tried to make my brother run away just like him. He said we would go to hell but that is not true.

"I am worried about my brother Shai. I hope someone can help us find him and bring him back.

"Thank you to everyone for coming and listening."

Raoul Felder, sixtyish, appears in his signature black cape and silver tipped cane, his short dark beard bobbing forcefully. Eloquently, he blasts the Brooklyn D.A.'s office for dawdling. He tells the crowd the case is plodding through "a lugubrious court system." He denounces the authorities. "It's an outrage." Why did they wait ten months before returning an indictment? "People came out for one woman. One child. But it's really for *every* woman. *Every* child."

It produces a communal shudder.

Rabbi Weinberg speaks from the heart. Shai was his bar mitzvah student before the kidnapping. "These are not the kind of acts God wants us to engage in in his name. I ask people of good will to speak out."

But it is Hana, fine-tuned for this occasion, who turns the crowd misty-eyed. "I am not able to describe what I've gone through. It's very difficult to live without Shai." Head down at first, she draws herself up, a petite woman. Pathetic, really. "We do not know where he is. We do not know what happened to him." A sigh. "It's very difficult to go to sleep at night. To wake up and know my son is somewhere in this world . . . and he does not see you . . . or feel you . . ." She pauses trying to gain control. "Within my heart, the heart of a mother, I sense that Shai wants to return home."

Tissues come out to dab at noses.

"He was the big brother who watched over his younger siblings. Now Shai is the one who needs our help. We know Shai thinks about us and loves us."

Even reporters who've seen everything are touched by her tragedy.

"Last year it was Passover and my son was not with us. Now it is another Passover. And my son won't be with us."

Passover begins at sundown Monday.

# 23. ALAN VINEGRAD

Assistant United States D.A. Alan Vinegrad is an up 'n' comer. Relentless and committed, he has been working with the investigation since 1992 when the feds came in. Sharing his perspective with Larry Meyerson and Bill Plackenmeyer, he's been dogging every shred of evidence to build an airtight case. Hana has provided him with gripping and powerful details. This is his expertise: *details*. His preparation for the trial will leave no stone unturned. Preparation is everything.

Alan Vinegrad is young and vibrant. Fueled by ambition, he has the dark good looks of a young JFK Jr., though a smaller, thinner version. The crease in his trousers is sharp and his cordovan leather loafers shine. He pays attention to appearance. The appearance of his fifth-floor office at Cadman Plaza East, with its carpeted reception area, security guard behind glass, and the sign OFFICES OF THE UNITED STATES ATTORNEY, EASTERN DIVISION OF NEW YORK pleases him. His speech is fast clipped and intelligent, his words measured. The investigation has led him to believe the *state* should charge the defendants.

"The state, not the feds." He explains it to Hana. "It's *legally significant*." He talks to her often.

Legally significant? "The technic . . . the technical . . ." she stumbles over the word, "I don't follow. Only when will I get Shai back?" Can you do it? her eyes ask.

"My job is to see that justice is done, Hana. That the rabbi and others involved in the kidnapping are punished." He doesn't talk down to her, he is personable.

Hana is impressed with him. "Alan knows what he's doing," she tells Larry. "Now we got a case."

Hana's dreams bounce from sweaty nightmares to sweet snippets of wish fulfillment.

In one dream, Alan Vinegrad is brutally cross-examining a squirming Helbrans on the witness stand, attacking his lies, until the rabbi jumps up and blurts out where he's hiding Shai.

In another dream, Bill Plackenmeyer leads NYPD patrol cars to Shai's secret address. Radios squawking, light bars flashing, they pull up with guns drawn in a rescue that ends with Shai running out the front door into her outstretched arms.

Alan Vinegrad and Bill Plackenmeyer couldn't be more different. Plackenmeyer, the street-smart Brooklyn cop with his tie loose, is the antithesis of cool, button-down Vinegrad. Yet both men bring dedication to finding Shai. In Hana's dreams, each plays the hero.

Of course it's Larry who keeps the wheels spinning, bugging them, doing the behind the scenes work that has to be done. Of the three, Larry is the only one not getting paid. And with the investigation intensifying, it's Larry and Elaine who keep Hana's spirits up on a daily basis.

"Justice will prevail," Larry assures her. "We'll get Shai back for you. Hang on, Hana."

"That's what I tell *her*," he admits to his wife with a rueful grin. Then his eyes dim. Jesus, who knows what the hasidim can pull off in Brooklyn. Larry can identify with Hana. Their son David will be bar mitzvahed in October of 1995. What if it happened to them? Hana Fhima has reversed their decision not to take their work home. Hana Fhima has changed their lives: she's part of every day.

In pillow talk, Larry explains convoluted legal procedures to Elaine. Updates her on meetings he takes in jeans, on phone calls he squeezes in transporting David to soccer competitions. His fury for Hynes's failure to move for conviction has festered to a boil. Why isn't the legal system working? Where the hell is justice?

None of this does he say to Hana. Instead, though impatient himself, he makes the case for Hana to be patient. "The wheels of justice move slowly, gotta roll with it." Does he fool her?

She smiles. "Sure." She wants to be hopeful.

When she bathes Shiran, she leans over the tub and sings her Israeli songs in Hebrew. She watches *Jeopardy* on TV with the boys and even guesses a few answers. She's learning American slang. She phones her mother often, the hell with the long distance bill. She puts new spark plugs in her ailing car. And she goes on a diet—well, sort of. Too much Entenmann's over the winter has strained the top button of her jeans. She vows to lose five, six pounds.

On days when a surge of good spirits feeds her, she goes down her list. D.A. Alan Vinegrad. Captain Bill Plackenmeyer. Rabbi Milton Weinberg. Attorney Raoul Felder. Elaine Meyerson and Lil Corcorhan. Larry Meyerson. America is full of good people. A hundred and fifty came out for Shai's rally. She is still bathing in the glow of their support.

With the boys in school, she takes Shiran shopping in the mall. The store windows are full of bright yellow daffodils and Easter bunnies. She treats her to pink barrettes, snaps them into her silky baby hair. "Beautiful."

Her eyes slide over to a basket of costume jewelry at 50 percent off. She tries on a pair of sleek hoops with golden balls like the Jerusalem sun. She strikes a pose in the mirror, tilts her head critically this way and that way. Trim your bangs. Wear brighter lipstick. Polish your toenails red like the girls on the beach in Tel Aviv. And buy a plant. Purple. For the kitchen window sill.

The mall offers distraction. Takes her mind off Shai.

"Wanna skip?" Shiran asks, pulling her along.

Shoppers smile at them. Such a carefree young mother.

At the outdoor garden center, she hands an African Violet to the guy with the mustache at the register. "You can spare me a little ribbon?" Flirting, a charming tilt to her chin. It is the Israeli tick to ask for something extra, a better price.

"For you?" he flirts back. "Absolutely." Then he whips a red lollipop out of a jar and hands it to Shiran. "For your little sister."

"Say thank you," Hana prompts her.

But Jacky always brings her down. He can't deal with her exuberance. He bullies her over the smallest thing. Good news from Vinegrad or Plackenmeyer he turns sour.

"Hana, you're a fool. They only want a piece of Shai for the publicity. It's what Americans call their own agenda."

"But . . ."

"Don't be stupid."

She has gone back to her apartment in New Jersey. But after school on Fridays, she arrives with the three kids for the weekend. Today, her toe nails are freshly polished, her bangs trimmed and her new earrings tossing their golden suns. She will cook him a nice dinner: a flanken with potatoes and figs, how he likes it.

But within ten minutes, the kids get on his nerves, they're in his face. Hana's good spirits offend him.

"Shut up," he screams, "my head is killing me." Hana is a pain in the ass. All the time Shai, Shai, Shai, all she gives a shit about is Shai. The kid is probably the darling of the weirdos. How he bragged to Osheri: you need money, ask me, I got plenty. I got a computer, too.

To outsiders, Jacky can be dark and pouty. Or ardent and expressive. And though he's not tall, he is compact and sexy. Like other Israeli boys and girls, he went into the army at eighteen. He was good at fixing things and building things with his hands—he'd get by.

Before he married Hana, he set her straight. Kosher was for rabbis to make money. "Sure we're Jewish. Torah is our history. But the rest is garbage."

"He's not a spiritual person," is how she explained him.

In the early years, he frightened her, but he never hit her. Only put his foot down and controlled her. One wrong word could set him off. He was strict with the kids, everything his way. His rules.

Finally, all she wanted was to keep peace and be a good wife. "Sure, Jacky, sure." She gave in for the children's sake.

After he lost the tile store, it got worse. He slapped her around, his tantrums erupting frequently. Though he apologized and brought them all little gifts and swore he'd never hit her again, she walked on eggs, tiptoeing around him.

Well, maybe it's my fault, maybe I make him go off the deep end. She blamed herself and tried harder. The children need a father.

At SOS, she learned she was not alone and she was not crazy. American women, professional women, even rich women have abusive husbands. It's all luck. The rally for justice has turned it around. *Hana Levi Reuven Fhima—your luck is changing.* Like Ema says: "What you need, *mamala*, is a little mazel." *Mamala.* It's what she calls Shiran.

Does she neglect the other three by spending so much time on Shai? Shiran is whiny, she can't fall asleep even with her stuffed animals in bed, the kittens and teddy bears. Eliran gets earaches: twice she rushed him to Urgent Care. And Osheri—so serious, so quiet—who can say what goes through his head? How much it took away from them?

Do I hurt my kids? Am I a bad mother?

With each piece of news, her mood swings. Bill Plackenmeyer is working to find Shai. But he could get buried under homicide cases, gang wars, and Saturday night shootups. He's on her side now, but for how long? Larry Meyerson is working already a year without a cent. Won't he get tired? On the good side, Alan Vinegrad gets paid good, so he won't give up.

The rally for justice gave us another chance.

But, ironically, it is not the rally that jumpstarts the investigation.

It is the arrest of Tobias Freund.

# 24. WOODWARD AND BERNSTEIN

On June 27, Tobias Freund is apprehended at his father's kosher food processing plant in the Bushwick section of Brooklyn. The short indictment charges that he lied when he told a grand jury that he hadn't seen Shai Fhima since late March of 1992. Perjury before a grand jury is a major crime.

It is Freund's telephone records, meticulously tracked down, that blast his testimony. Carelessly and imprudently, he used his business telephone calling card to phone people involved in Shai's disappearance.

Alan Vinegrad, working with U.S. District Attorney Michael Vecchione, have the records to prove it. Together, they have amassed every phone call *to* Helbrans and *from* Helbrans. *To* the yeshiva and *from* the yeshiva. *To* Weiss and *from* Weiss. Building their case with precision, they put it together one toothpick at a time.

Vecchione, forties, good looking, with salt and pepper hair, is as indefatigable as Vinegrad.

In the beginning, Hana didn't like Michael Vecchione. She was suspicious: he's working for Hynes, isn't he? So how can she trust him? Hynes is playing both sides of the street. Trying to keep the hasidic community happy and at the same time trying to appear even handed in prosecuting Helbrans. At every pretrial meeting, she can't erase that Vecchione works for Hynes. The arrest of Freund diminishes her distrust. Well, maybe he's okay. He's with Alan and Alan's on her side.

Hana takes Freund's arrest as a sign that Shai must be hidden somewhere in Brooklyn. The NYPD seem to agree. They focus fresh search efforts on heavily hasidic communities. Plainclothes officers and detectives roam Williamsburg, Crown Heights, and

Boro Park searching for clues, hanging out, asking and watching. Though Helbrans, his wife and Weiss are the chief suspects, Freund's involvement convinces authorities there are others. Perhaps many others.

Felder hops right on it.

"This shows that the government is not going to let this case go away," he tells the reinvigorated journalists. "And it sends a message to followers of this rabbi that this is serious."

That other Helbrans followers are in on it, that an organized plot may have pulled off the kidnapping, only adds to Hana's victimization role in the press. She is alone: one mother trying to find her child. They are many out there, conspiring against her.

Reporters ask her what she knows about Freund.

"Yes, Tobias Freund was one of them. A Helbrans follower. He's the one who drove Shai back home. I remember. How he came to Ramsey from Brooklyn when Shai stayed overnight with Weiss." She didn't pay much attention to him, but now the pieces are coming together.

Freund's arrest is called a "key link" in the investigation.

Helbrans, free on bail and awaiting trial, is the leader and the one indicted, along with his wife and Mordecai Weiss. But there are others. Tobias Freund was in on it, and others are part of the the kidnapping plot, too.

*There are others* swells like a chorus. Speculation grows that many hasidim, acting in concert, commit kidnappings like Shai's. It's an organized group. Ostensibly, the sect is small and obscure. But where and how far do their tentacles reach? To what extent do other religious sects support Helbrans? Who are the families that assist in the kidnappings of young boys? How many are in the conspiracy to snatch children and "save their souls"?

What provoked Freund to lie before a grand jury? He is no yeshiva bocher, no innocent boy. An adult, he is employed by his father's VIP Kosher Food processing plant. And federal perjury charges are no parking ticket. What kind of loyalty to Helbrans made Freund cover up his involvement? What allegiance to Helbrans led him to risk federal charges?

In the capable hands of Vinegrad and Vecchione, the kidnapping probe now takes on a formidable boost. A possible conspiracy? This goes beyond Helbrans. If Freund is involved, others may be covering up for the rabbi. Where are they hiding the boy? What families are housing him? Are there homes designated to harbor stolen kids? Where? Who? How many?

Indeed investigation into the phenomenon discloses that it is not uncommon for hasidic families with ten or twelve children of their own to "take in" another child transported from another city. From another state. Even another country. It is considered a mitzvah, a supreme good deed, to provide a child with a strict orthodox upbringing and teach him God's revelations and God's will. The means justify the ends.

"Whatever families are harboring Shai, they ain't gonna come forward," Larry tells Steve, pulling up a chair.

Steve's office, the largest and sunniest in the suite, has the miniblinds drawn to shut out distractions, a sure sign that's he's up to his ears in work. "What's up?" He palms his eyes, time for a break.

"They admit to nothing. Tell the authorities? C'mon, they're goyim, what can cops know about saving a child's soul? To them it's a holy mission." Larry is both elated and dismayed. "Sure, they nabbed Freund. But Jesus, Steve, there could be a hundred Freunds out there."

Steve nods. "Yeah." The break in the case indicates that the web reaches out. Helbrans is at the hub of the sect, their typical charismatic leader. A rebbe of such godliness that whatever he asks of his followers, they gotta do. "Freund lied to save Helbrans."

Mockingly, Larry bows his head low. "To whom all loyalty is due."

"Yup," Steve agrees. "It's all for the glory of God and not to be questioned. That's why I'm an atheist. It turns my stomach to watch the pious ones, such hypocrites."

Larry nods, he's heard Steve before. "If you're summoned by the rebbe, hey, there's no higher honor. The closer you get to the leader, the closer you are to God." He pauses. "Pulled the same shit on the kid. Told a child of thirteen: '*I see a light shining in your face. Come, sit near me, my son.*' Made him feel chosen. Convinced him his soul would be saved."

Steve's fingers drum the top of his desk. "Maybe the plot began that night. Isn't that what Hana's been telling you all along? How he *mesmerized* the kid. Step one of the conspiracy. Freund came in later. After Weiss . . ."

"There's a whole slew of hasids in on it. For Freund to lie to a grand jury, shit, that's no small potatoes. He's no kid like Weiss, barely out of his teens. Freund is thirty-five, a man."

Under questioning, Freund denies either seeing Shai or speaking to him on the night of April 5. The boy's disappearance? He knows nothing about it, nothing. That is his testimony.

When prosecutors ask him about telephone calls charged to his business card on that date, he simply repeats like a mantra that he never saw Shai Fhima or talked to him after March. He can't explain the phone records. It must be a mistake. Was he involved in spiriting the boy away? Does he know of Shai's whereabouts? No. He is innocent.

Reporters now demand answers to old questions about D.A. Hynes. Why were criminal charges brought against the rabbi *after almost a year had elapsed?* Why the delay? Wasn't there a recorded conversation between the rabbi and the boy's father? A tape when the NYPD wired the father?

Same questions. Same nonanswers. Same stonewalling.

More doubletalk from the D.A.'s office. "A redeveloped investigation has produced appropriate information. . . ."

✡  ✡  ✡

Like the Yosele Schuchmaker story from Tel Aviv, another story has come out in the *Post* on May 8 with the headline MOM GETS BACK HER KIDNAP KIDS. Patricia Heyman at Kennedy airport gives reporters a tearful interview before flying back to Belgium with her kids after searching the globe for six years. The emotional reunion came after the FBI made a predawn raid on a compound owned by a Satmar hasidic yeshiva in Bedford Hills. The FBI—using computers to update old pictures of the three children now thirteen, twelve, and ten—found them in the home of Herschel and Rachel Jacobowitz and their eleven children.

Another conspiracy. It's what religious cults do. Steal children. Turn them against the parents. Hide them. Isolate them. Always in the name of God. *Their* brand of God.

Which is exactly what Larry Meyerson has been screaming for over a year. "Pious people are *not* above the law. Kidnappers are felons," he tells the press. "Dangerous people. A menace to society. It's gotta stop."

He says it over and over. To friends at dinner parties. To colleagues at the courthouse. To rabbis like Weinberg who are revolted. But he's preaching to the choir.

Last month, the New York Board of Rabbis sent a letter to D.A. Hynes asking for developments in the Shai Fhima case. The board is the world's largest rabbinic organization embracing Orthodox, Conservative, Reform, and Reconstructionist rabbis.

"Quite some time has elapsed and we have not heard a word about whether the boy has been found and returned to his family and whether the culprits are going to be prosecuted." The language is polite. An inquiry, not an accusation.

Rabbi Weinberg received a copy of the letter on May 19 at his office in Temple Beth Haverim and he called Hana.

"Maybe it will do some good," he told her hopefully.

But the letter didn't make a ripple.

Hynes didn't move. Though the tabloids continued to chew it up. Secular Jews slugging it out with orthodox Jews? Jews against Jews?

Larry tosses the newspaper aside. "Don't they get it? It's a crime." His fist punches the sofa pillow.

"I know, I know." Elaine is as frustrated as he is. She feels an obligation to support Hana. "The woman has been through hell, Larry." She shakes her head sadly.

"It's a plot. A conspiracy."

Sometimes when he thinks about David's upcoming bar mitzvah, he feels ambivalent. You look at this and you get disgusted with religion. But Elaine would kill him. Not have a bar mitzvah? You're talking homicide.

"You see what Vinegrad told the press?" He grabs the paper.

"About Freund? What?"

He reads it to her. " 'He faces up to five years in prison on each of four counts.' Typical D.A. talk. Short, no comment."

Almost every day on and off the record, Larry is talking to Vinegrad. Talking to Plackenmeyer. Keeping Elaine up to speed, she wants to know everything.

Even in bed, she's got questions to run by him. Comments on how it's likely to play out. *"Give me your tired, your poor.* Know who wrote that, Lar?"

"Yeah, yeah. You forgot *your huddled masses yearning to breathe free.*" He pulls the covers up.

"Emma Lazarus. It's the inscription on the Statue of Liberty."

"Thank you, sweetheart, I never knew that." Long day, he wants to catch some zzzs.

"A woman. A Jew. Did you know that? Emma Lazarus was a Jew."

"Gimme a break." He closes his eyes and spoons himself against her. Hana Fhima, get outa my bed.

"She came here to breathe free and all she got for it was a mother's worse nightmare."

"I'm sleeping."

"Don't let go of this, Lar. We have to help her."

"We are. We will. Go to sleep."

But how long will Steve put up with it? He's gotta be getting pissed. Chunks of time cut out. Not a cent in billable hours. Can you blame the man if he squawks? He's running a law firm, not the UJA.

Steve looks up at Larry from behind his desk. "You nuts? I'm gonna pull rank and tell you to quit because my name comes first?"

Larry tilts his head, a gesture of you-got-the-right. "You sure this Hana thing is okay with you? It could drag on for months. Who knows what's coming down the pike? I got over a year into it, you got a right to pull the plug."

"You crazy?" Sure it's a drain on the firm, but there's the matter of principle. Integrity. You don't quit because things aren't going your way. You sign on, you do it, you don't back off. "C'mon," he responds to Larry's long face. "What's cooking with Felder? Is he gonna stick with it?"

Larry shrugs. "Wait'll he sees the kind of hours it burns up. Lotsaluck, Felder."

"He's smart, he knows what he's doing."

"Maybe he's tired of it. Maybe he doesn't think it's worth pursuing anymore. Maybe he's thinking it's not winnable."

"Mmmm." Steve purses his lips. "Too much work for too little return." He sits up straighter in his leather swivel and plants his elbows on his desk. "Which proves one thing."

"Yeah? What?"

"He's smarter than us," he jokes. Usually Larry dishes up the one liners. But this time, Steve's got a doozy. "Who appointed us the Woodward and Bernstein of the nineties?"

Larry stands up and roars. Helluva guy. For every Helbrans in this world there's a Steve Rubenstein.

"Get outa here." Steve points to the door. "I gotta get to court. Get out, I already gave at the office."

"Hey, Woodward and Bernstein. I like that. Only I'm the good looking one. Robert Redford."

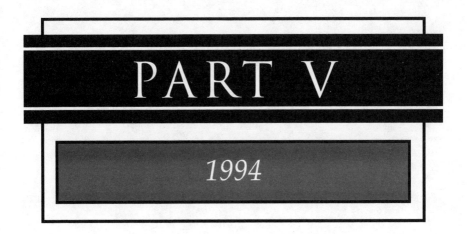

# PART V

## 1994

# 25. A CUSTODY BATTLE

Hana looks out the window. No, not more snow, not another blizzard. Snow everywhere. New snow falling over dirty snow. Mountains of snow. It is everyone's conversation. When will it stop? Which highways are closed, Route 17 or Route 4? Will school be canceled or have delayed opening? How many snow days will be lopped off summer vacation? She peers down the street. Can she shovel a path to the sidewalk? Get to the supermarket? Better stock up on canned soup and macaroni and cheese.

By January's end, the brutal storms have left ten-foot-high piles of snow. The city plows are out every day. She hears them in the middle of the night, too, scooping and gobbling up snow.

The only bright spot to the winter of 1994 was reading in the paper that Freund got convicted in federal court on three counts of perjuring himself before the grand jury and one count of obstruction of justice.

Wonderful. But is she any closer to finding Shai? No.

It makes her crazy. April will be two years.

Larry continues to be her major support. Right after Shai disappeared, he even called his friend Bob Miller from Channel 9. Told him the whole story after their Sunday ballgame.

"Ya gotta do this, Bob. Break it on television. How she's getting nowhere with the police." He has the videotape in his office.

Did it do any good? No. *Nothing does any good.*

Then Larry got Lyme disease. Went to the hospital, was on IVs, the man was really sick for months. Still, he never gave up. He even made her laugh. He still does.

"He's the King of the One-Liners," Elaine boasts. "Even in a crisis, he can make you crack up. Coulda been a stand-up comedian."

Almost two years.

Did it do any good? No. *Nothing does any good.*

By the end of January, the blizzards bring public transportation to a halt. Nobody can move. Hana and the kids watch the six o'clock news. Exhausted commuters and angry truckers. Emergency vehicles out rescuing people in twelve-car pile ups.

It is a winter of weather watches, a winter that shakes its fist at mere mortals and lets them know they are not in charge. Ten-foot-high mounds of snow block the streets and parking lots shrink, forcing drivers to weave around the stuff and maneuver into any available space. Housebound, kids get on your nerves and winter depression sets in. Even jokes about the storms, recycled too often, have grown stale.

Hana is despondent. She won't go to Jacky's apartment. She blames the weather, knowing the marriage is over.

Will I ever see Shai again?

The people she counted on, despite their good efforts, have been unable to get results. He's still hidden somewhere with the hasids. The rabbi and his wife and Weiss are free on bail.

*When will they make a trial? When?*


In February, Shai turns fifteen. To mark the day, she bought chocolate cupcakes and birthday candles. Up at five-thirty, she flicks on the kitchen light. A thick darkness gives no hint that the sun will rise. She sticks a candle into one cupcake and lights it. Alone, before the kids get up, she sings to him.

*Happy Birthday to you. Happy Birthday to you. Happy Birthday, dear Shai. . . .* She chokes on it, she can't finish. *Shai? Can you hear me? Can you see me? Happy Birthday, my son. I love you, my son.*

It is the children who force her to stay on track. Meals to prepare, clothes to wash, homework to be done. Only yesterday she found a red checker under the sofa—they were using a quarter. It is the kids and their incessant demands that keep her sane. Stirring the soup, scouring the bathtub and changing the sheets keep her going in some addled way.

Maybe she should go back to Israel. Divorce Jacky and start over. Ema would help her. But not now, you can't leave now. *After the trial. After* she gets Shai back.

A wild panic grips her throat. *Suppose they never find Shai?*

She waters the African Violet on the window sill. Look how it's growing. How every living thing fights for life, even a little plant from the mall.

At police lockers and urinals, even New York's finest are shaking their heads. Hynes has painted himself into a corner.

"In my book," a young rookie gives his opinion, "what ya got here is a fuckin' weirdo. Hynes got rabbi shit all over him. Wanna talk motive? It's a cult thing. Like David Koresh, like the Branch Davidians in Waco. Only this is Brooklyn and the rabbi wants the kid's soul."

The kid's right, let him talk.

"Hynes gonna get his balls on a plate for this. He had the evidence all along. Had the tape. The case was solid. He can't bury it anymore."

With jury selection for the trial about to begin, Hynes has to act. To extricate himself, he comes up with a plan. *Plea bargain.* Cut the charges against the rabbi to a misdemeanor *contingent on the kid's return to Brooklyn.* The boy will be returned and the rabbi will get a lighter sentence. Poof—the incident will blow over.

"What? What?" Hana screams. "As long as they bring back Shai. I don't care they give him a lighter sentence. Just bring back Shai."

"The deal is this," Bill Plackenmeyer explains on the phone. "They'll turn him over to the Brooklyn District Attorney in return for reduced criminal charges. Friday. At noon."

"I'll be there. I'll be there."

✡   ✡   ✡

Hana sits and waits. Watches the wall clock ticking.

Twelve. Ten past twelve. Twenty past.

She paces. Where is he? They said noon. Wait here in this room. Something went wrong? Silence. One o'clock. Ten past.

"I can't take this." She bolts off the chair and runs out past the line of reporters in the hall.

"Hana?" they yell at her. "Where's your boy?"

A law enforcement officer comes forward. "Meissner was to give us the kid back and they would cross the street, enter a plea, and get probation." His frustration level is apparent. "We worked on this in good faith. Now all bets are off," he huffs and turns away.

Driving back to New Jersey, Hana is seething, shaking, her hands clenched around the steering wheel. The vise around her chest clamps tighter. *Liars. Liars.*

"What happened?" she screams at Larry on the phone.

"Jesus. We don't know, no one knows."

"Liars, they're liars."

"Even the prosecutors don't know. They simply don't know why he never arrived." Clearly, Hynes's plea bargain deal has evaporated.

Larry maneuvers his car around the ten-foot-high piles of snow. His parking lot is shrinking. When's it gonna end? It's the last week of February, looking at March.

He grabs a coffee to start the day. Brings it to his desk. Gets to work on another case.

His intercom rings. "Who? Rockland County Sheriff? Sure. Put him through." He takes a sip of coffee and picks up the phone. "Hello? . . . What? He's there now?" He grabs a pad. "Right. Right. Rockland County family court," he repeats. "I'll get back to you. Thank you." *Holy Shit. They got Shai, he's there, just walked in, like that. Holy Shit.* Call Hana.

*"Where? Where?"* Her heart is thumping into her molars.

"In Rockland County. New City, New York."

"We can go? We can get him? He's okay? Is he okay? *Shai is there now?* Tell me again."

"Ab-so-*lutely.*" His voice is triumphant. "Let me call you back, Hana, let me get on it, okay? I'll call you back."

"Call me, I'll go, I'm ready, call me back."

Larry heads straight for Steve's office. He falls into a chair. *"They got him, Steve."*

Steve looks up. "They got the kid?" Astonished, he pushes the file folders aside. "Where?" He's been hearing it for two years. Larry arguing on the phone, the walls are thin. Giving him updates, dishing out drips of frustration and chunks of anger. "So why aren't you smiling?" His partner's face is sober.

"Here's what happened." He reports the sheriff's phone call. Then, hands cupping his knees, he leans forward with an intensity Steve recognizes.

"What?"

"Let me give you this."

"Okay. I'm listening." He sits up straighter.

Larry takes a breath, he's gotta lay it on him big time. *"It's a custody dispute now.* I need your help, Steve. I can't do this alone. This is your bailiwick. This is yours, your expertise."

"Hold it. Wait." Steve doesn't blink. "What's it doing in New York? I can't imagine any judge in New York getting involved. It's a New Jersey thing. The New York courts are gonna want to get rid of it."

Larry crosses his arms. *You with me?* his eyes ask. *I can't do this alone.*

"Okay. Okay. We do it."

Larry sighs. "Great."

Steve picks it up. "We go in *pro hace vice.*" He's mapping it out. "Shouldn't be a problem." *For that case only* is the first step. "What do you want to do?" he hands Larry the lead.

"Got to call Hana back. Maybe we can meet on Sunday at my house. We need to plan strategy."

"Sunday, huh? Let me check with Susan, I think it's okay."

"Great." His burden is lifted. "You know anyone up there in Rockland County?" It would be a help.

"No."

"A Judge Stanger?"

"No." Steve shakes his head.

"Anyone who knows him? Anyone up there?" He looks sternly at his partner. "We could get blown out of this case. Michael's going to fight Hana for custody, he's going to want his own lawyer. It's going to be a mess. We're looking at one helluva custody battle."

Steve pushes his chair back and stands up. "Woodward and Bernstein, that's us. Only *I'm* the good looking one, I'm Robert Redford."

"No way." Larry's on his feet. "I'm taller. You're Dustin Hoffman."

"Robert Redford."

"Dustin Hoffman."

"Redford."

"Hoffman."

Larry phones Felder. A lawyerly matter to clear up. Could be touchy. "We got the kid. You want to come up to Rockland County? Now is the time," Larry tells his colleague who understands immediately the gist of the call.

"Rockland County?" Hesitation.

"Yup. You're looking at one helluva heavy custody battle. The parents are going to be at each other's throats, it's going to break wide open." His question hangs in the air. *Are you prepared to continue representing Hana Fhima?*

"Mmmm."

"It's going to be a long uphill fight. Could drag on for years." He pauses. "You want to go on with it?"

They both know what they're talking about. A pro bono custody battle that could drag on for years?

"Felder's out." Larry reports it to Steve. He takes a breath. "So it's you and me, Steve. Mostly you at this point."

"Hey. Gotta do what we gotta do. The system failed her. The woman deserves to get her kid back. Woodward and Bernstein will uncover the conspiracy."

Larry's thumb pokes his chest. "Just remember who's Redford."

"Get outa here."

# 26. SHAI APPEARS IN ROCKLAND COUNTY COURTHOUSE

I t's Monday, February 28. Snowing again. New City crosswalks are piled high and the Rockland County courthouse parking lot is a disaster.

Steve and Larry flank Hana as they head for the front entrance. Tension tugs at Hana's mouth. Is it really true? Or another trick? Shai is in that building?

The courthouse is a veritable circus. They can hardly get up the steps past the media people. Video cameras. Flashbulbs going off. *Newsday* and *Post* reporters swarming like bees. Journalists from the Jewish press. People shoving and yelling.

Inside, Alan Vinegrad is walking up and down the hall like a detective, trying to pin down what's happening. Who is there in the crush? The Rockland County sheriff is standing against the wall. Rabbi Aloney, the chaplain from his department is there. Bill Goldberg, a therapist who deals with kids and cults, is there. Elaine found him, she was worried about how to deal with his psyche, a kid snatched from his home and brainwashed. Rabbi Weinberg and his wife are there. Lil from SOS. Michael is talking to his lawyer. Hasidim are pressed against the walls. The hallway is rumbling.

*A spectacle is about to begin.* Any minute Shai Fhima, the little kidnapped bar mitzvah boy will be brought in. After two years, the kid's here.

Hana's eyes, searching the crowd, are hungry for him. *What does he look like? How much taller?* The last time she saw him he was thirteen, wearing a baseball cap and a T-shirt. Will he run to me? Oh God, just let me see him, hold him, press him against me. See how nothing bad happened to him, they didn't hurt him.

*"There he is!"*

An explosion of screaming and yelling announces his entrance. A mob of media people are shoving for position. Shouting questions at him. *Hey Shai. Where were you? Who took you?*

Surrounded by rabbis is an expressionless fifteen-year-old in a black suit, yarmulke, and long sidecurls wrapped around his ears, his eyes downcast.

*It's Shai?* Shocked, Hana's mouth drops open. Oh my God, he's so tall, so big, so . . . so . . .

Pandemonium erupts. People yelling to capture his attention, pushing wildly to get a closer look.

Above the din is Michael, waving at Shai and screaming in Hebrew: *Shai I love you, I love you. My son, my son. It's me, Shai. Aba, Aba.*

"Which one's the father?" a reporter pokes Larry.

He points to Michael. "The one with the brand new yarmulke with the price tag on it." What a farce. Is Michael trying to convince the rabbis he's on their side? Show them how religious he is?

Hana can barely see him though the mob, rabbis are all over him, encircling him. "Shai, Shai," she calls.

Incredible. He hears his mother's voice. His head swivels, then jerks back. *No.* He won't acknowledge her. He turns his face away. Eyes glazed over, he is taken into the courtroom.

Judge Bernard Stanger is a kindly grandfatherly type. Small, frail, with thin white hair, he seems nice. He has no trouble with *pro hace vice.* "What's going on?" he asks.

Not knowing anything about Rockland County, not the judges, nobody, Steve and Larry have decided at their strategy meeting to present the case plainly.

"Judge," Steve buttons his jacket, "this should be in New Jersey. It's a New Jersey case, not New York. This child says he's a runaway. We say it's a kidnapping. Either way it's got to go back to New Jersey." That is Steve's position and he's confident the judge will say yes.

Judge Stanger takes it in. "Since there is a family offense petition—an allegation that Hana Fhima beat her son, I have jurisdiction to dispense of this and that's what I'm going to do. Decide
if it's a danger for Shai Fhima to go back to his mother."

Larry approves. He's exactly correct at this point. So let's see
how we can resolve it.

The judge wants more information. Fine. Child Protection
Services (CPS) in New York is appointed to do an investigation,
like New Jersey's Division of Youth and Family Services (DYFS).
But didn't Detective Kevin Kelly of the Ramsey Police already do
that? Way back when Shai ran to his friend's house because Hana
wouldn't give him permission to go to the mall on the bus and he
told the police Hana beat him. Kelly's report said Shai admitted
he lied. *No* abuse, just a typical teenager rebelling. But okay let
CPS do their thing, let them investigate.

What about right now?

Everyone wants a piece of Shai. Hana. Michael. They are the
parents. In order for Stanger to act, he has to take away custody
from Hana. But right now, after a two-year disappearance, both
parents are sitting in court waiting. Waiting for a chance to be
with their son.

The judge allots Hana forty-five minutes of private time with
Shai.

"Thank, thank you."

In a small private room, mother and son meet again. How can
she recapture the lost years?

"I love you, Shai, oh God, how I missed you."

He warms up a little. Alone together, he embraces her. Then,
remembering something, he steps back.

"I left home because you weren't religious." It sounds rehearsed. Robotlike.

"It's okay, it's okay," she coos, brushing it aside, she only
knows he's here now, he's alive, the nightmare is over. "We'll
make peace, everything will be good again." She believes it. To

Hana it is clear. Her child was kidnapped and now he's found.
Shai will come home with her and they will be a family again.
What else to say?

Does she notice that he backs off? That his eyes float to the
wall avoiding her? No. So flooded with relief, so overcome with
the sight of him, little registers except: *I got Shai back.*

"You'll come home with me," she declares. "We'll straighten out."

Family court Judge Bernard Stanger grants Michael the next
forty-five minutes. Like Hana's reunion, it is highly charged with
emotions bursting to be expressed. A father's concern and anger.
The boy belongs to him. He has filed an application to be his cus-
todial parent, he'll negotiate a visitation schedule. But Shai
belongs to him.

Michael, overwrought, piles up details to prove how dearly he
missed him. How much he loves him. "Shai, you know how many
times I came from Israel? How many yeshivas I searched? Every
yeshiva in Brooklyn knows your father's face."

Shai tells Michael he loves him, too. They have not seen each
other for four years. A lot to make up for.

Michael's reunion with his son unleashes a deeper fury
against Hana. All her fault. Everything bad that happened to his
son, Hana did it. "You are my son, you'll live with me. I swear it.
I'll get custody," he repeats.

Perhaps, like Hana, he does not notice that Shai retreats and
averts his eyes.

What neither parent knew when they arrived is that a black
stretch limousine has delivered yet another player in the custody
battle about to unfold. The man waiting his turn for a private
meeting with Shai is Rabbi Aryeh Zaks. He is not a hasid, he is an
orthodox Jew. Calmly, quietly, he sits in the sheriff's office,
waiting his turn.

Shai, accompanied by his lawyer, has petitioned for Judge
Stanger to appoint Zaks his guardian. *Not* his mother. *Not* his
father. *Rabbi Aryeh Zaks.*

Zaks has his own story to tell the judge. Why *he* should be Shai's guardian. Why Shai wants to live with *him*. Not either one of his parents. His English is excellent. He is extremely polite. Though a young man in his thirties, he looks older.

"The boy ran away because his home was impossible to live in. Mrs. Fhima hit him with the flat side of a knife and his step-father hit him with a bat. He left Brooklyn shortly after April 4, 1992, on a bus headed for Monsey."

The judge nods, he knows Monsey. He's been a Rockland County family court judge for years. He's an orthodox Jew himself.

"It's a town," Zaks explains with a small smile, "that's home to a community of about 6,500 orthodox and ultraorthodox Jewish families. Shai lived with different families in the Monsey area under the name *Avraham* because he wanted to avoid discovery. And to live as an orthodox Jew."

Rabbi Zaks speaks like a reasonable man; his beard is neat, he is soft spoken. Clearly not *ultra*orthodox like Rabbi Helbrans. Judge Stanger understands the distinction. He himself follows orthodox traditions, he observes the rules of kashruth and he honors shabbat.

"Shai felt Rabbi Helbrans was too strict, so he came to us."

Judge Stanger nods his head. "When?"

"To me he came about eight weeks ago, your honor. He said he heard Rabbi Helbrans was about to go on trial. He wanted people to know that he was not abducted in any way."

"Rabbi Zaks," the judge asks sternly, "do you know Rabbi Helbrans?"

"No, your honor. I don't know the man. I never met him."

Judge Stanger seems satisfied. He allows the new contender for Shai an hour visit with the boy.

"Lies. All lies." Hana shrieks in pain and confusion. "My son doesn't want to come home to me? I'm his mother. He wants Rabbi Zaks? Who's Zaks?" she screams at the judge.

But Shai's lawyer has made a motion for protection against her.

Against *me?* Hideous. Cruel.

To Larry and Steve it's perfectly clear. It's a set up.

*By turning up in Rockland County family court and by filing an application for Zaks's guardianship, Shai has effectively avoided being returned to his mother.*

Poor Hana. Poor, poor Hana.

There is little comfort they can offer her. Not now. Not while she's screaming, "Who's Zaks? He knows Shai a few weeks so he should be his guardian? I'm his mother, I'm his mother."

On the way back in the car, Larry reviews the events for her. "We have to be back in court after CPS finishes their report. Then . . ."

"Who's Zaks?" Hana repeats like a broken record. "Where he came from?"

"He has a yeshiva in Monsey. Shai lived with him in his house. We don't know much more." Now there's a *third* contender for Shai's custody. The mother. The father. And the rabbi. *Another* rabbi. A *different* rabbi. Not Helbrans. A rabbi who claims he never set eyes on Rabbi Helbrans. Where the hell is this going? How did they drag in Zaks?

In Brooklyn, Rabbi Helbrans sits quietly in a fourth-floor court-room as Judge Thaddeus Owens hears pretrial motions and prepares for jury selection and Malka Helbrans rocks in her chair, her eyes closed, praying silently.

Reporters ask him: "Did you know where Shai was?"

He smiles benignly. "I don't know. I can't talk about it."

And he bends over his religious scriptures, a pious man.

"What can you do?" Hana moans to Steve. Rejected by the son she fought to find, she is at her wit's end. The walls of her body are collapsing on each other. All she has thought about for two years is Shai, Shai, Shai. Where he is. How he looks. What he eats. Does he think of her? All she has longed for was to get him back, to hold him, to be his mother again.

And now, after two years, after she held him in her arms and he told her he loved her and she smelled his sweet young flesh and felt his long bony arms embrace her, *he wants Zaks?*

Impossible. It's a trick. A blow so incomprehensible, so vile, she can hardly breathe. How can it be?

"Explain me," she begs Steve over and over. "How can he want Zaks? Who's Zaks? Who's Zaks?"

In a few days, it registers with clarity. What happened at the Rockland County courthouse comes into focus. They are going to attack her from all sides. The ultraorthodox have called in the orthodox rabbi.

For years the enemy was Helbrans. The kidnapper, his wife, and Weiss, the three of them were the enemies, the ones who hatched the plot. Stole him away and brainwashed him. Changed him to a different boy. Made him turn against his own mother.

*Now, a new enemy.* Rabbi Zaks wants him. And Shai wants Zaks. How can it be?

"A rabbi he met eight weeks ago, he wants *him* for his guardian? Not me? Not Michael?"

"That's what they're saying." Steve is patient though he's gone over it a dozen times.

"What it means—an order for protection against me? I'm his mother."

Larry denounces the abuse charges to the press. "They are categorically untrue and unfounded." He points out that federal investigators have found *no evidence* that Shai was abused. "Why are abuse charges made now, instead of twenty-two months ago?"

Judge Stanger's family court is closed to the public. And will remain closed for however long the custody battle rages. Justice dispensed behind closed doors?

What emerges in the next week is clear. The kidnapping trial will take place in Brooklyn. The custody fight will take place in Rockland County. Different battles. Different enemies. Different judges.

Unless Steve can move it to New Jersey.

"I understand, I understand," Hana tells him. "Shai, he showed up to defend Helbrans from kidnapping charges. To testify for him at the trial."

She's got that right. But does she have a clue how long and vigorously this custody battle can drag on?

"Zaks is part of the plot," Larry tells Steve. They are holding another strategy-and-bagels meeting at Larry's house. "I'm convinced of it. He's in their pocket."

"Who was that other rabbi at Zaks's elbow? Older. Fatter. The guy sticking to Zaks like velcro."

Steve shrugs. A lot to find out. And as predicted, Hana and Michael, once allies, are at each other's throats.

Michael will fight Hana to the end for custody. Even if he has to pretend he's on *their* side, like he wants Zaks to have custody. Maybe make a deal with Zaks. Con him. Whatever he has to do to take Shai back to Israel. Michael is a canny player—he'll figure it out.

Hana now grasps what she's up against. The manipulation of the hasidim to keep control of Shai. So many of them, families hiding him. Who else after Rabbi Aryeh Zaks? The older rabbi whispering in Zaks's ear—who is he?

To the press, Larry puts it succinctly. "What a coincidence that on the very day that the kidnapping trial is supposed to start in Brooklyn, Shai Fhima shows up in Rockland County."

But it is Judge Owens whose remarks turn out to be the most cogent. The black judge, a veteran of the bench for decades, has a sense of humor. Also a literary flair.

"If this isn't like Alice in Wonderland! It gets curiouser and curiouser."

# 27. JUDGE STANGER

O n March 7, while the complex custody battle swirls around Shai in Rockland County and his fate seems uncertain, in Brooklyn, D.A. Hynes concocts yet another plea bargain deal: a second one.

His deal is to drop the kidnapping charges against Rabbi Helbrans to *conspiracy to kidnap in the fourth degree*. The sentence? Five years probation and 250 hours of community service. *No jail.*

"No prison time for Helbrans? He don't go to jail, Larry?" Hana is frantic.

"They won't get away with it. It's a sellout if Judge Owens allows this."

Larry gets on the phone to Vinegrad, demands to be put through. "I know we're not talking Richard Nixon, Alan, I know that. It's not Watergate, not the White House. But it's a *conspiracy plot*. Hynes can't plea bargain it away."

"We're working on it." Vinegrad replies.

In Brooklyn, clutching a prayer book to his chest, Helbrans testifies before Judge Owens and declares he had nothing to do with the boy's disappearance. He has no idea where he has been for two years, he even tried to find him.

In Rockland County, Rabbi Aryeh Zaks sings the same song. He has no idea where the boy has been. "Shai didn't divulge his whereabouts out of fear it would bring repercussions to the families who sheltered him. Shai told Rabbi Helbrans about the abuse in his home and simply ran away. He was afraid if he went home he'd get the beating of a lifetime."

✡   ✡   ✡

Hana Fhima embraces her daughter Shiran, 4, and son Eliran, 7, as her older son Osheri, 9, sits nearby. October 1992. *(AP Photo/Ed Bailey)*

# MISSING

## Shai Fhima

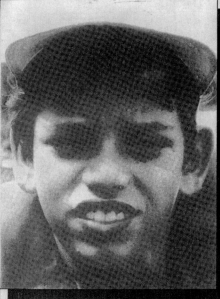

**Male**
**Age: 13**
**D.O.B.: Feb. 8, 1979**
**Height: 5 Feet**
**Weight: 105 lbs.**
**Hair: Lt. Brown**
**Eyes: Brown**
**LAST SEEN IN**
**NEW YORK ON 4/5/92**

*May be dressed in garb*
*of an Hasidic Jew.*

If you have seen this person, please contact:
66th Precinct in Brooklyn, N.Y.
Phone: The Hotline

The poster of missing Shai Fhima distributed
by the 66th Precinct in Brooklyn, N.Y.

RETIRED
CAPTAIN

PLACKENMEYER
WILLIAM     F

TAX
855129

1252     RETIRED 03-12-98

NYPD Captain Bill Plackenmeyer who pressed
for the investigation of the kidnapping and
gathered the evidence.

Larry Meyerson (right) and Steve Rubenstein (far right), the New Jersey attorneys who battled the court system for four years pro bono to achieve justice for Hana Fhima.

Brooklyn District Attorney Charles J. Hynes in his office. January 1994. *(AP Photo/Ed Bailey)*

Schlomo Helbrans arriving at State Supreme Court in Brooklyn to face kidnapping charges. October 1994. *(AP Photo/J. Kirk Ondyles)*

Indicted Rabbi Schlomo Helbrans (foreground) and yeshiva student Mordecai Weiss at a news conference in Brooklyn after their release on bail. February 1993. *(AP Photo/Mario Cabrera)*

In Brooklyn, Hana appeals to Judge Owens.

"Judge, if they get away with it, who's going to be the next victim kidnapped?"

Michael jumps to his feet. "Judge, I have evidence that Rabbi Helbrans wanted to buy my son from me. These people are criminals." He storms out of the courtroom.

Is Judge Owens taken in by their lies? Does he believe Hana was such a terrible mother Shai ran away to Helbrans?

Hynes's response to the press is that his primary concern has always been the safe return of the boy. "I call my decisions based on what I think and the law, and the facts are . . . there's no way of pleasing everyone in this case."

Nevertheless, inquiries to Hynes's office confirm that they've been deluged with telephone calls *denouncing* the prosecution of Rabbi Helbrans. Flyers are circulating, plastered all over Boro Park. The hasidic communities are out there working to make Hynes's new plea bargain stick. Can they do it?

Shai is insisting that he left home to escape his parents' abuse and he denies that Rabbi Helbrans held him against his will.

"He said this? My Shai said this?" Hana's reddened eyes widen with disbelief. Her son is now her adversary. He defends his kidnappers. "Dear God. How did they make Shai like this?"

Worse. Hynes's new deal includes the unusual condition that the defendants do not even have to state in court that they committed a crime. *No allocution*: They don't have to give a factual foundation of guilt. Helbrans will plead guilty only to *conspiracy to commit a crime*. All charges against Malka Helbrans will be dropped. Meissner, Helbrans's lawyer, feels confident it will fly.

Larry and Steve are on the phone every day. Calls are flying back and forth. Clarifications. Modifications. Negotiations.

"No." Hana won't budge. She is adamant against any suggestions to work out a compromise. "I won't make a deal with the rabbis. Zaks is part of this. Let Michael make a deal with them. Not me." She stares Steve down. "I got custody. Me. I got custody from Israel."

"Right." Steve's checked it. It was docketed in New Jersey and filed and got a New Jersey docket number. In order for Judge Stanger to act, he has to take away custody from Hana.

Scary. Very scary.

Because at a minihearing before Stanger on March 3, a sea change occurred. The kindly grandfather evaporated. Another Stanger appeared. A custody battle? Custody? No, no. He calls it *visitation* and he orders Zaks to have *visitation*. Shai can stay with him.

"You won't believe this." Now it's Steve's turn to dump his frustrations on Larry. "Stanger's going through more mental hoops than I ever saw. He's creating his own fictions. He's redefining words. He's bending over backwards. He's making up things."

They stare at each other.

"You mean . . ."

"Stanger's got his own religious agenda."

"Waddaya mean? Cause he's orthodox?"

"All he lets me do is question Shai. But he won't let me introduce any evidence to show the kid's testimony is incorrect. So now he's created his own reason to keep Shai from Hana."

"Give me more."

"Shai says she beat him every day. She beat him when they were in the shelter. Lil is sitting there waiting to testify that it never happened. Detective Kevin Kelly is there, too. But all Stanger will hear is the ammunition he wants to keep Shai away from Hana. He won't let them speak. He's creating his own case."

Larry shakes his head slowly. "We're in deep shit."

In Brooklyn, Helbrans's trial is supposed to start March 7, but it's put off. They discover that the fat man sticking to Rabbi Aryeh Zaks like velcro is Lieb Waldman, Zaks's father-in-law. Was he in on the plea bargain deal for Helbrans to get five years probation and walk? Who is he? And why is he at the criminal case in Brooklyn with Helbrans's lawyer Meissner?

The convoluted plot and new players are coming at them from every angle. Each day uncovers a new twist, another enemy, another miscarriage of justice.

Michael is frantically trying to make a deal with Zaks to wrest custody from Hana.

Larry and Steve are on the phone, consuming the entire week.

It's falling apart on both fronts.

In Rockland County, Stanger's doing a new dance to keep Shai from Hana.

In Brooklyn, Owens's deciding on the plea bargain to let Helbrans off.

"Yup. We're up shit's creek." Larry scratches his beard.

"Jesus. What do we tell Hana?"

But Hana knows where it's going. When Stanger sets another hearing for March 17 and issues a gag order on all parties in the case, she worries that Stanger will do anything to keep Shai away from her.

"Shai will remain with Rabbi Aryeh Zaks," Stanger rules.

She leaves his court in tears. "The court's helping those people kidnap my son for the *second* time. This is not justice."

How can it be? How can the law say this is fair?

Michael is enraged. Neither he nor Hana are one step closer to getting their son back. Stanger has sliced the legs from under them. Cut out *both* parents.

Sobbing hysterically, Hana phones Steve. "They just made a deal. Stanger gave him to Zaks." She is devastated.

No place to go.

It is a watershed event.

# 28. SHARED CUSTODY

**H**ana and Michael decide the world is against them.

They might as well join forces. Make peace and try for shared custody. Will it work?

The brilliance of the deal Steve works out is that on March 17, he is prepared to walk into Stanger's court with only two things to address. With satisfaction, he describes his strategy to Larry.

"Tell me, I'm all ears."

"*One:* The CPS investigation of a family offense petition—we know we can slam-dunk. Not a prayer it will fly."

"And the custody petition?" That's the crux of it. He's been hearing Steve hammering it out, arguing on the phone, every hour a new twist, another fax.

"That's *two*. Here's what happened," he leans back in his swivel. "I'm getting conference calls coming in from Zaks. His father-in-law, too, Lieb Waldman is calling. I remain very circumspect, I say nothing. It makes them suspicious. We're supposed to be back in court March 17 and they're getting nervous, very nervous."

Larry is grinning, he can guess. "You got a new deal."

Steve snaps him a circle of thumb and forefinger. "We reach an agreement. Zaks will withdraw his petition for guardianship. Hana and Michael will share custody."

"Helluva job." He leans across his desk and slaps him a high five.

"Just one little zinger," Steve adds. "They tell me Shai's sick, he's going to the doctor."

"Sure. Sure." Larry rolls his eyes.

✡   ✡   ✡

Snow. More snow.

On Thursday, March 17, the custody tug of war takes a breath in Judge Stanger's chambers.

"We got a deal, Judge," Steve announces. "CPS has determined there's no family offense, abuse charges are dropped. No basis in fact. They are unfounding the case. These proceedings are dismissed." He takes a step closer. Now for the biggie. "Rabbi Zaks has withdrawn his application. The parents have reached an amicable agreement. You have to give this child over to them."

Stanger is stymied. He frowns. "Where's Shai?"

"They tell us he's sick," Steve says severely.

"Sick? Sick?" Reluctantly, he sends the sheriff to bring him in. The delay is irritating.

When Shai arrives, he's fine.

"Let's proceed." Stanger runs his hand through his wispy white hair and massages his forehead. He leans on the palm of his left hand and studies his papers. "Wait. You have to deal with the religious aspects."

*The religious aspects?* Steve contains himself. Where are we? Is this a court of law in the United States of America? Do we have separation of church and state? What's he going to lay on us now?

"The parents agree to address Shai's religious needs, Judge. We have everything in place. We have an orthodox . . ."

"Wait," Stanger interrupts. He sees what's on the table. He coughs and takes a drink of water. Puts the glass down and continues. "I only have jurisdiction over the family offense petition. Since that's unfounded, the parents can make their own deal, any deal they want regarding custody. I'm releasing Shai to his father. But," he adds, "the parents must deal with his religious concerns."

"Thank you, thank you." Hana can hardly breathe.

"Thank you, Judge." Michael is almost jumping.

Stanger nods. Another miracle in his chambers. Parents and

child are talking and actually agree to make peace. The parents are secular, but the boy wants to be orthodox. He looks at them sternly. "Shai will go home with his parents. He will be educated in an orthodox Jewish manner."

Shai leaves Rockland County courthouse arm in arm with Hana and Michael. He also leaves with a new name. Henceforth he will be *Shai Fhima Reuven*. He wants his father's name: *Reuven*. A victory for Michael.

For Hana, also a good thing.

In August 1993, she secured a *gett* from Jacky—a Jewish divorce obtained by a rabbi. Jacky was a mistake and Steve is taking care of the legal divorce. Michael is Shai's real father, he'll always be his father. It's what Shai wants. To be *Shai Reuven*.

As they sprint across the parking lot to the car, they hardly notice that another blizzard is piling up new snow. Their hearts are warm. Rabbi Zaks is out of the picture. It went perfect. Perfect.

"Thank you, Steve," they wave at him as he unlocks his car door. "Thank you."

He waves back as the snowflakes stick to his lenses.

The winter of pain is over.

To celebrate their bonding, they go out to a kosher restaurant. They are a family again. It doesn't matter that the parents are divorced, lots of parents are divorced. They both love him, they want his happiness. And in that glow, on that very afternoon, a healing begins.

"We want a nice table," Michael tells the waiter.

*"You see? God was watching. Thank you, God."* Hana's smile lights up her eyes as she hands Shai a menu.

Initially, Shai is very quiet. He toys with his paper napkin, eyes downcast, folding and refolding it. It is a lot to take in. Perhaps he doesn't grasp what is happening; he's fifteen.

Today he is reunited with the mother he hasn't seen for two years. Reunited with the father he hasn't seen for four years. He has been the subject of a fierce custody battle in Rockland County. And a kidnapping trial in Brooklyn. A child swept up by the eye of a tornado and dropped. Stunned. Disoriented. Not once. Many times in his fifteen years.

But then he lightens up. His parents are kissing and hugging him and joking together. He looks up and smiles.

They tell him stories about the day he was born. About his grandmother and grandfather and Uncle David, Hana's brother, in Israel. About the day he got his first shoes. How Osheri and Shiran and Eliran are waiting for him back in New Jersey. It feels like a beautiful mending.

Hana teases him. She tells him how blonde he was as a baby. So cute, so adorable, so sweet. How much they loved him. The funny things he did and said, the time he got his first tooth. Family stories. So dear, so private, the intimate depository of every loving family. The silky ribbons tie them together.

And Shai warms to their praise and their embraces.

In this conciliatory and joyous mood, Hana and Michael vow to do what's good for Shai. Share custody amicably. Be good parents and restore him to normal family life. No intruders are in their midst. Only mother, father, and son. How good it feels.

A new life for Hana. Shai's back.

# 29.  A TROUBLED BOY

Parched by his two years absence, Hana drinks in her son as the car pulls out. *He's safe. He ate good. He'll be okay.*

She gazes at him watchfully. What is he thinking? What does he want? "So tonight what do you want to eat?"

Shai taps his belly. "Eat? I'm full."

"Tonight you'll be hungry." Michael is exuberant. How can he please his son? So handsome, eyelashes a girl would die for, and taller than Hana already. "So? Where do you want to go?"

"I don't know."

"And tomorrow? Saturday? You want to go to the mall?"

"Sure."

"I know. Let's celebrate!" Michael is full of plans. "Let's check into a motel." He turns to Hana, her children are with a neighbor. "It will be okay?" he asks her.

"Absolutely." The kids will devour Shai when he gets to the apartment. Better to give him a little time alone, he should be reacquainted with his parents. Full attention to him.

"We'll pick up milk and kosher food, we'll bring it to the motel. You want cupcakes? Chocolate?"

"Okay."

"A wonderful idea, Michael." They understand, without speaking, that there must be no conflict. No controversy. No mention of Helbrans or Zaks. Wrap him in love. Blanket him in approval. Win him back. A weekend to remember.

By Friday, the blizzard has worsened. Fierce wind-powered snowflakes are whipping against the windshield as Michael heads back to New Jersey. The driving is hazardous with backups of crawling vehicles and the afternoon is already darkening into dusk.

200

At an Exxon station, Hana calls her neighbor. "It's pretty bad up here, very slow. You have enough to give them supper?"

It's dark when they open the front door.

Shai's arrival is marked with screaming and tumbling. Three puppies are all over him. Right off, he and Osheri have a water pistol fight and Eliran tackles him. His little sister, shy at first, stands to one side, watching. But then they're all chasing him and he's playing into it, and the horsing around is getting so loud, Hana's sure the ceiling will fall from the jumping.

*Shai's back.*

On Saturday they drive to the mall in Wayne, with Michael, too. He has checked into a motel. "Maybe I'll bring Lilit and the kids over. I got a lot to celebrate." He is glowing.

Shai has shed his hasidic garb. With his father's arm draped around his shoulder, they window shop through the mall, Hana and the kids tagging behind munching Mrs. Field's chocolate chip cookies.

Hana catches up to them at Video World. "You want a video? Something special?" She gives Michael a knowing poke in the ribs. Look, he's a boy again, normal. Shai picks out two action movies with Steven Seagal.

At Foot Locker, the Nike display captures Shai's attention.

Michael squeezes his son's shoulder. "You like those sneakers?" He's still wearing his black leather shoes. "C'mon, we'll go in. You'll pick out something." *My son loves me, he took my name. Whatever he wants, anything.*

It is four A.M. Does she hear a car pulling out of the driveway? Her eyes fly open, she runs to the window. Sees the taxi. And she knows. *Shai's gone.*

"Please, please," she cries to 911. "My son ran away, he took a taxi."

"Yes, ma'am," the Ramsey police officer says. "We'll contact the cab company."

He orders the dispatcher to instruct the driver to take the boy to the police station. All she can do is wait, they'll call back as soon as they find him.

Knuckles pressed hard into her teeth, she paces. Stands at the living-room window, pacing, waiting, pacing.

At six A.M., sobbing hysterically, she phones Larry at home. "Shai's gone, he's gone, he ran away."

Larry gets the Ramsey police on the phone. Then phones Steve. "They caught him on the way back to Zaks. Can you believe it? He was going to Zaks's house. To Zaks."

"Where is he now?"

Larry emits a long sigh. "A snafu—don't ask. Instead of returning him to Hana, they sent him back to Rockland."

*"To Rockland?"* Steve is aghast. "Major disaster."

"Major. Big time."

"Back to Stanger." Steve slaps his forehead.

On Tuesday, they are back in Judge Stanger's courtroom.

Hana and Michael sit next to Steve on one side of the aisle. Shai, barely visible, is on the other side of the aisle, obscured by Thorsen, his New York attorney.

Eric Ole Thorsen, forties, is dressed nattily in an expensive business suit, button-down white shirt and silk tie. Tall and sleek, thin to the point of gauntness, he speaks with a sharp bite of arrogance, a thoroughbred demanding attention.

"Look at that snake," Hana whispers to Michael. "They're paying him plenty."

"Who? Who's paying him?"

"Lieb Waldman. Zaks's father-in-law."

Adjusting his aviator glasses, Thorsen makes much of this runaway incident. Shai's escapade has handed him fresh ammunition to impress the judge.

"The boy's taxi was headed for Monsey and Rabbi Zaks, Your

Honor. He wants to live with Rabbi Zaks and be orthodox. He wants to practice his religion."

On Shai's behalf, Thorsen files a petition asking the judge to reappoint Zaks as Shai's guardian. No joint custody. No parents. "The boy wants Zaks, *not* the parents."

The judge hesitates. "What I need . . . I'm going to order a psychiatric report, I'll rule on it Thursday. Until then, I'll assign him to stay in a private home."

"This is ridiculous, Judge," Hana stands up and cries out. "How can you tear him away from us? We're his parents."

"This is a joke," Michael yells as they leave.

But it is not a joke. It strikes terror, a familiar terrain, in Hana's heart. "It means I lose him again?" she asks Steve in the hall.

"Just another roadblock, Hana. It's not over til it's over."

Privately, Steve and Larry exchange views.

"The kid's a little shit," Larry says.

"He's eating her heart out." Steve shakes his head sadly.

On Thursday, March 24, Judge Stanger listens to Shai contend that he cannot live with his parents.

"Why not?" The judge presses his palms together.

"They violated the sabbath by driving a car," Shai says. "They are not religious enough. I want to live with Rabbi Zaks in Monsey."

The psychiatrist's report describes a troubled boy. He sees unbelievable anger and there's no reason to send the boy back to his parents because he'll run away again.

Now the craziness begins.

On the one hand, Shai seems invaded by an angst of metaphysical proportions. Genuinely torn between the secular life of a teenager and the rigid life of an orthodox Jew. On the other hand, does he *know* what he wants? Is he making choices free of rabbinic pressures or is he brainwashed?

At best, the teenage years are a period of deep questioning. Why am I here? Who is God? Why do good people suffer? Why does God allow it? Which rules should be obeyed? Which flouted? The challenges to a child can be overwhelming, a heavy burden. Add to that the physical changes the adolescent experiences. A body assaulted by pumping hormones and leaps of growth. Puberty is galloping across Shai's face, pimples cover the boy's cheeks.

Perhaps Stanger takes this into consideration. Nevertheless, Thorsen's plea rings louder. The boy only wants to be *orthodox*.

"You violated my orders on religion." He glares at Hana and Michael. A child wants to observe the Sabbath and respect orthodox Jewish laws—why should he be denied it? A boy past bar mitzvah is countable as a man, acceptable in a minyan.

"We're not religious enough?" she puts it plainly to the judge, then bites her bottom lip, hate washing into her mouth, flooding her . . . *I hate you, Stanger. Thorsen. Hynes. Zaks. Waldman. I am his mother!*

Steve calls on Rabbi Aloney to testify. He is the chief rabbi of the Concord Hotel and the rabbi with whom Shai stayed over the weekend. Surely, he can provide expert observation on Shai's religiosity.

"For three days all he wanted was videos and movies and to play on the computer," the rabbi says. "When he stayed with us, Your Honor, my family would go to shul, we wanted to pray, and he refused to go." He pauses. "Shai has a very weak religious commitment."

Judge Stanger rubs his watery dull eyes. "The parents violated my orders. They drove on the Sabbath." His decision will come April 4.

"Driving on the Sabbath, that's my sin? For that I'll lose my son?" Hana moans to Steve on the way home. "My poor Shai, he's so mixed up," she says. She refuses to believe he wants to be orthodox. "He's not my Shai, they talk to him on the phone, Zaks is running him on remote control."

Steve drops her off and vents his rage in Larry's office.

"Stanger's eyes glazed over when Aloney testified. *You drove on the Sabbath*, that's all he hears. All he knows is: *You drove on the Sabbath*."

Larry squirms. "Me? I couldn't deal with the rejection. If David ever did it to me, I'd go ballistic."

"Yeah." Steve has doubts about Shai's sincerity, too. "He's tearing her heart out."

It's Larry's quote to the press that relieves the tension. When asked about his response to Stanger's ruling, he shoots back his one-liner: "So who appointed *him* the Sabbath cop?"

But the sobering truth is they're facing two uphill battles.

The custody fight in Stanger's court. And Hynes's plea bargain deal in Owens's court.

# 30. JUDGE OWENS RULES

Elaine Meyerson and Rabbi Weinberg organize a letter writing campaign. They ask people to write to Judge Owens. Tell him *Don't accept Hynes's plea bargain. Make Helbrans face kidnapping charges.*

Hana's own letter is enclosed.

"Please express your outrage at the light sentence for such a hideous crime. We didn't see our son for almost two years—we didn't know if he was dead or alive. We hope to persuade Judge Owens to give a tougher sentence. Our boy was deprived of normal family life and a regular public school education."

Will it do any good?

Rabbi Weinberg is optimistic. "Look, Hana. Helbrans acted like a vigilante," he tells her on the phone. "Who gave him the right to take matters into his own hands? If Shai wanted to be orthodox, Judaism could have provided it." There's more to it than that. He's worried. "This case can set a dangerous precedent. Religious kidnappings violate any sense of righteousness."

"It's plain kidnapping," she nods.

"There are limits to legitimate interference. The Torah portion of Pinhas, Numbers 25—the religious right uses it *incorrectly* to support zealots who step in. But according to Jewish law, zealots can't act violently on their own. You follow me? That's exactly what Helbrans did."

"He did, he did. He tore my son away from his home."

"Pious acts for the honor of Judaism? No. They can't be condoned. We have to stop them. They're dangerous people."

The pressure is building on both fronts. If Stanger awards custody to Zaks, if Owens accepts Hynes's plea bargain—it's all over.

The craziness is getting to them.

The weariness. The sleepless nights. The fear and rage.

"Suppose Owens accepts the plea bargain?" Hana puts the question to Larry for the umpteenth time.

"You should have grabbed Shai when you had him," he scolds her. "You should have shoved him on the first plane back to Israel," Larry tells her in his office.

"Shoulda, shoulda: don't tell me shouldas. Don't talk to me like I'm stupid," she lashes out, hands on her hips. "I know what I'm doing."

"Okay, okay," he backs off grinning. It is this side of Hana Fhima he admires. She takes no shit. Not from lawyers. Not from judges. On the other hand, she can be exasperating. A royal pain-in-the-ass. Incredibly naive one moment. Extraordinarily manipulative the next. Lacy innocence in steel determination.


On April 4, the custody fireworks erupt in Stanger's courtroom. Shai's suit claims his parents refused to let him practice his religion—*a condition required by Stanger*. To punish them, Stanger awards *joint* custody to Zaks and Hana. Sort of. Shai will *live* with Zaks, but Hana can *visit* him. Under restrictions.

Shai *lives* with Zaks in Monsey? And I have to call Zaks and arrange to visit? This is joint custody? I gotta get permission to visit my own son?

Leaving court, Hana screams at the triumphant rabbis waiting outside. "You are religious garbage! We are not Jewish enough to raise our own son?"


A week later, on April 13, Hana and Michael drive into Brooklyn for hearings before Judge Thaddeus Owens. Hana has carefully constructed her plea: how politics dampened Hynes from pursuing Shai's kidnapping. *Politics*. Rabbi Weinberg's warning sits on her tongue: *a dangerous precedent*. But when she speaks to the judge, it comes from her heart. The prepared words slide away: her fuel is her pain.

"They kidnapped him, Judge," Hana implores Owens. "They brainwashed him. They gave him a new name *Avrahami* and they called him *Yishi*. They gave him new clothes, they hid him for two years."

Judge Owens gets off his bench and paces—a tall, lean handsome man, keen of mind and straight of back. It's a habit that helps him think. Perhaps it crosses his mind that in this courthouse Lemrick Nelson Jr. faced federal civil rights charges in the killing of hasidic scholar Yankel Rosenbaum. Perhaps he sees again the Crown Heights riots of 1991 and Nelson's acquittal. Perhaps the contradictory stories from a stream of hasidim who testified before him play in his mind. Perhaps he senses the public disgust at what passes for justice. Or perhaps it is Hana herself. So believable in her grief.

What rings in his ears is how human beings claim to be civilized and act like animals. From the bench, you see it all.

He returns to his chair. Let the mother say her piece.

"He made me live in hell, Your Honor. I remember nights I wished to sleep forever and not wake up in the morning to this nightmare. Please Judge, if you accept this plea bargain, these criminals will get exactly what they wanted in the first place. They will get my son and they will walk away from this crime."

He nods to excuse her. "Mr. Reuven?"

It's Michael's turn. "Your Honor. Hynes bent to the pressures from the orthodox right. They control the D.A.'s office." His voice is shaking with emotion. "Someone stealing a VCR would get more time than these defendants who are charged with kidnapping my son."

Judge Owens lets him go on a bit, then excuses him and asks Rabbi Helbrans to speak.

The rabbi has two sentences. "I never met such strange and terrible persons as these two people, they told so much lies. My English is too poor to answer." Nothing more.

"Thank you. Where's Shai? Where's Shai?"

Shai stands up and reads a prepared statement in a rehearsed monotone. "I ran away because of abuse. I never saw Rabbi Helbrans or Mordecai Weiss after April. I am not a victim. I chose to leave my parents. Rabbi Helbrans and Mordecai Weiss are victims." He sits down.

There is a fearful silence. The sound of the judge drumming his fingers. All eyes on him, waiting for him to speak.

"Rabbi Helbrans." He fastens his gaze on the black-shrouded figure. "There's a perception that you have political connections and that justice was not even handed."

Meissner objects wildly, but the judge rebuffs him.

Owens clears his throat. "I am convinced," he speaks forcefully to the rabbi, "you should let twelve impartial people make a determination as to what occurred here." He crosses his arms.

Is he rejecting the plea bargain? Saying *No Deal*?

Hana and Michael lock eyes.

Meissner is jumping to his feet again, objecting, "Your Honor, Your Honor . . ."

"Hold it. I've been on the bench a long time. And I do what I think is the right thing to do. And then I look for the law to back me up." This judge will not budge.

On that day, he reinstates the kidnapping charges and orders a June 20 trial date. No plea bargains. No deals. *A public trial.*

A public trial? Hana and Michael are pinching themselves.

Judge Owens looks out over his courtroom. "It will be the best forum to determine guilt or innocence."

The rabbi now faces up to twenty-five years in prison.

Outside on the courthouse steps, reporters mob Hana and Michael. "Were you expecting this? Didja think the judge would turn the deal down?"

Hana lifts her head to the sky and lets the sun fall on her face. *Thank you, God.* Smiling, she holds court with the reporters, pushing her silky hair behind her ears, glints of red shining through. "Pictures? Okay."

"Howdaya feel now, Hana?" A reporter stands one step below her next to a photographer clicking away.

"I really appreciate what the judge has done. This is the first time I see justice in the last two years. We got a chance now. We got a chance."

"You ready for this trial?" Another reporter gets in her face. "You ready for this fight?" He's been covering the case since day one, it's his baby. And this mother has captured people's hearts. He'll be assigned to the trial.

"I'm a fighter. I'm Israeli. Waddaya think? We're only big as New Jersey so we have to know how to fight." She's gushing, she can't help it.

"C'mon, Hana." Steve takes her elbow, urging her to leave.

Steve and Larry: two years. Not paid a dime. Should she say something?

"America is wonderful," she tells them. "You know, you got a big heart."

# 31. JUDGE SWEEN
# VS. JUDGE STANGER

Larry stops Steve as he returns from court. "You look beat."

Steve plops his attache case on his desk and thumbs through messages, then he looks up. "Stanger claims," he rolls his eyes, "adjournment's in the best interests of working out an amicable agreement."

"Sure, sure. How many adjournments?"

"Got a scorecard?" Steve rubs his forehead. "He's getting advice from the rabbis. He gets away with it because no one sees what goes on behind closed doors."

"Know what Plackenmeyer told me?"

"What?" Steve asks.

"He says what Stanger's doing is *criminal*. It scares the shit outta him that something like this could go in the United States court system. He says it's the most terrifying thing he ever saw. A judge out of control—those are his words, Steve—*out of control*. Justice blatantly subverted. A judge doing whatever the hell he wants to do. No checks on him. It's cloak-and-dagger stuff."

Steve nods. "He's right. Plackenmeyer's just one of those honest-to-God decent cops who wants to see the kid back with his mother. He says it over and over: *It was a kidnapping*."

"We got Hynes playing ball with the hasidim. And Stanger playing ball with Zaks and Waldman. Watta they gonna come up with next?" He pauses. "And Thorsen? Slick, very slick."

"C'mon, Lar, give him a break. He's a very effective lawyer, he's doing his job. I even sent him a client way back."

"Yeah? Hana calls him a snake." He drops it, so they disagree about Thorsen. It doesn't matter.

"She doesn't understand the process." Steve folds his arms and sighs. "Right now I gotta play by Stanger's rules. But I'm going to move it to New Jersey, get it out of his jurisdiction."

Steve's bulldog strategy pays off.

In Bergen County Superior Court in Hackensack, New Jersey, Judge Birgen M. Sween orders Zaks to return Shai to his mother's home in Ramsey. "This child is from New Jersey. He's a New Jersey child. We have jurisdiction over him."

But Judge Stanger will not budge. He refuses to release the case to Judge Sween. Two states are now fighting over jurisdiction: New Jersey and New York. A tug of war between two judges. A bistate feud that only slows down the proceedings.

It demoralizes Hana.

Waiting outside Stanger's courtroom, she often sees another rabbi, his scruffy greying beard and face turned to the wall, his mouth barking orders in Hebrew into his cellular phone. "Who is he?" she asks Steve.

"Lieb Waldman? He's Rabbi Zaks's father-in-law."

"Why does he come here, what does he want?"

"Waldman says he's a businessman. Real estate. We think he's the point man, he's footing the bills for the hotshot lawyers."

"What's hotshot?" Hana asks bewildered.

"They're bringing in big hitters, expensive lawyers out of New York and Washington."

He's already filled in Larry.

"Nat Lewin?" Larry whistled a long low one. "They're going to use Nat Lewin? Really? A crackerjack on constitutional law. ACLU stuff. Speaks Yiddish and Hebrew."

Steve nodded. "Yup. He defends First Amendment issues, so you know where it's going if they're bringing him up from D.C."

"Hey, this has gotta cost them big bucks. Where's the green coming from? Waldman?"

"Hey. Didn't they deliver for Helbrans's bail? They've got their sources."

"Who else?" Larry asked. He looked worried.

"Eleanor Alter."

"Holy shit. She represented Mia Farrow against Woody Allen. Canny, ferocious. They're bringing *her* in?"

Steve nodded. "She bills out at $400 an hour, Lar. Mia Farrow's tab was around $1.6 million. Waldman's gotta be paying her tab. A custody battle for a kid is not exactly Woody Allen and Mia Farrow. So why?"

They looked at each other searchingly. Alter and Lewin. Big guns that cost big money. And Stanger and Sween at each other's throats. "We're about to play hardball," Steve predicted.

Larry shook his head dolefully. Then he stood up, hands thrust deep into his trouser pockets. "That's why Waldman's always in court. To see where his money's going. The man who pays the piper calls the tune."

Waldman's presence frightens Hana. One afternoon at a break, she passed him in the hall. "Whore," he hissed at her in Hebrew.

*What? What?* She turned, rolled up her newspaper and chased him down the hall. Raised her arms, aimed, and whacked him on the back with the full force of both arms.

The other person she fears is Judge Stanger. He has the power to take Shai away from her. "What Stanger is doing is helping the criminals, not the victim," she cries to Steve.

Alone, she asks God to right these wrongs. "Please, God, please take Stanger off the case because I can't get a fair trial. I don't want to lose Shai, please make someone else to be appointed." Hana believes in God. Believes that whatever happens comes from God. "Please God, help me. Get rid of Stanger."

So many enemies. Stanger. Zaks. Waldman. Thorsen. And now more lawyers to tell lies. Hotshots.

To retain some degree of sanity, she also counts her heroes.

First is Captain Plackenmeyer. If not for him, there'd be no investigation. He stuck to it, never gave up and kept his men on the job, saying: *it's a kidnapping.* Expect phone calls. *You're dealing with a kidnapping.* He never let up.

She remembers the day he sort of bowed his head and told her his own story. "I know what you're going through. I lost a son, he was a little past four years old. You never forget it. You go through an experience like that, you're never the same." Then he straightened up and cleared his throat. "If there's anything humanly possible, I'll do it." He stroked his reddish mustache, a bit embarrassed. A Brooklyn cop with his tie hanging loose. It came from his heart.

Alan Vinegrad is another hero. From June of 1992 when the federal government got involved with Shai's disappearance, she knew he was her ally. Smart, so smart. He was the one who said *the state, not the federal government, should charge the rabbi.*

"My satisfaction will be if justice is done, Hana." His crinkly eyes smile so nice, like a magazine ad.

So she has two good people fighting for her. She calls them her heroes, her angels. Two angels on my side. If God will help her and get rid of Stanger, she'll get Shai back. Even with the hot shots, she'll get him back.

Over the months, Judge Sween in New Jersey and Judge Stanger in New York wrestle it out in a series of bitter motions over jurisdiction. Which produces another long trail of papers, phone calls, and reappointments.

"This is a New Jersey case," says Sween to Stanger.

"*No,*" says Stanger to Sween, "it's *my* jurisdiction."

"*No,*" replies Sween, "he's a boy from New Jersey, it's *my* jurisdiction."

All of this is executed in perfect judicial language.

Papers filed. Duly recorded.

But where's Shai? No one will produce him.

When Stanger orders the next hearing for April 11, Larry and Steve look at each other and wince.

There goes opening day at Yankee Stadium.

# 32.  HANA MAKES A DEAL

Jacky Fhima, watching the battle from the sidelines, does not sit idly by. On April 4, he executes his own insidious plot. It comes at the end of a long day that has been particularly devastating to Steve. In Stanger's court, he has been beating his brains out against Eleanor Alter.

"This is a New Jersey case, Judge. Shai hasn't lived in New York for six months," he argues.

Alter is jumping up at every word. "No, no, Judge. It's a New York case. No, no, it belongs in New York."

Larry, sitting beside him, slips Steve a note. *So where was he? Ask them.*

"Then *name a name*," he challenges. "Tell us who Shai lived with in New York. We want the names."

The answer comes back from Thorsen. "We can't. People would be implicated."

*Implicated? Implicated?* Isn't this a court of law?

The judge lets it go by.

Weary and frustrated, getting nowhere, Steve and Larry decide to have a late afternoon strategy meeting at the Pearl River Hilton and to consult a law school dean on constitutional law. For four hours, from four-thirty to eight-thirty, they bat it around. It's dark and they're getting nowhere.

Larry takes a break and calls home. "A lousy day in court, no solutions in sight," he tells Elaine. But now David's on the phone crying because he got moved off one baseball team to another and he's not with his friends. And it comes to Larry as he slaps his forehead: *What am I doing here at night, I got a kid who's unhappy, I should be home.* Elaine's back on the phone. "You got an emergency call from the Ramsey Police."

215

"Emergency? The Ramsey Police?"

He punches in the number.

"We got three kids here," Kevin Kelly tells him. "Osheri, Eliran, and Shiran Fhima. They walked into the station house. Alone. Said their mother abandoned them. We called DYFS. The kids say they want to live with their father Jacky Fhima."

*What?* Immediately, Larry and Steve pack it in and head for the station house. In the car, Larry runs down scenarios.

"It's Jacky. He told the kids to make the complaint. I called Hana, she said they had a baby-sitter. He did it to show how neglectful she is, how she's a bad mother."

"Jacky's a thug," Steve adds with disgust. "And this is a two-pronged sword for him. One: to show he's the better parent when he files for custody of his three kids. And two: it plays right into the hands of the rabbis. I bet they put him up to it, to gain control over Hana, to distract her from Shai. They'll do anything, they'll stop at nothing. There's no question in my mind, it's Zaks and Waldman behind this Jacky thing."

The station house is pure bedlam.

Hana is there. Jacky is there. Rabbi Weinberg is there. Kevin Kelly is there. DYFS is there. The kids are crying. Everyone is screaming. And in the background on television is the NCAA finals. The University of Arkansas Razorbacks beating Duke University Blue Devils. Bill Clinton at the game.

Larry dives straight for the DYFS woman. He draws her aside, he's dealt with the Division of Youth and Family Services before.

"You understand what's going on here," he tells her. "Jacky Fhima put the kids up to this. He's working with the rabbis and they'll do anything. These kids were *not* abandoned. You talk to them?"

The DYFS woman nods. "Yup. It's clear to me after talking to the kids, they were put up to it. It's the father talking, not the kids."

Hana, distraught, takes them home.

✡   ✡   ✡

On that Tuesday, May 24, both sides in the custody war—Hana and Rabbi Zaks—lay down their arms. It's over. Lewin and Alter go back to greener pastures. Shai's custody is settled.

The final five-hour battle ends in Rockland County. On Stanger's turf. In his courtroom.

On that day, Hana and Rabbi Zaks finally consent to share Shai. He will live in an orthodox yeshiva in Rockland County, New York. And they will take turns on holidays.

"I'm confused," Hana says after signing the agreement. And she bursts into tears. What has she done? Was it right? She seems bewildered. "I can't fight everybody for my son. I want to start having a life with him again." She dabs her cheeks.

It is the lawyers on both sides who emerge smiling.

Thorsen hails the agreement as "a means of rebuilding the parent-child relationship."

Larry and Steve hug Hana. To the press they say, "This agreement is in the best interests of Shai and Hana." They truly believe it.

To Hana they say: "Now you can begin a new life."

Hana gazes at Shai. Let him be what he wants. Orthodox is okay. Fine. *"We'll begin a new life."*

Since February when Shai turned up, the lawyers have been negotiating at urinals, in parking lots, in hallways, and in judges' private chambers. Now both sides have hammered out the best deal possible. The lawyers are punching each other's shoulders. Hurrah, it's over.

Michael Reuven, standing on the side, alone, watches this. His back pressed to the wall, he sees them congratulating each other and his lips curl into a snarl.

*"What new life?"* he demands in a booming voice that resounds down the hallway. Every head turns. He moves in closer, he's in their face.

Larry and Steve step back, they can see the veins popping purple at his temples.

"*Me* you cut out?" he glares at Hana. "I am the father. I will not share my son with anyone!" he roars.

Scorned for doing what few divorced fathers do, he is bitter. He left his family in Israel, his wife and kids. Stayed three months to find Shai. Stalked yeshivas all over Brooklyn. Finally, brought Lilit and the kids over, everyone in a motel room.

*Once* he said, "I intend to stay here until everything is finished. How long it takes, I'll be here."

*Once,* he asked Larry about hiring a deprogrammer. "Me and Hana, we'll take Shai to this guy in Boston, he get kids deprogramed from the brainwashing in four, five days. Then we'll take him back to Israel."

*Once,* wearing a yarmulke like an orthodox Jew, he had even pretended he was on Zaks's side. His plan was to gain the rabbi's trust and trick him. Make a secret deal for Shai to return to Israel.

Nothing worked.

Now, Michael hurls his fury at Hana. She has made her own deal with Zaks. Cut him out. He's been duped, conned, a father used like a tissue and tossed aside.

Didn't he tell her all along: "Don't make deals with them, you can't trust them, you can't trust Zaks." Didn't he scream at her for months?

Now look what she did.

"*Hana has made a deal with the devil,*" he shouts to the press.

Then he storms over to Larry and Steve. "I put a lot in. I'm done. I'm washing my hands of it. I'm done. *Done.*"

Michael returns to Israel.

# PART VI

## The Trial

# 33. PARIS

With Shai's custody settled, Hana feels free to focus her attention on the kidnapping trial. It is slated for June in the Brooklyn courtroom of Judge Thaddeus Owens. A very different kind of battle, not hidden behind closed doors like Stanger. A public trial. The press there every day. A trial by jury.

Her anxiety level rises. Will I get nervous on the witness stand? Will I tell it right? Will I get scared and flustered? Can I stand up to their fancy lawyers when they cross-examine me? Will the jury believe me?

"What chance we got?" she asks Larry. In America, justice seems to come out out drop by drop, so slow, so much waiting, until one side, exhausted, gives up: the weaker side. "What do you think?"

"You're gonna be okay, Hana, just tell your story. Judge Owens runs a tight ship. Remember: he didn't let Hynes get away with the plea bargain."

So Hana allows herself to hope. With a judge who is fair, we got a chance. With a public trial, we got what Steve calls accountability.

To understand Shai's new orthodox life, she spends a weekend next door to Zaks to see the lifestyle he's experiencing. She watches the women on Saturday come home from shul and, in strict observation of the Sabbath, they sit around waiting for the TV timer to go off. The timer is their *shabbos goy*, turning on their programs to avoid the sin of working. Not a life for me, she thinks, I couldn't live like that. But if it's what Shai wants, okay. This summer, Shai and me, we'll talk, we'll be together, we'll make up. We'll be mother and son again.

✡   ✡   ✡

Another small victory comes on the heels of the end of the custody battle. On Friday, May 27, Tobias Freund is sentenced to fourteen months in prison. In a courtroom packed with hasidim, Judge Raymond Dearie orders Freund to surrender to federal authorities on June 24.

Alan Vinegrad issues a statement to the press. "Freund's perjury hindered attempts to find Shai and the family will certainly never get back the two years they lost with their son. The mother was betrayed by Freund. She trusted him and she was duped."

"See, Hana," Larry phones her. "Our luck's changing. Maybe we can arrange connecting cells," he chortles. "Freund and Helbrans in the same slammer."

Freund's sentence puts light back in her eyes. "Good. They convicted Freund, they'll convict Helbrans, right?"

"Doesn't work like that, Hana. But it's sure a point for our side."

However, the June 20 trial date comes and goes. No trial.

July. No trial.

August. No trial.

"October third is looking good," Steve tells her.

The summer is over. And with it, Hana's high hopes have evaporated. The shared custody agreement has turned out to be a farce. She has had no access to Shai.

"I don't see him. They're hiding Shai," she complains to Steve. "Every time I call, Zaks got another story. He's sick, he's studying, he's not there. We had a few visits, it was terrible: in a room with someone there." Frustration in every word. "I won't do it like that no more," she balks. "They tricked me. This is shared custody?"

Steve's words of comfort are tinged with regret. "I know, I know." When he persuaded her to sign the custody agreement with Zaks, he truly believed it would usher in a new life. How could he have trusted Zaks? Ironically, Larry, observant Jew, had warned him: *Don't trust the rabbis.* While he, the atheist, argued for trusting the rabbis and signing.

"You know what Shai told me one visit?" Hana has more to add. "He said: *if you drop the kidnapping charges against Helbrans, I'll come back. I said: no, Shai. Helbrans kidnapped you, he has to pay.* After that he was never available. I asked Zaks: why can't I see him? How come? Where is he?"

Steve shakes his head sadly. "And?"

"He's in camp in the Poconos, he says. So I say what camp? I want to write to him. And he says, I don't know the name."

"They're liars." We shouldn't have trusted them.

"Michael was right. *I made a deal with the devil.*"

The next day, Larry phones her, excited.

"No more delays. Judge Owens's courtroom in Brooklyn. October third. Can you make it?" he jokes.

Hana brushes her bangs off her forehead. "It should only be true. October third."

*But where's Shai?*

✡    ✡    ✡

The answer comes by phone in September. A long distance call from Orly airport in Paris.

Steve takes the call at his desk. It's barely nine in the morning, afternoon in Paris, and he's trying to follow the thick French accent of the caller.

"Shai Fhima Reuven was picked up as he was trying to board a plane back to the United States," says the French authority.

"What?" Steve grabs a pen.

"The passport photo, it did not match the boy's face. Our immigration officers spotted it. A false passport, understand?" says the French officer. "We had to detain him."

"You're holding him right now?" Steve asks all the right questions, gets the facts down.

"We'll keep him in custody until you arrive."

"Thank you." He's writing as fast as he can. Thinking: Call

Sheriff Kralick. Alert Rockland County. Phone Hana. A phony passport? How'd he get there? How long has he been in France?

Larry is asking the same questions. "How'd he get to France? Who got him a false passport? How fast can Hana get out there?"

"In Paris?" Hana shrieks. "He's in Paris?" She takes the next plane out.

She arrives at Orly and reports to the proper authorities.

"Gone? What you mean gone? You were supposed to hold him in custody. Where is he? My son is fifteen, where is he?" she screams at immigration. At airport officials. At anyone within earshot. "Where is my son?" she demands. "You had him, you let him go, you know where he went. *Where is he?*"

Immigration shrugs. "Sorry, madame."

She runs from one airline's counter to another. "Sorry, madame." "Go to this office, madame." "Try over there, madame." "Inquire in that department, madame."

"Did you see my son?" She waves his photo in their face.

They smile. "No, madame, regrets."

"He just vanished?" she screams.

A woman in uniform pulls her aside, her eyes sympathetic. "Maybe he went through ECC. For French, Belgium, German, Danish, Dutch, you just walk through." She's pointing to the sign European Community Control. "Understand?" She means he's gone. He slipped away.

Defeated, stymied, and disoriented, she takes a taxi out of the airport. Think what to do. Stop at a park, sit on a bench. Go back and talk to them tomorrow. Try again.

Outside, a light rain is falling. She walks aimlessly, mumbling, confused. *Shai. Shai. I'm in Paris. Where are you, my son? Aren't you tired of running? You can't run and run and run. I'll find you.*

A sidewalk artist, with a navy beret at a saucy angle, approaches her. "A portrait, mademoiselle?" Quickly, he goes to his easel and pulls out pastel chalks.

"No, no, no." She hurries past him.

"Five minutes," he calls after her. "A memory of Paris."

It stops her cold. She turns and walks back. Why not? *Proof.* I'll show him the portrait. See, Shai? I flew across the ocean to find you.

Hana thumbtacks the Paris sketch to the wall of the bedroom she shares with Shiran. One day, I'll show Shai.

"How did he get to Paris?" she asks Steve. "How long was he there? Where did he stay? Zaks knew it? Thorsen knew?"

"The circumstances are cloudy."

"What means cloudy?"

"Zaks admits he knew about Shai. Knew he was in France for a month this summer."

"A month? Shai was there a month?" She could kill Zaks. All the time with the lies: he's in camp, he's sick, he's studying. "These people don't know how to tell the truth."

"Thorsen said . . ."

"Thorsen knew, too? He's a snake."

"So Zaks knew where he was. All summer he lied to me." Hana takes a breath. "What are you going to do?"

"Thorsen's position is that Zaks made a mistake in judgment. He committed a technical violation of Stanger's order, only technical. They're saying Shai's a strong-willed kid used to being on his own and not following anyone's directions. So . . . according to them, you can't control him."

"No, no. They arranged. They sent him. Waldman, he fixed it. With his money and his lawyers, he . . ."

"Of course, Hana, we know it was Waldman."

"He paid for Shai's ticket. He made him a false passport. He arranged."

"It was a conspiracy to hide Shai. There are yeshivas in France, ultraorthodox. He probably stayed there." Steve's anger is past the boiling point. "It's a blatant disregard of a court order.

Let's see what Stanger does with it." A flight to Paris. A phony passport. No fifteen-year-old does that without help.

Zaks was covering up while Waldman pulled the strings and got the kid out of the country." Larry's frustration is over the top. "Christ. How do you beat them?"

"You gotta do something, Larry," Hana wails. "Steve, you gotta do something. *Do something!*" Two years ago, Hana Fhima was a mild-mannered woman of some naivete. Now she is unstoppable and demanding.

Shai's trip to Paris reopens the custody battle. A boy fifteen running around the world on his own? No supervision? A court system that claims to protect the interests of the child? This is justice?

"Don't you see?" Larry has decoded their strategy. "Why was Shai hidden? Why is he coming back now? Only one reason. To defend Helbrans at the trial."

"Absolutely." Steve's head is bobbing up and down. "Don't worry, Hana, you'll see Shai in a few weeks in Owens's courtroom."

Which is exactly what happens.

# 34. THE TRIAL BEGINS

**H**er temples pounding, deep in thought, Hana walks past the ornate old post office building with its castle turrets. Past the government buildings, cold and imposing. Past the strip of neglected weeds that run alongside the Brooklyn courthouse.

Today the trial begins. October 3, 1994.

At the foot of the wide staircase to the main entrance, she stops and looks up. SUPREME COURT STATE OF NEW YORK is etched in stone over the entrance doors. She climbs the steps.

The courtroom of Judge Thaddeus Owens looks like the other courtrooms: wood-paneled walls and fluorescent lights. Except Room 438 is a sea of black. Rows of hasidim are packed tight on spectator benches—five rows on the left, five on the right, all glaring at her. Two bearded men hiss as she enters and a woman mutters *shame, shame* in Hebrew.

Hana takes a space next to Michael. Despite his parting shot last May, *Hana has made a deal with the devil*, he has returned for pretrial hearings, determined to see that his son's kidnapper is punished. He has left his home in Arad and left his family again to testify against Helbrans. They sit together now, as Shai's parents. Glum. Anxious. Tense. Hana exudes a woeful distress from head to toe. Michael shows a grim restraint, his armor against the world.

Rabbi Helbrans, meek and mild, hands one of the young yeshiva boys in the front row his coat. Clearly it is an honor and the boy actually blushes as he receives the garment. A beatific smile plays on the rabbi's lips and he offers a pleasant *good morning* to each person who greets him. It worries Hana. This chubby Buddha isn't threatening or menacing. Will the jurors believe he kidnapped Shai and hid him for two years? Will they send a gentle, pious man to jail?

With a racing heart, she searches for Shai. Not here. Is Thorsen bringing him? What will Shai say when he's called to testify? So much is about to happen. Two and a half years to prepare for this day.

At the prosecution table are Alan Vinegrad and Michael Vecchione. To Hana, they look splendid. Both have been taking testimony from the hasidic community: boxes and boxes. They have taken on heroic proportions in her eyes.

"Alan will make him pay," she tells Larry and Steve.

"We won't be at the trial," Larry tells her, "we got a practice to run. But I'll be on the phone every day talking to Alan." Larry is willing to give the D.A. credit. Since June 1992, he's been gathering evidence and planning his strategy. "Alan's totally prepared," he assures her. "On top of it."

Next to Vinegrad sits U.S. Attorney Michael Vecchione. Very presentable business suit, his salt and pepper hair well cut. Taller and older than Alan, a figure of pure professionalism.

Taking them in now, both D.A.s so classy and smartly dressed, makes Hana feel better.

In the beginning, it seemed pretty simple to decide about who was on her side. Everything boiled down to one question: *"Is he sincere?"* she asked Larry early in the investigation.

"Vinegrad? C'mon, he's getting paid," he shot back. Larry is not crazy about D.A.s; they're often stuffy and impressed with themselves. "Prosecutors are not interested in justice, Hana. All they want is a conviction. Forget sincere, okay?"

"Vecchione. Is *he* sincere?" Sincerity was her litmus paper, it gathered the good people into a pile on her side.

"C'mon, Hana, wise up, it's a job. Vinegrad's getting paid. Vecchione's getting paid." Christ, we're the only shmucks *not* getting paid, he thought. Even Woodward and Bernstein got paid. Sometimes it gets to him. She repeats the same question over and over, she only hears what she wants.

Days later, she asks Larry, "You think Judge Owens is sincere?"

"Hana, *pull*-ease. Gimme a break."

Hana Fhima is exasperating. Maddening. But she's also a pretty woman and very appealing. This will not go unnoticed in Owens's court.

All rise as the honorable Judge Thaddeus Owens enters.

The handsome black judge, with the well-trimmed silver hair and small mustache, enters briskly, belying his seventy-plus years. He looks over his courtroom, his kingdom, his turf. Feels the rush of opening day. They're all here, all the players. The do-or-die, win-win attorneys. The flamboyant D.A.s on the way up. Heroic young lawyers hungry for justice. Political pawns, liars, murderers, rapists, weirdos, sycophants—he's seen them all. Seen a lawyer grandstand. A client lie. A wife exact vengeance. A black brother jockey for a spiff. Victims and victimizers.

Next year will be his last year on the bench. Maybe at this closure he's mellowing a bit. Ronnie Schwartz, his superb right hand, teases him about it. Hell, one thing Thad Owens knows is people. "I know people and their problems," he likes to say.

Today, he wears snappy suspenders, a striped shirt with white collar and cuffs, a print tie, and gold cufflinks. His black robe flaps open giving everyone a peek. Hey, he still works out at the St. George, he's trim, he's sharp and he knows his reputation: Thad Owens? Piece of work. Approachable, funny, a man of the people. But, warning: play by his rules.

Asked by an aggressive D.A., "Sidebar? May I approach the bench?" he's likely to snap back. "About dispositions, yeah, not to shoot the breeze." Often, he stands up as he deliberates, plunging his hands deep into his pockets, pacing or turning to check the calendar on the back wall, then swinging around. "You're not hearing what I'm saying. Get this straight."

He knows Michael Vecchione, he has appeared before him. Alan Vinegrad, cross-designated for this trial, has not.

Opening statements begin.

The prosecution and the defense paint sharply contrasting pictures. A boy, kidnapped and brainwashed by an ultraorthodox rabbi, was hidden away for two years in a conspiracy of religious zealots. *Or* . . . a boy in an abusive home ran away and was taken in by a kindly rabbi, then the boy became religious.

Hana sits spine straight. Concentrating. Watching Judge Owens. Weighing his expressions. Did he grunt? Sigh? When he pulled out the pen clipped to his shirt pocket and wrote something down, was it a bad point against us?

It's a game she can't follow, with rules she doesn't know. *Objection, sustained, denied*, she understands those words. But after that, a lot gets away from her. Her knees are shaking and the aspirins aren't working. Alan has told her she will be the prosecution's first witness. First witness is hard.

*Just tell the truth, tell the story*: Larry's advice reverberates in her head. Vinegrad and Vecchione have prepared her, too. But sitting here now with Judge Owens presiding, it feels worse than she imagined. She feels small and helpless. Only a few of us against hundreds of them. She glances at the jurors—how will they vote?

To calm herself, she goes over her list of angels and devils. Captain Bill Plackenmeyer was her first angel. He fought to keep the investigation alive and he really cared about finding Shai, his heart was in it. Alan Vinegrad, once he was called in, he wouldn't let go of it. He was determined to get a conviction so he became her second angel. Now Judge Owens. Will he be her third angel? He didn't bow to pressure from the hasids and he turned down Hynes's plea bargain.

"Owens is a hero, Alan. Right?"

Vinegrad was amused when she put it to him. He understood her need for heroes. "There are many heroes in this case, Hana. But there is *one* hero," he held up one finger for emphasis, "and he's responsible for bringing the trial about. Thad Owens. He rejected the plea bargain." Alan gave Owens the most credit.

She calls them *my three angels*. Where would she be without them? Plackenmeyer. Vinegrad. Owens. They made today happen.

At the defense table sit the devils. Lawyers who defend kidnappers and help religious zealots go free. She'll have to listen to their lies.

On October 11, the state of New York calls Hana Fhima to the witness stand. First witness against Rabbi Helbrans. Mother of the missing boy. Reporters press forward in their seats, pencils out, craning not to miss a word. A hush of attention falls.

*Do you swear to tell the whole truth and nothing but the truth, so help you God?*

"I do." She sits down, skirt over her knees.

A cold suffocating tightness falls on her chest. Every muscle tenses. The skin on her face grows tight.

Hana pours out her story like a river that knows its path. Her testimony is unswerving. In a quavering voice, she tells it from the day she sent Shai to the rabbi's lecture. How he came back to her aunt's apartment hypnotized. How the rabbi told him: *Come sit by me, my son,* and everyone turned to look at him.

"He was only thirteen, a kid in sneakers and jeans. They wore black coats and white socks and long curls hanging down by their ears."

She tells how the rabbi told Shai: *I see a light in your face.* How Mrs. Helbrans invited her to tea the next day. How the rabbi took her downstairs to a room and they sat separated by a curtain. How she had to read from a book, read and stop, read and stop. "It was about ghosts in the forest. Devils in hell." How the rabbi told her Shai was special. Very special.

"He wanted to make my boy a *zaddik*. It's . . . a holy person, very holy, very close to God. He talks directly to God and God hears him."

Can the jury understand *zaddik*? Understand the mitzvah to change a secular boy to God's messenger? Can the jurors understand the craziness that controls the ultraorthodox?

Who are the jurors? What are they thinking?

The jury consists of eight blacks, two whites, one Asian and one Latino. A jury of your peers: the American system. What chance I got? The O. J. Simpson trial is blasting on every channel, with the white Bronco and the bloody glove. Car chases and a double murder, Americans love it. Who cares about a Jewish boy from Brooklyn, a rabbi kidnapped him? A football star and two dead bodies, this is more America.

Testifying, she faces the sea of hasids. With weathered Hebrew prayerbooks clutched to their chests, they stare venomously from the benches, their contempt spraying her like bug killer.

In a small, frightened voice, she tells the story, halting at times because her eyes fill up and it comes from her heart. There is restraint, no uncontrollable sobbing, no cheap shots. She starts again. She explains. The story is powerful and she tells it simply, forcing the jury to lean in to catch every word.

"And then what happened? Go on."

She tells how her aunt pressured her to send Shai to the rabbi for bar mitzvah lessons. How she had to call the police to get her son out of Lev Tahor when she changed her mind later on.

" 'If you don't want your son to be religious, I have the right to take him away,' Helbrans told me, and one of them twisted my arm and held me back. I couldn't go inside to get Shai. Helbrans explained me: 'It's not good for Jewish kids to go to public school with black kids and Italians, other Christians.' "

"Objection! This is inflammatory." Paul Rooney, Rabbi Helbrans's attorney, jumps to his feet.

"Continue," the judge rules.

Her concentration is broken, she's flustered. "Mrs. Helbrans grabbed me. She was screaming Shai belonged to them, he was her son and she would raise him. She yelled, 'You'll never see him again.' " She stops. She feels herself losing control. The grief and the sorrow hang on her like bricks. Will they believe me? You can hear a pin drop.

The jurors are listening intently, concentrating on this heart-broken mother with her Israeli accent. An astonishing story. Chilling. But not one juror blinks, no indication.

"Then Mordecai Weiss, he called and called. He persuaded me I should let Shai stay overnight with him in Brooklyn. 'We'll study together,' he told me, 'and I'll drive him back home to Ramsey. I promise.' It seemed okay." She shakes her head as if admonishing herself for her own stupidity.

"Please describe the circumstances that led to the day of your son's disappearance."

She rearranges herself in the chair, swallows, and gathers strength to go back to it.

"It was April 4, 1992. Two and a half years ago."

She tells how Weiss took Shai for an overnight to study together. How he told her to meet them on Sunday in Brooklyn and she would drive Shai back home, that was the plan. How she went to the designated location and waited and waited. How Shai and Weiss didn't show up. How she called the police and they arrested Helbrans for kidnapping.

"But then . . . , D.A. Hynes . . . he, he just let him go." A voice full of pain. But she does not break down. Does not wail or weep. She just tells it.

How Michael came flying from Israel when he read about it in the paper. How he called Rabbi Helbrans's parents in Israel and they said: "Yes. Yes. We lost our son the same way. We understand. When he was a teenager, just like your boy, he turned ultra-religious from a weekend yeshiva camp. We were secular. He turned against us, it was terrible fighting. *The same as your boy, the same.* They turned him against us."

She is twisting a tissue in her lap, but now she looks up.

"I know this is true because Helbrans once, he phoned me. He told me how Shai reminds him of himself. How when he was the same age, he went through the same thing. He found religion and his parents fight with him, so he just ran away. He ran away again and again until his parents give up. Same as my Shai." Not coached. Not rehearsed. It just pours out. Eyes on the twisted tissue.

"And then?"

She tells it step by step. How Michael was wired by the NYPD to get the rabbi's bribery offer on tape. How Jacky's finger was sliced off.

"For two years, I went through hell." Her eyes are misting, her throat catching. "I didn't know if my son was dead or alive. Michael and Jacky and me, we searched everywhere. They went out every night looking in yeshivas, hiding in cars." She shakes her head, fighting back the tears. "It don't do no good."

Do the jurors see what she went through? Do they understand how hard she fought to find him? If Shai hears, will he love her again and come back?

But Shai is not present in the courtroom. Where is he? No one knows. Not even Thorsen, his attorney.

She tells about Osheri and Eliran and Shiran, how they wake up in the middle of the night. "My children have terrible nightmares. They wake up screaming, they think they'll be kidnapped like Shai. They went through plenty from this. We were living in a battered woman's shelter because . . . my husband Jacky . . . he hit me." She is ashamed, her shoulders sag. Hundreds of eyes are peering at her shame.

Hana Fhima is that utterly credible person whose testimony is riveting. It has the ring of truth.

She pulls herself together.

"I came to America for a better life. What happened . . ." her head slumps, her eyes fall into her lap. "I lost my son. Nobody cares they stole him. Two years I was without my son. D.A. Hynes, he don't care, he only wants votes. Even when we give him the tape from the NYPD—how the rabbi said he'll pay Michael $50,000 for the custody papers . . ."

*"Objection! Hearsay! Irrelevant!"*

She stops.

She starts again. Judge Owens's rulings puncture her testimony, she follows his instructions. Lawyers approach the bench for private conversations with the judge. She waits. She proceeds. She does what she's told. Continues the story. Tells it, and tells it, and tells it.

Then . . . *something happens.*

This time, the telling feels different. The same words, the same events. But this time Hana Fhima is fed by a different fuel. Up to now she was an object, the loss of Shai happened to her. She was a butterfly caught in a net. Flaying and flapping, out of terror. Reading about herself in the media. Their facts. Their editorials. Their headlines. *Religious War. Political Payoffs. Secular Jews Fight Devout Jews. Rabbi Spends Sabbath in the Slammer.* Shai's kidnapping belonged to *them.*

Today everything changes: it belongs to *her.* Her story is the state of New York's most important testimony. It has power, and she can feel it. She has to make the jurors believe her. She has to show them how Shai was kidnapped. She has to make Helbrans pay. Give him back suffering like what he gave her.

It is a turning point, this realization that Helbrans is in her hands, she cannot afford to botch it up. For Shai's sake, for other boys like Shai torn away from parents, she *has* to make the jury see what happened. How religious cults steal children. How they get away with it. How they cover it up.

Bringing Helbrans to justice is her mission. She was a good mother. What happened bad to Shai was not her fault. It could happen to any child.

"They kidnapped him," she concludes, wringing her cold sweaty hands. "They turned him against me. They brainwashed my son. Made from him a different child."

That difference is now offered brilliantly in the state's exhibits. *Before* and *After* pictures of Shai.

*Before Helbrans.* Shai romping in the park. Grinning at a

birthday party. Horsing around with his brothers and sister. A kid in sneakers and baseball hat, an adorable little boy.

*After Helbrans.* Shai, dressed in black suit, black fedora, and black shoes. Gone is the baseball hat. Gone the sneakers and T-shirt. Gone, the carefree grin. A somber face, unsmiling, with long sidecurls dangling at his ears.

The difference is so dramatic, two jurors draw in their breath.

# 35.  HANA TESTIFIES

Now comes the cross-examination. Their turn.

"The cross, that's the hard part," Larry had warned her. "Their job is to drag you though the mud. Trash you, understand? They'll say ugly things, they'll lie . . ."

"I don't care what lies they tell," she interrupted him. "I know what happened to Shai."

But now it feels different. Her heart is racing. What will they say?

Paul Rooney rises. He is middle-aged, pleasant, and earnest. He questions her closely about boasting that she'd sell her story for a book or movie. "Are you sure you never said you're going to make $10 million on a book?"

She smiles ruefully. "Shai accused me. And me and Michael joked about if Helbrans is convicted, we'd make $10 million."

It goes nowhere, so he attacks her on another issue. "Did you ever strike Shai with a broom or a knife?"

"No. Shai ran away because I refused to let him take a bus to visit a friend. I didn't hit him," she responds full of conviction. His jabs make little headway so he passes her to Joyce David for further cross-examination.

David is Malka Helbrans's court-appointed attorney. She pushes her chair back from the defense table and walks toward Hana. The two women face off, the air between them emotionally charged.

Joyce David is a fortyish woman with a sparkle in her eyes. She knows she was asked to take the case because: one, she's Jewish, and two, she's a woman. She took it because she likes the challenge of defending difficult clients. The man who stabbed

Reverend Al Sharpton. The hit man "Baby Sam" who worked for a drug ring.

David has an excellent mind. She has authored a 1986 booklet *What You Should Know if You're Accused of a Crime*. She didn't get to read all the pretrial stuff and the secret tape Shai made of his fight with Hana, but she's confident. She really believes the rabbi was railroaded. Doesn't the record show a troubled kid in a dysfunctional family? The kid ran away, the rabbi didn't kidnap him. What she has to do is break the mother down, impugn her credibility. Chew up her testimony and spit her out. David knows exactly what she's doing.

"Tell us, Mrs. Fhima," she closes in on the witness stand. "Didn't you tell Shai you were in love with prosecutor Alan Vinegrad?" It sets the tone. A sleazy affair?

Hana's head drops, she is embarrassed. "I love him like a friend. But not romantic."

She moves on. "Didn't you share a hotel room with your ex-husband in April, 1994 . . ."

Hana's throat closes up.

Judge Owens bristles. He is tweaked by David's line of questioning. He sends the jury out.

"Ms. David," he speaks sharply. "This is not the Reverend Pat Robertson or Rush Limbaugh channel. We do not care who slept with whom, we care about what Rabbi Helbrans did."

Vecchione, feeling Owens's support, asks the court to limit questioning about the April 14 tape the defense is using to drum up a romance with Alan Vinegrad. Come on, he argues. Shai was angry with his parents for scuttling the plea bargain deal. The boy made the tape *secretly*. He had instructions. His job was to bait his mother and father into saying things that could be used against them on cross-examination. He baited his mother about Alan Vinegrad. Baited her into calling him garbage. Baited her into saying he needs mental help and she's sorry she had him. Shai deliberately engineered a screaming fight to discredit his mother and father.

"Hmmm." Judge Owens frowns. "I'd hate to be held responsible for some arguments I may have had with my children in 1994 over something in 1991 or 1992." He scowls at David. "I'm not allowing it. You're talking about 1994. Forget about it."

David tries to make the point that a mother who would call her child garbage and who tells him she should have aborted him probably abused him and made him run away. But Owens will have no part of it, he cuts her off saying they are irrelevant.

"Let me explain something to you, counselor. You're talking about two years after the alleged kidnapping. You're asking the jury to speculate. I'm not going to permit it and that's the end of it."

Vecchione jumps on it and asks the judge to strike all references to 1994 and to instruct David not to go into any evidence that stems from the tape. "Is your Honor striking references about France in 1994?" he asks.

"That has nothing to do with the case either," Owens snaps.

Rooney disagrees. "Judge, part of our defense is to show this young man is very willful and has taken off a number of times. . . . There's a pattern here."

"Well . . ." Judge Owens will not be bested. "He showed up in Paris and the jury might start speculating where he got the money from . . . how did a fifteen-year-old get to Paris? He didn't accumulate frequent flier miles. . . . You open up a Pandora's box." *This case is like Alice in Wonderland! It gets curiouser and curiouser.* "Bring the witness back. Bring the jury back."

Now he turns to the jury. "Any rulings I make, any reprimands or admonitions I give the attorneys, I don't want you to think I have a slant on this case. I have no slant, I have no opinions, that's entirely up to you."

Hana bites her lip. The victory for the prosecution does not erase Shai's betrayal. He secretly set her and Michael up. Pretended to come for a nice visit. Only he was wired and he had a purpose: to push them into a screaming fight and bring back a tape against them. What parent hasn't had a terrible fight with their teenager? Yelled words they didn't mean? But to tape it for a trial? Shai needs psychological help.

Later, in Steve's office, she cannot hold back the flood of tears. Watching her, Larry and Steve squirm. "A child, he acts against his own flesh and blood?" she wails. "That's what the rabbis teach him? What about the commandment *Thou shalt honor thy mother and father?*" This is what they teach my son. The righteous ones, the religious ones. Eh!

"It's what cults do, Hana." Steve tries to soothe her. "It's how they operate. They separate the kid from the parents and break the bond. This way they hold ultimate power, they make the decisions. It's mind control."

"Yeah, it's an old trick," Larry's voice is full of disgust. "Satmars. Hasids. David Koresh. Jones. They use the same tactics. They disconnect you from your family and make you rely on them. They become your family, you do whatever they say." It's hard for him to see Hana crying, she's held up so well up to now. "They pick out a vulnerable kid, an angry kid, a troubled kid. It's the way they operate."

She sits there weeping, shaking her head. "I don't understand. I don't understand. This is not my Shai."

"C'mon, Hana." Larry pulls her to her feet. "You're doing great. By my count, we're ahead." He wants to make her feel better.

"C'mon." Steve stands up and lays a solicitous hand on her shoulder. "Let's grab lunch." Food: it's the great comforter.

The prosecution goes on for days. Vinegrad and Vecchione have built a thorough case. They call witnesses who saw Helbrans talking with Shai. Who saw Shai after the alleged kidnapping. Who testify against Malka Helbrans. More and more evidence.

Sometimes a joke breaks the tension and everyone laughs except Hana because it's an American expression she doesn't get.

"I don't understand," she admits, tipping her head to one side. Which only makes her more believable.

"The thing about Hana," Larry pinpoints it later for Steve, "is that she's so damn sympathetic you want to help her. Lift her burden. Open the door for her. Pull out her chair. Take her pain away. Rub the spot that hurts."

"But the problem . . . the problem," Steve weighs the downside, "is that it's a convoluted case for a jury. Conflicting evidence. Cross-referenced dates that span two and a half years. Complicated events to line up chronologically. You got locations that bounce from where? Starts out in Ramsey, New Jersey, goes to Boro Park, New York. From the Brooklyn Police to the Ramsey Police."

"True," Larry nods, "a lot to keep straight. Shai's custody battle's bounced from New City in Rockland County, New York, to Hackensack in Bergen County, New Jersey. He disappeared twice and turned up twice. Last February in Rockland County. And last month in Paris. A lot to sort out. A lot for a jury to follow."

On Friday, October 14, New York City Police Officer John D'Onofrio testifies about the tumultuous scene in 1992 at Helbrans's yeshiva after Hana called the police to take Shai back.

"I was trying to break it up, calm everybody down, but they were all yelling at once," he tells the court. "So I took out my whistle and blew it like a referee."

"And what happened?"

"Me and my partner escorted the Fhimas out of the apartments. As we walked away, Mrs. Helbrans opened the windows and shouted, 'You can't take my son. You can't take my son.' "

The week ends strong. Two weeks into the trial, the prosecution's case looks good. Hana has done well. She is credible and she is the spine of the prosecution's case. The cross-examinations didn't turn out too damaging.

"She's so believable," Larry observes exuberantly to Steve. "You let her go and they eat her up, they love her."

Steve remains wary. "You never know, you never know. Juries are full of surprises."

Adding it up, Larry takes a deep breath. Two years of phone calls, letters, leaning on Plackenmeyer, leaning on Vinegrad, holding Hana's hand, thinking, planning, reacting to Hynes's stonewalling, issuing statements to the media, facing a system that failed, time stolen from his own kids, boxes of records all over his office floor. Jesus. The emotional toll. The financial loss to the firm.

"Are we *nuts?*" he asks Steve.

*"Now* you're asking?"

# 36. SHAI TESTIFIES

Mike Vecchione calls witness after witness:

A reporter from *Yediot Ahronot*, the Israeli paper, testifies that Helbrans told him in an interview on April 12, 1992: " 'I had something to do with the fact that the boy disappeared.' The rabbi said it was a mitzvah to take someone who was secular and make him a religious Jew."

A floor waxer, Jesus Rivera, testifies that he was working at the Kasho Yeshiva in Bedford Hills and he saw Shai there in 1992 just before Passover. In January 1993, he also saw Helbrans who came to teach there and was well known at Kasho.

An engaging Belgium boy, Simon Edwar, thirteen, testifies that he lived at Kasho for four years after he and his sisters Moriah, eleven, and Marina, fourteen, were kidnapped in 1986 from a schoolyard in Belgium. He saw Shai at Kasho just before Passover which began April 18, 1992.

On Monday, October 24, the prosecution calls Michael Reuven to testify. The jurors sit up straighter: now the father's side.

Michael testifies about his phone conversations with Helbrans. How the rabbi asked him to write a phony letter and back-date it to April 1, before Shai disappeared. How he met with Helbrans at Lev Tahor and the rabbi told him to get Hana to forfeit her legal rights to her child. How the rabbi claimed he saved Shai from an abusive mother and stepfather and Mrs. Helbrans told him he was lucky she took Shai in.

Michael makes a strong witness; he is passionate and convincing. Every juror's attention is fully on him.

On Tuesday, he concludes his direct testimony and the cross-examination begins. But the defense team fails to rattle him. He comes across as a father who dearly loves his son.

Finally, the prosecution shows the jury a series of charts detailing telephone records which substantiate that Helbrans was in constant touch with other suspects during the days and nights of Shai's disappearance on April 5, 1992. The telephone records are damaging evidence.

And then it's over. On Wednesday, October 26, Mike Vecchione turns to Judge Owens. "Your honor. The prosecution rests."

At this marker in the trial, Owens declares he will set aside any conviction against Malka Helbrans. "I have misgivings that the People have not made out a legally sufficient case." However, his views do not extend to the rabbi. Outside the jury's presence, he says: "I think the prosecution made out a case against Rabbi Helbrans, there's no question about that."

Now it's Helbrans's turn. The defense team.

*Their* witnesses. *Their* chance at bat.

On Monday, October 31, the defense calls Nachman Helbrans to the witness stand. The jurors are attentive, ready to hear the other side.

The rabbi's oldest son is twelve. He says Shai slept in his bedroom and he never saw his father alone with Shai, refuting Hana's claim that Helbrans instructed him almost exclusively and brainwashed him into staying. But yes, he went to bed at ten, so he doesn't know what happened after. He is excused.

What everyone is waiting for is Shai. Where is he? When will he testify? What will he say about Helbrans? Whatever witnesses the defense totes out, it is the boy's testimony that will speak to the heart of the matter.

"So where the hell is the kid?" Larry asks Steve first thing Tuesday morning. He and Elaine have taken a long weekend and he wants to know what happened in court. "He show up?"

"Nah." Steve pushes a file across his desk, he's got more to say. "He's probably out raising money for Helbrans, he's their star attraction. It's a dog 'n' pony show, Lar, they got flyers out . . ."

"Flyers?"

"Yup. I hear they're asking people to cough up at least $100."

Larry's eyes turn serious. "No shit."

"Yup."

"Maybe Waldman pays the lawyers up front, gives them a decent retainer to get started, then he stiffs them." Larry holds up three fingers. "Rooney is Helbrans's third lawyer. First George Meissner. Then they got a lawyer from the Assigned Counsel 8b panel. Now Rooney."

In private conversations, the two partners often speculate about money for the defense. "Is Lieb Waldman the money guy?"

"Hana says he's there at the trial almost every day. You gotta ask *why*. What's his stake in Helbrans? Why is this man showing up at a kidnapping trial? Successful business man. Multimillionaire. *Why?*"

Larry emits a long sigh. "It figures. Zaks is very involved. A lot of people are involved, they hid Shai."

Larry gives Steve a dark look and shakes his head. "Funny how money subverts the system." It saddens him. He believes passionately in a justice system that works. Laws to protect the innocent and punish the criminals. That beautiful instrument called The Constitution of the United States. It galls him to see justice subverted. "Know what?" He shakes his head despondently. "The corruption probably stretches through Europe, Israel, everywhere."

"What burns me up is how they're using Shai," Steve drums his knuckles on the desk. "The kid's a cash cow, he delivers money after they parade him at the temples. I heard he brought in $60,000 bucks. Hey, Lar, put it together. Nat Lewin flew in from Washington, right? That's air fare, hotels, legal fees: Nat Lewin had to get paid. Eleanor Alter had to get paid. Thorsen had to get paid. Guys like Waldman probably launder money and get away with it."

Larry slaps his thighs and stands up to leave. Enough. They've been over it a hundred times.

On November 2, a Wednesday morning, Shai Fhima Reuven appears in court, seated next to Thorsen. His face is barely visible under his fedora, his head is down and his eyes are pasted to his black shoes. Electricity sparks the courtroom. *He's here. There he is.*

Hana is so nervous, she cannot control the twitch in her mouth. Her throat is burning and her teeth feel tight. Because when she looks back on it, the four weeks in October are all blurred, all of it. The witnesses Vecchione called to the stand and what they said. The arguments about admissible evidence. The rulings by the court. Objections sustained and objections denied. Times when the jury was dismissed and when it was recalled. Even the lies Paul Rooney and Joyce David told about her. *It don't matter, they can't hurt me. Only what Shai says.*

He is sitting only yards away, she can feel him. What she knows absolutely is that *Shai alone can hurt her*. No witnesses, no testimony, no exhibits, no cross-examinations, nothing can devastate her. Only Shai. For four weeks, she played her part and did what she was told. But now, the only thing that counts is *what Shai will say*. Because a child who tears his own mother's heart out is an abomination.

Her eyes rest on his seated figure, a view obstructed by hasids squeezed into every inch of benches. If only she could sweep him into her arms and crush all that went bad between them.

Up half the night, her mind racing, she stared at the alarm clock: three-fifteen, almost five-thirty. Is my son my enemy?

Or, maybe . . . facing his mother on this autumn morning, swearing to God in this Brooklyn Supreme Court, he'll speak the truth. Tell what really happened.

She phoned Larry late last night. "Is it possible . . . I mean, you think maybe Shai could change his mind? He was a good boy, a loving child. A sweet nature. Maybe he'll, you know . . ."

Larry's heart went out to her. Can she really be so naive? "Hana." His voice offered no hope. "Don't count on it."

Sometimes Hana Fhima is charming. And sometimes she's so irritating, he wonders how he ever got roped in. It galls him that she's got three heroes: Plackenmeyer, Vinegrad, and Owens. All getting paid. Me and Steve, pro bono, are absent from her list. So okay, Owens deserves the lion's share of credit for not accepting the plea bargain. But wasn't there some underlying feeling that the ultraorthodox get treated different and they get all the perks? Didn't Owens believe it was a political deal and it would be an outrage to let the rabbi walk?

Larry put the phone down and turned to Elaine. "Owens deserves to be on her angel list. But how about me and Steve? A simple thank you is rare. A tie from K-Mart maybe?"

Elaine defended her. "What do you expect? Low esteem is typical of abused women. Inability to make good decisions is . . ."

"Drop it, Elaine." The last thing he needed to hear was more battered women stuff.

"Shai Reuven to the witness stand."

A hush falls.

Hana swallows.

With his black suit in full view, his fedora squarely in place and his sidecurls brushing his cheeks, Shai testifies. His voice is flat and unemotional as he answers Rooney's questions.

"My mother beat me every day with a broomstick when I lived with her in the battered women's shelter."

"Where were you beaten?"

"Everywhere."

Hana's face crumbles. Her chin falls on her chest.

Court reporter Nanette Cantwell, her hands flying to get it all down, feels sorry for Hana; her heart goes out to the woman. The son so nasty to his mother, and the mother just sitting there taking it.

"Were you kidnapped on April 5, 1992?"

"No. I decided I was going to run away because I couldn't live that way anymore. Because after you've seen a normal life, you can't live an *un*-normal life."

Hana shudders and clasps her hands tighter. Tears roll down her cheeks. The jurors take in her despair. A mother suffering at her child's hands.

"Did you report those beatings to the authorities?"

"I told the shelter workers, but they didn't do nothing." Sullen. Annoyed.

Hana, head bowed, takes the blows. But her carefully constructed exterior is crumbling.

*This is not my son nomore.*

*He's brainwashed.*

*They stole his soul.*

There is profound sadness in the courtroom throughout the grueling morning of direct testimony. Shai is becoming testy. Even under Rooney's polite questioning, he hisses contempt.

By one fifteen, Judge Owens has had enough. He calls for a lunch break. "All right, be back here, let's see . . . you should be on the elevator by two-forty-five."

The afternoon session opens with the clerk's announcement: "Case on trial 1533 of '93. *People* v. *Schlomo Helbrans and Malka Helbrans.*"

"All right," Judge Owens quips. "Bring in this erudite group which is known as the jury."

# 37. VINEGRAD QUESTIONS SHAI

The court officers escort Shai in. He is seated.

Alan Vinegrad now rises for the cross-examination.

Hana stiffens. This is the defining moment of truth. If Alan can get Shai to stop lying, if Alan can make him say the truth, then it will be over.

"Shai," Vinegrad begins pleasantly. "I want to ask you about the time you were living in New Jersey, before you met Rabbi Helbrans, all right?"

He establishes that Shai liked to play volleyball and basketball, Nintendo, and video games; he was a regular kid.

Q: Did you keep kosher before you met Rabbi Helbrans?

A: No.

Q: Did you observe the Sabbath?

A: No.

Q: Were you religious?

A: No.

Q: Do you love your sister?

A: Yes.

Q: Do you love your brothers?

A: Yes.

Q: Do you love your grandparents, your mother's parents?

A: Yes.

Q: Do you love your mother?

A: *No!*

Hana flinches, every muscle tensing. It's going to get worse. He started out stone faced, now he's defiant.

A male juror clenches his jaw. A woman juror, pained, looks away.

Vinegrad moves in closer, still polite.

"Isn't it a fact that you wrote an essay in 1991 that you were willing to die for your mother?"

"*No!*" A sharp denial. Emphatic.

Vinegrad marks People's Exhibit 73 for identification and hands Shai a paper written in his own handwriting.

Q: Read line eighteen.

A: But I don't mean what I'm saying!

Q: Read line eighteen.

A: All right. I'll be willing to die for my mother.

Vinegrad is satisfied.

Q: You and your family moved to a shelter because your stepfather Jacky was beating your mother. Correct?

A: Yes.

Q: You testified that when you were living in the shelter, your mother hit you every single day, right?

A: Yes.

Q: Did you tell anybody about it?

Shai hesitates.

Q: Haven't you testified before that you told Lil numerous times that your mother was hitting you on a daily basis?

Shai is resistant. Antagonistic.

A: I don't remember.

Q: It was your testimony that you told Elaine, the head of the shelter, that your mother was hitting you constantly. But she did nothing, right?

A: Yeah.

His voice sinks to barely audible.

Q: And once you told the police in Ramsey you were afraid your mother was going to hit you because you snuck out of the house without permission and the policeman said, "There's nothing I can do, Shai, go back to your mother." Right?

A: Yeah.

Shai grunts.

Judge Owens turns to Shai. "You have to speak up so they can hear you."

Vinegrad shows the jury an angry teenager who has changed his earlier testimony and denied what he wrote about his mother. A boy who claims his mother beat him daily at the shelter. All unsubstantiated by investigative teams, documented reports, and earlier testimony. Who is this defiant teenager who can't keep his story straight? Shai's testimony on cross-examination is precisely the effect Vinegrad wants. The kid's a liar. Look at his mother, look what it's doing to her. Tearing her up, she's dying inside.

Nimbly, Vinegrad moves the cross-examination back to the four weeks Shai spent at Rabbi Helbrans's yeshiva before the police were called by Hana.

Q: Isn't it a fact that Rabbi Helbrans stopped in the middle of the service and spoke to you? And he said . . . he could see a light shining from your face?

Shai shifts in the chair. About his mother he knew exactly what to say. About the rabbi . . . He sneers at Vinegrad. He's not going to let anyone push him around. No way.

A: I didn't understand what he said.

Q: Now the day the police came to the yeshiva, March 15, 1992. You were on the third floor, sitting on the bed, crying, right?

Vinegrad's voice is more insistent, his questions become more direct.

A: Yes.

Q: Followers of the rabbi were talking to you in there, weren't they?

A: I don't remember.

Q: You don't remember?

A: I told you I don't remember!

Q: They were whispering in your ear, weren't they?

A: I told you I don't remember. Don't tell me what they were doing!

Shai is rude. Disrespectful. Several jurors shift uncomfortably in their seats, watching this boy, so bad mannered.

Q: You left with the police, they physically had to drag you down the stairs and out of the building. And you were screaming. And while you were in the street, the rabbi's followers were out there yelling at you, telling you to run away from your parents and come back.

A: I told you, I don't remember!

Vinegrad moves to testimony about Mordecai Weiss and Tobias Freund, reestablishing their contact with the boy, driving him up and back for overnights in Williamsburg. The day Weiss didn't bring him home. April 5, 1992.

Q: So he put you on a bus, right?

A: Yes.

Q: And for a day or two you stayed in Williamsburg? Then took a bus to Monsey?

A: Yes.

Q: One time you went to Kasho and went back to Monsey?

A: Yes.

Q: And you stayed in Monsey about two years.

A: No. I was there a month and a half.

Q: And then you left and went somewhere else?

A: Yes.

Q: We'll get back to it.

Vinegrad has now positioned him exactly where he wants. Caught in his own lies.

His questions, pleasant at first, come faster, a series of short jabs calculated to bring the boy to this point and show the jury the tangled web of his testimony. A story full of denials, false accusations, changed testimony, and a string of *I don't remembers*. Judge for yourself, jurors.

He moves in closer now to corner Shai in his own lies. Graceful and calculating, like a matador maneuvering the huffing bull into position so he can plunge in the sword.

Q: Do you remember signing a document . . .

A: I signed a lot of them.

He interrupts. He sneers. He glares back.

Q: In late February, you were the one who started a Family Court case. And in that document you said you went to Williamsburg for a visit and ran away on April 5, 1992, and never came back.

He asks that People's Exhibit 76 be marked for identification and shown to the witness.

Q: Look at the second to last page. Now do you remember you signed the document and affirmed everything in it was true?

A: Yeah.

Q: My question, Shai. Rabbi Helbrans arranged for you to go to Monroe so the police wouldn't find you at his yeshiva. *Isn't that what happened?*

A: *No!*

Q: You stayed at Michael Apter's house, right?

A: *No!*

Q: And Tobias Freund drove you up there.

A: I told you! It didn't happen.

Q: When the police started looking for you in Monroe, he took you over to Kasho.

A: *No!*

Q: It's your testimony that you never saw or spoke to Rabbi Helbrans on April 5, 1992, right?

A: Yes.

David: Your Honor, I object. The D.A. just made a face. I think it's improper to try to . . .

Owens: Come on, you object to what?

David: To the D.A. making a face that telegraphs his feelings to the jury. I consider it totally improper.

The judge takes a breath.

Owens: Jury, step out please.

The jury exits the courtroom.

Owens: I'm going to call the jury back and ask each one if they saw the D.A. make a face. Bring them back.

The jury returns.

Owens: There's been an accusation that the prosecution, the attorneys who represent the prosecution, were making faces. Did you see them making faces? No 1?

A: No.

Q: No. 2?

A: No.

He ballots all fifteen of them. Fourteen say no. One juror says: Possibly, an expression of doubt and the expression varied.

Owens: All right. In other words, you're saying it's a level field.

That out of the way, Vinegrad's cross of Shai continues.

Q: You were never in Monroe. Ever?

A: Ever.

Q: You stayed at Kasho the week of Passover, how did you get there?

A: Somebody was going there.

Q: Who was someone?

A: It's somebody.

Q: Does the person have a name? What is the name?

He has to drag it out of him.

A: Shmuel Minsky.

Q: At Kasho you stayed with the Benedikt family, didn't you?

A: No.

Q: Look at the picture of the man on the wall, do you recognize him?

A: No.

Q: That's Mr. Benedikt who you stayed with at Kasho, isn't it?

A: No.

Q: Where did you stay?

A: Somebody else, not Benedikt.

Q: Who?

A: I don't remember.

Q: You don't remember? Or you don't want to tell us?

A: I said I don't remember!

Q: And you stayed a week.

A: Yes.

Q: Did he have children?

A: I don't remember.

Q: Anybody else?

A: Probably his wife, I don't know.

Q: Probably? Shai, you were *there*, weren't you?

David: Objection as to form.

Owens: Overruled.

A: It was him and he had a wife, that's all I remember.

Q: Passover is an eight day holiday and you can't remember whether there were children in the house? Is that your testimony?

A: Yeah! That's my testimony.

Rooney: Objection. It's argumentative.

Owens: Overruled.

A: I stayed in people's houses for two years. I was there eight days.

Q: Isn't it a fact when you were interviewed by Agent Savnik on March 1, 1994, you told him *you were never at Kasho?*

A: I don't know what you're talking about.

Q: Isn't it a fact this interview took place in Rockland County Sheriff's Office and Agent Savnik and myself and you and your attorney were there?

A: Yeah. I don't remember.

Q: But you remember saying *you were never at Kasho, right?*

Rooney: I object to this, it's been answered.

Owens: Overruled.

Rooney: I object to these theatrics, Your Honor.

David: And I object to the form.

Owens: The form is bad. Sustained as to form. Go on.

Vinegrad picks it up.

Q: Is there a reason why you denied before being at Kasho? And now, today, you're admitting it?

A: Yes.

Q: And the reason is, you knew that there were witnesses who saw you there, right?

With this, Vinegrad clearly establishes Shai has lied. Has changed earlier sworn testimony to FBI Agent Savnik. Has denied documents he signed at Rockland County court. Can the jurors believe a boy who flies in the face of written documents? And then, caught in the web of his unbelievable lies, lies again?

Vinegrad glances at Hana in the spectator section. She is weeping softly. Not lost on the jurors.

Now he picks up the thread. He is gathering names, pulling out identifications from Shai. Going up and back to trip him up. Under Vinegrad's expert hand, Shai has grown increasingly belligerent. Snappish. Nasty.

Q: Well who did you stay with in Monsey?

A: Some family.

Q: What was the name?

A: I'm not going to tell you!

Q: You're not going to tell me. Is that your testimony?

A: Yes. I'm not going to tell you names of families, so it doesn't worth asking.

Q: So if I go on asking . . . you're not going to tell me a single name?

A: *No!*

Vinegrad sinks his teeth into this.

Q: You won't tell me the third or fourth or fifth or anybody else, will you?

A: *No!*

Q: But it wasn't Helbrans, it wasn't Benedikt, and it wasn't Apter. Right?

The list of conspirators is growing. Add Weiss and Freund to the list. Who else?

A: Yes.

Q: How many different families did you stay with in Monsey until you resurfaced in February?

A: Nine or ten.

Q: You told the FBI you stayed with 2,573 families, right? You were being a wise-guy, right?

A: No.

Q: And you didn't use your real name? You used a false name, right?

A: Right.

Q: And what name was that?

A: Avram Meyer.

Q: And you made up stories about who you were. Where you were from, right?

A: Yes.

Q: And you were very good at that, weren't you?

A: Probably, if they believed me.

Vinegrad doesn't permit a hint of a smile to reach his lips.

Q: For two years, none of these families with whom you stayed ever said: *Aren't you the boy who disappeared? The boy the police are looking for?*

A: No.

Q: None of them ever said: *I saw a picture in the paper and you're the boy, you're Shai Fhima. I heard this in shul, he's thirteen, that's you, isn't it?*

A: I told you it never happened! No!

Q: By the way . . . are you aware that since January 1993, Rabbi Helbrans and his wife and his yeshiva have been located in Monsey?

A: Yes.

Vinegrad moves in.

Q: You stayed in Monsey. In Kasho for a week. Where else?

A: France.

# 38. A GOOD DAY IN COURT

Vinegrad gives the jurors time to take this in. Didn't the kid say he was in Monsey, in Rockland County? Stayed with nine, ten families? Didn't he say he was there for two years? What's this all about? Whatta kid. What stories.

Q: You were in France before February of 1994?

A: Yes.

Q: And when you were in France were you with hasidic people?

A: No.

Q: Who?

A: I stayed in a yeshiva.

Q: What yeshiva?

A: Novardok.

Q: How long?

A: Over a year. It was since the middle of July.

Q: Until February of 1994?

A: Yeah. Until a couple of days before I showed up in court.

Q: That's about a year and a half, right?

A: Yeah.

Snotty. Doesn't like being corrected.

Q: How did you get there?

A: Somebody helped me get there.

Q: Who is somebody?

A: Shmuel Minsky.

Q: He paid for you to go to France?

A: Yes.

Q: How did you get back to New York?

A: With a different passport.

Q: Using somebody else's name?

A: Yes.

Q: And you did that to sneak by the authorities, right?

Rooney objects.

David objects.

Owens overrules.

Q: You used a passport with someone else's picture and someone else's name so you could sneak by the authorities back into the country? That's why you did it?

A: Yes.

Vinegrad lets that sink in. He is building the case one brick at a time. Showing them who Shai Reuven is. A boy, who disappeared at thirteen. Changed his sworn testimony, can't remember documents he signed, and has an attitude a mile long. Hidden by members of an ultrareligious sect, he was sent to France on a phony passport.

Despite the surly resistance, he's pulling names out of the boy. Weiss: tried separately. Freund: found guilty of perjury. Add two new names from Shai's testimony: Minsky. Benedikt. Plus the rabbi and his wife and nine or ten other families who hid Shai, names unknown. Minsky arranging for a false passport. Nice. Very nice. The case for the kidnapping conspiracy is coming sharply into focus.

Okay. Time to move on.

Q: When you were staying with these nine or ten families in Monsey, did you go to school?

A: I had a private tutor.

Owens: I didn't hear you, speak up.

A: It was done in the synagogue.

Q: I see. What synagogue?

A: I don't remember the name.

Q: You went there for about three months, is that fair to say, from April to July. And you don't remember the name?

A: No.

Three jurors shift in their seats, tired of this cat and mouse game. A kid who won't answer. Who is he protecting? What is he hiding? Vinegrad doesn't miss this. He asks another question he knows Shai won't answer.

Q: These nine or ten families that you lived with, where in Monsey did they live?

A: Around Maple Avenue. I don't know the exact address.

Vinegrad asks for Exhibit 9, 10, 11, and 12.

Owens: How long are you going to be?

Vinegrad: I'm well over halfway done.

Owens: All right. Take a ten minute recess.

The jury is excused and Shai steps down.

Ten minutes later, Owens calls the jury back.

Vinegrad's cross-examination continues.

Q: Shai, when you were in Monsey studying in the synagogue with this tutor, it was the same tutor?

A: Yes.

Q: And who is that?

A: Shmuel Minsky.

Q: The guy who took you to France?

A: Yes.

Q: When is the last time you saw or spoke to Mr. Minsky?

A: Before I went to France.

Q: Back in 1992?

A: Yes.

Vinegrad asks for People's Exhibits 9, 10, 11, and 12 to be placed before the witness.

Q: When you were interviewed in the Rockland County Sheriff's office, you were shown those same four letters and asked if you wrote them.

A: Yes.

Q: You said you wrote the first two, which is a letter to the rabbi and a letter to your mother. Also a second letter to your mother, right?

A: Yes.

Q: But you denied writing the second letter to the rabbi, People's Exhibit 11, isn't that right?

A: Yes.

Q: And the reason you denied it is you did not want to say anything to the authorities that could show that you wanted anything to do with Rabbi Helbrans or his yeshiva once you disappeared. Isn't that right?

A: No, it's not the reason.

Q: And the reason you're admitting that you wrote that letter now is you realize how ridiculous it would be to deny it?

Rooney objects.

David objects.

Owens overrules.

Q: The date on that delivery receipt there, the date of delivery to Federal Express is April 14, 4/14, you see that?

A: Yes.

Q: Where were you when you wrote the letters?

A: Monsey. I told you I'm not going to tell you the name.

Defiant. Contemptuous.

Q: Whose idea was it?

A: Mine.

Q: And I take it from your testimony that Rabbi Helbrans had absolutely nothing to do with your writing those letters, is that your testimony?

A: Yes.

Q: By the way, I take it that your reason you wrote those letters was because you knew the police were looking for you and you wanted them to stop, is that right?

A: Yes.

Q: It didn't work, right?

A: No.

Q: The police kept looking for you, right?

A: Yes.

Q: And your mother kept looking for you, right?

A: Yes.

Q: So a couple of weeks later you wrote two more letters, right?

A: Yeah.

Q: Exhibit 11 and 12, right?

A: Yeah.

Q: Where were you when you wrote those letters?

A: I think in Kasho.

Q: And what did you do with the letters after you wrote them?

A: I gave them to somebody to send it.

Q: Who is somebody?

A: I'm not going to tell you his name.

Scornful. Angry.

Is the jury getting tired of this brat?

Vinegrad has more to show them.

Q: Did anyone ever tell you, Shai, that on April 27, the day before you wrote those letters, your father, Michael Reuven, spoke to Rabbi Helbrans for an hour and a half and asked if you were okay? Did anyone ever tell you?

A: No.

Q: But it's a complete coincidence that the day after that phone conversation you wrote those two letters?

A: Yeah.

Court Officer: They still can't hear him.

Owens: The lady in the corner can't hear you at all. You have to speak up, please.

Q: How did the somebody that you gave the envelope know to put the name Shay Sima?

A: I don't know.

The jury has heard the boy say it over and over. *I don't know. I don't remember. I won't tell you.*

Exactly what Vinegrad wants.

Q: You were calling yourself Meyer Avrim, weren't you?

A: Yeah.

Q: And the other somebody who you gave the second set of letters to, how did that person know to put the name Yishai Reuven on the envelope?

A: I don't know.

Q: And in that very same letter you say at the bottom: "If you become religious, eat kosher foods, observe the Sabbath, etc., there is a chance that maybe I will come back." Don't you?

A: Yeah.

Q: And the reason you say that is because your disappearance was all about religion and had nothing to do with abuse. Isn't that right?

David objects.

Owens overrules.

Q: In fact, what was happening here was your mother was not raising you to be a religious Jew, like Rabbi Helbrans wanted. So he took you from your parents. Isn't that what this is all about?

Rooney objects.

Owens: Sustained. Sustained. That's for the jury to decide, not Shai, not you.

Q: Rabbi Helbrans was the one who orchestrated all the sending of these letters, isn't it?

A: No it, he's not.

Q: It was all his idea to get the police off his back, wasn't it?

A: No.

Owens: Jury, questions are not answers, I mean are not evidence. It's the answers to the questions, that's evidence. You understand that, don't you? All right.

Q: Shai, what is *msira?*

A: It sounds like the name of somebody.

Q: Let me try it a different way. Are you familiar with a rule of Jewish law that it is wrong, it is forbidden under Jewish law, to say anything to the authorities that would get a fellow Jew in trouble?

A: Yes.

Q: And is the name of that rule, the word that's used to refer to that rule, *msira* or something like that?

A: Yes.

Q: Pronounce it for us.

A: *Msira.*

Q: And that's the rule that all religious Jews have to follow, right?

A: Yes.

Q: And you consider yourself a religious Jew, correct?

A: Yes.

No further questions. He returns to the prosecution table.

Rooney's turn. He approaches the witness stand for redirect examination. His voice is pleasant, a lion tamer, calming the irritated beast who has been poked and prodded all day.

Q: Now, you were interviewed by the FBI and other people in the early part of this year, were you not?

A: Yes.

Q: And is it your testimony you did *not* tell them the truth?

A: Yes.

Q: Now, are you testifying here today and giving untruthful testimony to protect Rabbi Helbrans?

A: No.

Hard to follow? Not really.

What Rooney wants is for the jurors to believe that Shai *lied* to the FBI. But today, the boy is telling the truth.


Will they buy it?

Clearly, Shai's testimony has been the highpoint for the jurors. Perhaps even more revealing than Hana's heartfelt testimony.

If the jurors felt mildly sympathetic to Hana before laying eyes on her son, now they feel intense pity for the woman. Look at that boy of hers. What's the matter with him? Can't remember, refuses to name names, a nasty, sneering attitude. Isn't he protecting Rabbi Helbrans and the other hasidic people?

Something feels wrong.

Shai's testimony, followed by Vinegrad's cross-examination, has introduced too many holes. He has damaged the defense's side. The prosecution's contention that hasidic people conspired to cover up Helbrans's kidnapping—what part of the boy's testimony refutes it?

Hana has been phoning Larry and Steve daily with reports of the trial. Asking, "So what do you think?"

"What every trial comes down to," Larry has told her, "is *who do they believe?*"

Shai Reuven? Or Hana Fhima?

*Because Rabbi Helbrans does not testify.*

"All right," Judge Owens rises. "Try to get here ten o'clock tomorrow morning."

As Judge Owens adjourns court until Thursday, November 3, Hana feels sure that Shai's testimony has weakened the rabbi's defense. Alan has made wonderful points for their side. Then why is pain throbbing into every bone? Why is her flesh burning? *He hates me. My son hates me.*

As Hana rises to make her way past the sea of black coats, her eyes fall on both D.A.s, their eyes bright with satisfaction as they snap their briefcases closed. *Their* success. *My* pain.

Clearly Alan Vinegrad owns the day. His brilliant cross-examination will be remembered. His day in the sun.

Outside the court, reporters rush to Hana for a quote.

"Look at what they did to him," she mumbles weary. "He's brainwashed. It really hurts me to see what this child has become." Tears well up. "This is a different Shai. They changed him and turned him against his family."

Which is exactly what she tells Larry on the phone that night.

"Hana, I know how you feel about Shai. But it was a good day in court, wasn't it?" Upbeat, that's Larry.

"Yeah. Alan, he was wonderful, he was."

"Listen. It's important to stand up for the truth and that's what you're doing."

"Yeah." Listless.

"If you let it go, religious cults will keep on getting away with it. Whether it's a small hasidic sect in Boro Park or as widespread as the Moonies, it's mind control."

"He's not my Shai, he's brainwashed," she mumbles.

"*Someone's* got to stop them. Today was successful, Hana. Concentrate on the good side."

"I'm trying. But it really hurts me."

# 39. VECCHIONE'S SUMMATION

Thursday, November 3 marks one month since the opening day of the trial.

Looking every bit the small-town cop, Detective Kevin Kelly is called as the prosecution's final rebuttal witness. A shining young officer with an all American smile, he's a guy who wants to be helpful.

He testifies that he is a juvenile investigator with the Ramsey Police Department and on January 20, 1992, he was summoned to investigate Shai's charges that his mother beat him. But when he examined the boy, he found no marks and no bruises.

"No marks and no bruises." Vecchione repeats it for the jury.

"Shai finally confessed he'd fabricated the whole story because he left home without permission."

"Thank you. No further questions, Your Honor."

He returns to his seat at the prosecution table. Another record of how Shai lied.

With this last witness, both the prosecution and the defense rest their case. Done. Finished. Over.

All that is left is summations from both sides.

Judge Owens will give the jury final instructions before they begin deliberations.

*How long it will take?*

*Please God, don't make me wait too long.*


Tuesday, November 8 is election day and Nanette Cantwell takes her seat. She's not thrilled to have to come to work. Everyone else is off. Schools are closed. Banks are closed. Post offices are closed. Her luck, Judge Owens wants to finish it up, so he orders the court to be in full session. Busloads of hasids are already squashed into the benches, another day of standing room only. Her hands find the familiar position. Okay, let it roll.

The judge is in good spirits this morning. A nice plus. "Any Giants fans in the courthouse?" he asks.

"They lost again, Judge," says prospective juror no. 5.

The jurors like the man. He's one of the people, not one of the high and mighty.

Paul Rooney rises for his closing statement. He's wearing the well-suited attire of a fiftyish Fortune 500 executive and he is neatly turned out.

He approaches the jurors.

"May it please the court, counsel, Madam Forelady, ladies and gentlemen of the jury. The kidnapping victim has come in here and said *there was no kidnapping*. That should be the end of it. But there seems to be a story. I submit to you this is the odyssey of a young person trying to survive. It's a sad story. And why?"

He recaps earlier testimony, making his point that Shai suffered at home at the hands of a mother who abused him.

"This boy couldn't take it anymore and he says, 'I'm going to run away because I never really had a chance to realize what a normal family is like.' His mother says, 'If you leave, I'm only going to beat you . . . so hard you'll never want to leave again.'

"The indictment charges that my client prevented this young man's liberation by secreting him in a place, allegedly up in Monsey or Kasho." He steps closer, to engage the jurors' attention. "Nothing like this ever happened.

"My client extended himself to try to help out another human being. That's all. There's no issue of brainwashing here. The hasidim is not on trial here."

He takes a step back. Too authoritative? Lighten up, make them trust you. He shifts to a casual stand.

"Look, I'm not hasidic, I'm not Jewish, I'm not orthodox. I happen to be a Catholic. Some of their ways I think are a little crazy to me. But the hasidim isn't on trial here. It's a free country."

The jurors register no response to this personal information. Not a blink, so he moves ahead.

"Essentially, it's a story about a boy and his mother. He says he's abused, the mother says he isn't."

Okay. Now show them the mother, the kind of woman she is.

"Hana Fhima is a very needy person, an abused person from this monster Jacky. That's our stage. Two needy people, two main witnesses. Hana Fhima and the boy. The boy grew up essentially with his grandparents until he's ten, and comes to this country. This clearly is a troubled home."

He recounts incidences. Shai running away. Witnesses' testimony. Moves into the crux of his summation.

"Hana Fhima *consents* to let him stay at Helbrans's. She *allows* that. She *agrees* to that." He drives home that point. Hana's consent.

"On April 4, Weiss goes to the apartment at 10:30 on a Saturday night. And she *lets* the boy go to stay overnight in Brooklyn, the night before he disappears. *She consented, she consented, she consented to this.*"

He pauses for effect, then moves in closer to the jurors.

"This has absolutely nothing to do with Helbrans."

Now he goes into Hana's meeting with Helbrans and his wife.

"Mrs. Helbrans says, 'I want to raise your son.' A little odd. The rabbi was talking about ghosts. But Hana doesn't leave, she stays. Why didn't she pull Shai out of there? No. She *lets* the boy spend almost a month there. She *consents*."

Hana's complicity is his theme. Complicity and abuse. A terrible mother. He reviews "lies" she told the court. Then he tackles the father.

"Michael Reuven, the wonderful father who hasn't seen this boy for years, comes over here. And I submit to you he told us a phony story. He comes because he figures he'll take a shot: See if he can make some money out of this deal. He goes to the rabbi. Why didn't he go to the police right away? This is absurd. He says

he wore a wire, then he gets Rabbi Helbrans involved in conversation about paying $50,000. This is craziness."

He measures the effect on the jurors. Are they with him? He
can't tell.

"About the letters Shai wrote. . . . What's clear is Shai Fhima
wrote these letters. He decided to write to his mother and Helbrans on April 14. And you're supposed to think the next letter
was occasioned by Michael Reuven's call on April 27 to the rabbi,
saying he wanted to come over here. That's why Shai writes again
to his mother."

He sidetracks to describe the rabbi. Kindly. Naive, perhaps.
But not a man who kidnaps.

"Rabbi Helbrans does not proselytize. He doesn't go out and
try to grab people in. What he does try to do is deal with those
who want to return to religion.

"About *the light in Shai's face*. You're supposed to believe this
is some hypnotic statement that puts people in a trance. This is
nothing but a colloquial expression. Like 'there's a glimmer in
your eye' or something."

He's covered the main points: complicity and consent. The
boy was escaping abuse. Time to wind it up.

"Ladies and gentlemen, please remember. *Shai testified for the
rabbi.* He insisted all along *he ran away* and the rabbi had nothing
to do with it. There is no evidence the rabbi ever hid the child. My
client had nothing to do with Shai going to Paris. Shai Fhima says
this."

He pauses to deliver his final message.

"What did my client do except lend this boy a helping hand?
It's clear, when you listen, that he wasn't kidnapped. The rabbi
says over and over he doesn't know where the boy is. So what this
comes down to is . . . it's a saga of a boy on his own journey. What
he did, he did on his own to survive.

"I urge you to acquit my client based on the facts in this case.
Thank you."

The jurors register no emotion as he returns to his seat. A few change position, uncrossing a leg, recrossing another, folding their hands in their lap. Not exactly a fire and brimstone summation.

But Hana's heart is beating wildly. His words strike fear. Suppose they believe him and let the rabbi off. Oh, God, dear God, I made mistakes, are they going to punish me? She clasps her hands tighter to stop the trembling. She struggles to compose herself. *Hold yourself together.*

Owens: "Miss David?"

Joyce David rises for her summation. She greets the jurors pleasantly and tells them her summation will be briefer than Mr. Rooney's. She takes a moment to make eye contact with each one.

"This case," she declares with certainty, "was about *a kidnapping that never was.* Hana Fhima is a mother who refused to take responsibility for Shai running away. So she blamed it on the rabbi and his wife."

She paints a devastating portrait of Hana: a mother who emotionally abused her child. A terrible woman. A mother who damaged her son.

Hana winces, biting the inside of her cheeks, not to scream back *liar, liar.*

"All Shai ever wanted," David concludes with dramatic flair, "was to be religious."

*Liar, liar, liar.*


Now Michael Vecchione rises for the prosecution's summation.

Handsome and polished, he stands before the jurors like an opera star about to sing his aria. His voice, clear and true, because he knows exactly where the music will take him. He will build to a stunning crescendo marked by brilliant high notes and sostenutos. The jurors will be swept away, every one of them.

What Vecchione wants is: *Guilty.* Twelve guilty votes.

If Alan Vinegrad owned the day last Wednesday, Michael Vecchione steps forward now prepared to own this day. He has rehearsed it with painstaking detail. A summation so spell-binding, so incisive, so logical, it will electrify the jurors.

They have sat through five weeks of testimony. Had a helluva lot thrown at them. Conflicting stories. Charts. Exhibits. Details. Instructions from the court. What to accept, what to ignore. What they need now is a clarity of vision. A narrative easy to follow. Rational. Convincing.

He has it all laid out for them. An aria so dramatic and ab-sorbing, so true and indisputable, it will bring them to their con-clusion: GUILTY.

The charts are correctly displayed. The visual aids properly assembled. The day is all his.

Judge Owens has advised the attorneys that the courtroom will be sealed. "I don't like people going in and out, I don't want the jury to be distracted. Proceed."

Vecchione's summation begins pleasantly.

"Justice Owens, Mr. Rooney, Miss David, Madame Foreperson and ladies and gentlemen of the jury, let me begin by thanking you on behalf of Joe Hynes, the district attorney of King's County, for your attention during the course of this long and sometimes tedious trial. We've been here almost five weeks and you have been a marvelous jury."

That said, he smiles. Ready? With me?

"I believe the indictment reads *The People of the State of New York against Schlomo Helbrans and Malka Helbrans.* I didn't see Hana Fhima's name. Isn't that amazing after listening to Mr. Rooney's and Miss David's summations? Hana Fhima and her life are not on trial here. And who said that consent to let Shai Fhima go to Brooklyn is equal to giving consent to anybody to take him forever? Because Hana allowed Shai to go with his friend Mordecai Weiss three times, that means there was consent on her part to lose her boy forever?"

He takes a breath, a quarter note of a rest, to let it sail through the air.

"This case is about individuals who, through their words and their actions, have said: the bond created by birth is meaningless. Because they have an interest, a precept, that transcends the bond between a mother and her son. And that's religion. And not just any religions. *Their religion.*"

He makes a sweeping gesture indicating the defendants.

"It's not good enough for the mother and son to follow any religion. It must be practiced in the way *they* practice it. *Their* way. And it's okay to even sever that bond to see the greater good accomplished.

"That's what this case is all about: the severing of the bond between a mother and her son. The kidnapping of a thirteen-year-old boy from his mother in the name of religion. It's not a Hollywood movie. No snatch off the street, no midnight calls demanding ransom. But what these defendants did in the name of religion, I submit to you, was criminal. *They committed a crime.* They seized an opportunity to bring a child into their religion despite his mother's wishes and in spite of the law.

"Yes, Hana and Shai Fhima didn't have an easy life. She married and divorced and remarried, and Jacky Fhima beat her. So she took Shai and removed him from that household because she was a good mother. And when Hana moved her family from Israel to the United States in search of a better life, she didn't leave Shai behind. Tough times, yes, but the bond between Hana and her kids stayed strong. In fact Shai became a normal twelve-year-old kid, the kind we see every day: junk food, Nintendo, basketball, movies.

"But then . . . suddenly everything changed when he met Rabbi Helbrans. And what began as simple training for the traditional right of passage for Jewish boys ended in the loss of her child. Helbrans has his own religious school in Boro Park called Yeshiva Lev Tahor. And when he sees Shai, he makes the comment *there's a light shining in your face* because he thought Shai was special. And with this meeting, the quest for Shai began."

He watches their faces: they are engrossed in his summation.

"From the very moment Hana and Shai met Helbrans and his wife, the defendants went out of their way to convince her to take Shai out of public school. In fact, Malka Helbrans says: 'Let me raise your son,' And Hana realizes she doesn't want Shai living with them and studying very orthodox religious ways. So on March 15, 1992, she goes to Lev Tahor to take Shai home. And they refuse to let him go, saying *the rabbi has the right to take him away from her because she did not let him be religious.*"

He pauses. Waits a full measure before he picks it up.

"Hana calls the police, the rabbi's followers yell at Shai: 'Run away from your mother and come back to the yeshiva.' And Malka Helbrans screams: 'You can't take my son!' In sum, it took the New York City police department's intervention to get Shai out of Lev Tahor and back with his mother."

Now his voice darkens and moves to a lower register.

"But unfortunately for Hana, the boy she brought home was not the same Shai who left in February. He had changed. In the space of just two weeks, thirteen-year-old Shai Fhima was transformed. He wanted to be strictly religious. He refused to go back to public school. He even refused to eat the food his mother prepared because it wasn't kosher.

"And because Rabbi Helbrans can't get Shai back, what does he do? He has Mordecai Weiss give it a shot."

Vecchione moves into a counter theme, a new melody introduces Weiss's part in the conspiracy. He sings it plaintively, evoking the sadness of duplicity.

"Mordecai Weiss and his associates came on the scene to convince Hana that Helbrans is not such a bad guy. They'll find a different yeshiva for Shai to attend. They call Hana almost every day, relentless, asking her to let Shai stay with them and be religious. Look at the phone records. Sixty-three."

He places People's exhibit on an easel.

"Here they are."

He points to phone call after phone call. Weiss to Hana with the dates noted, the lengths of each conversation recorded. Phone calls from Rabbi Helbrans to Hana. One, on March 26, for three hours while he tries to convince her to let Shai go. And Weiss's relentless pursuit of Shai, his phone calls to Hana's apartment, to Jacky's apartment, constantly looking for Shai.

He stops. Steps away from the easel. Speaks directly to the jurors.

"Don't be fooled. Don't be fooled. He's not doing it for himself. Because these phone charts show that in between his calls, Weiss is talking to Helbrans and Helbrans's yeshiva. In fact, Weiss calls Helbrans seventeen times at his apartment and four times at the yeshiva. Look at these records."

He has three full charts on display, with every detail of every phone conversation pinned down. Who made the call. Where it went. The date and time. Length of conversation. Indisputable evidence. Enormous impact. His aria so clear and true, it is a stunning performance.

"Ladies and gentlemen," his eyes sweep across the jurors, claiming their full attention. *"Rabbi Helbrans is the link between Weiss and Shai. Helbrans is the master manipulator, the puppet master pulling the strings on the stooge from Williamsburg: Mordecai Weiss."*

He will return to the phone charts later.

Time to knock out the defense.

"On April 4, 1992, Hana allowed Shai to stay with Weiss for a third visit. She did not see her son again until February 1994." A quarter note pause.

"Let's talk about the defense case."

# 40. THE VERDICT

"The defense case." Vecchione takes a few steps closer to the jurors. "Best described in *three* words. *Exaggeration, fabrication* and *cover-up*.

"The *exaggeration* is that Shai was physically abused and Hana is a merciless child abuser. There is nothing in the evidence from a teacher, a social worker, a friend, a counselor, a police officer or anyone to support that Hana ever beat Shai. This was an adolescent who disobeyed his mother, who snuck out of his house and fabricated a story. A complete *fabrication*." He smiles, establishing camaraderie: hey, we weren't born yesterday.

"Do they think all of you are fools? How can you believe this stuff? It stinks."

He moves to the *cover-up*, punching holes in the stories of hasids who testified for the defense with botched dates and conflicting stories. *Uh, 1993. No, I mean 1994.*

"Come on. They would have you believe that Shai gets off the bus, stays in the women's section of a synagogue for two days and finds a bus to Monsey. That Shai spent time there with people whose names he would not reveal, at places he doesn't remember, being tutored by Shmuel Minsky. And for the next year and a half, until he resurfaced in February 1994, he was in France."

A small wry smile. Are you with me? Good.

"You know what? There's not much I agree with with the defense. But I agree: *you don't get to France on fifty bucks.*"

He is building the case for a conspiracy and he can see that the jurors are following it.

"Now let's look at April 5, the day Shai vanished. Weiss claims he's too busy to see that Shai is safely returned to Hana. So he puts him on a bus. Why didn't he simply call Hana and say:

276

'Listen, my plans changed.' Why? Because Weiss was lying to Hana. And he lied to the police to cover up the fact that Shai had been taken upstate. It's clear the bus story is bogus.

"So who are these people? Obviously, in this conspiracy the most important task was moving Shai. It was Tobias Freund who did, in fact, move Shai out of New York on April 5. He drove him to Monsey. And what clinches it? The telephone records."

He steps over to the phone charts.

"There it is. Calls billed to Freund's calling card at 8:44 P.M. Two hours later, another call. There it is: 10:40 P.M. Then a series of calls that show the conspirators were plotting Shai's kidnapping."

He runs down calls lasting six minutes, eighteen minutes. And finally, Weiss to Helbrans for one minute.

"This entire period begins with a phone call and ends with a phone call. And in the space of twenty-four hours, Shai was gone."

He's got them entranced.

"On April 7, once the police get involved, the *cover-up* begins. The defendants and their co-conspirators begin to lie to the police. And I submit to you that they were so successful, *so successful*, that this boy managed to remain hidden for almost two years. In spite of the massive efforts by the New York police department. By the FBI. By the state police. By the Royal Canadian Mounted Police. And by other international police forces."

He moves away from the easel, he's done with the charts.

"Where are they hiding Shai? I submit they are at Kasho, the perfect hiding place. A small isolated hasidic enclave in the mountains. One road in, the same road out. We have witnesses. Jesus Rivera sees Shai at Kasho. So does Simon Edwar and we have phone records to support this as well. Even Shai was forced to admit that he was at Kasho. Originally, he *denied* it to the FBI. But when confronted with this overwhelming evidence, he begrudgingly admitted during cross-examination he was there.

"*Helbrans himself was there* in January 1993 while Shai was still missing."

He lets it hang in the air, his eyebrows raised. Helbrans and Shai? Both at Kasho?

"Now the cover-up doesn't end with Shai. Ask yourselves: is it simply coincidence about the letters Shai wrote to his mother and the rabbi? I think not."

With painstaking precision, Vecchione maps the trail of how the letters got mailed.

"How? By a conspiracy of best friends all loyal to Helbrans. Letters delivered to Federal Express *in a car from Rabbi Helbrans's yeshiva.*

"How does the defense counter this evidence? They get Shai to tell one of the truly absurd stories you will ever, ever hear."

The barest smile. Let me lay it out for you.

"Shai sees two hasidic men thumbing a ride and figures they're going to Williamsburg, they'll drop them off. But you are all too smart to be fooled by that. This is a thirteen-year-old boy who, they want you to believe, cooked this entire scheme up by himself. Remember Shai was using the fictitious name AVRAM MEYER. So how did they know to use the names SHAY SIMA as the sender on April 14? And YISHAI REUVEN on May 1? *Only the rabbi,* or someone close to him, would know to use those names."

He watches one juror square his jaw, another tilts her head to catch every word, a third squints his eyes for concentration. Then he hands them the only conclusion they can draw.

"*Helbrans was the mastermind behind the Federal Express letter scheme.* And that's why the second set of letters talks about the abuse Shai suffered at the hands of his mother. You can almost see the rabbi thinking maybe allegations of abuse will get the police off his trail."

He shakes his head sadly, closes his eyes briefly.

"What is more despicable than to have a child lie about his parent beating him? How would you feel if your kid went from loving you so much he'd be willing to die for you . . . to accusations you beat him every day?

"Well, that's what these defendants did. That's how low they stooped to see that their crimes remained covered up.

"And ladies and gentlemen, what has taken place between the rabbi and Michael Reuven is truly sad and totally devious. Because the rabbi used the distress of a father who lost a son to lure Michael to the United States with the promise he'd see his son. But once Michael gets here, the rabbi recognizes, 'Hey, Michael is here to help. I can use this guy. He's willing to play ball with us.' But things start to unravel when Michael goes to Lev Tahor *wired.*"

Time to reach for the high notes. To sing out the theme.

"Ladies and gentlemen, what has been presented over these last five weeks is evidence of an intricate, complex plan to kidnap Shai Fhima. It lays out the actual kidnapping, it lays out the cover-up. And the evidence leads you right to Rabbi Helbrans and to Mrs. Helbrans."

His eyes sweep across the jurors. They have to be careful. Two shift away promptly to convey no response. The others make their gaze seem neutral.

"To repeat, it's clear that acting with others, Rabbi Helbrans and Malka Helbrans conspired and did kidnap Shai Fhima by secreting him in a place he was not likely to be found, without the consent of his parents. The evidence could not be more clear.

"And it doesn't make a bit of difference what the defense says about what a terrible mother Hana Fhima supposedly was. And it doesn't make a bit of difference what Shai said. He said he was not kidnapped *because Shai is one of them.* He went from this . . ." He steps over to the pictures of Shai *before* Helbrans. "To this." He points to pictures of Shai *after* Helbrans. A different boy: one of them.

"Shai's testimony is the ultimate cover-up. He denies the defendants had any role in his disappearance, yet he refused to tell who did. You can't help but feel sorry for him."

A good touch. Two women jurors look down into their laps. Pity for this family, this mother and her boy.

"In the name of religion, Rabbi Helbrans and Malka Helbrans severed the sacred bond between a mother and her child. Shai doesn't seem to care. *But you must care.*"

His pause asks them: do you care?

"These are people who will stop at nothing to do whatever it takes to accomplish their greater good. It doesn't matter to them taking Shai from his parents. Hiding him. Making him an ultra-orthodox Jew against the will of his parents.

"They thumbed their nose at the police. At the FBI. At the law of this state. They imposed their will, their way of life. And to hell with the law."

His meticulous point-by-point recreation of the events is finished. He moves in closer. Pauses. And takes a dramatic inhale of breath to sustain the finale.

"I ask you to find Schlomo Helbrans and Malka Helbrans guilty."

It's pitch black when Hana arrives on her front stoop. A sharp wind whips the back of her knees. Head bent she fumbles with the key and unlocks the front door.

Ah, warm inside. She shifts her shoulder bag to steady it and climbs the flight of stairs to the apartment.

Vecchione's summation is still singing in her head. He was wonderful, wonderful. So many documents. Exhibits, phone charts, pictures. The juror with the tight thin smile and the one with the brisk nod, they're maybe on our side. The rest—who knows? What will be with me and Shai? If they find Helbrans guilty, he'll hold it against me. He's one of them now.

Reaching the last three steps, she calls to her children, "I'm home."

They don't hear her. The television's blasting and they're laughing at the show. After school Osheri watches them, a responsible boy, and her neighbor, a nice woman, looks in. Five weeks you neglected them, she scolds herself, the trial's over, take care of your children.

"I'm home," she calls louder. "I'm home."

For dinner she opens a can of ravioli. Skip the baths tonight, get them to bed early.

For dessert, she pulls a half gallon of ice cream out of the freezer. "Who wants chocolate chip?" She affects a cheerfulness she doesn't feel. What she feels is bone weary. With a soup spoon, she dishes out three portions.

"I want sprinkles." Shiran is whiny and she's pulling on her ear—another earache? "I want rainbow sprinkles."

"Here, Mamala. Rainbow sprinkles I got."


It's after ten. The apartment is quiet, but she's too wired to sleep. She sits down at the kitchen table. Call Steve. She phones him. "You think the jury will . . ."

"You never know. They like a witness, they don't like a witness. They believe the testimony, they don't believe the testimony. It's a tough call, Hana."

"Uh huh." She hangs up.

Tonight feels different. She ties her bathrobe belt tighter and calls Larry. It rings four times.

"I'm waking you up?" She doesn't care.

"No, no." He's watching a game.

"You think they'll take a long time, the jury?"

"A week, a month. You never know, Hana."

"A month?"


The jury's verdict comes the next day. In less than five hours of deliberations.

Judge Owens reads the message.

The jury convenes.

"Has the jury reached a verdict?" he asks soberly from the bench.

Madame foreperson stands up. "We have, Your Honor."

"How do you find?"

An intake of breaths.

Hana makes a silent prayer and closes her eyes.

*"Schlomo Helbrans: Guilty. Malka Helbrans: Acquitted on kidnapping charges. Convicted on conspiracy."*

Gasps slice through the courtroom. Then cries of outrage.

Hana makes a beeline for Vinegrad and hugs him. Then Vecchione. "Guilty, guilty," she sings into his lapels. "Thank you, thank you."

"This way!" Court officers rush the jurors out the back door. "Quick. This way." Could be trouble.

Malka Helbrans is screeching, sobbing, moaning, clinging to her husband as hasids rush toward her, swooping like noisy black crows, encircling her and protecting her, cutting her off from court officers who, under strict orders to prevent chaos, are pushing their way through to restrain her.

Helbrans looks stunned at the verdict, a deer caught in the headlights. As he's led away, Malka Helbrans collapses, her wrenching sobs pierce the air.

"This way, this way!" someone is yelling at Hana, a hand above the crowd, beckoning: "Follow me. Quick. Get out."

She can't see, but she obeys the hand, inching away, sensing danger all around her. One of them could go after her. Punch her or hit her like the day at the yeshiva. Burrowing like a small animal, she follows the hand and works her way out the courtroom. Larry and Steve and Elaine behind her.

Out in the hallway, a crush of hasids pushing and shouting. Is Malka Helbrans in the middle? She can't see because reporters and television crews are shoving and shooting questions.

A reporter spots her and breaks away from the crowd. Immediately, the others lunge after her and a wall of microphones appears in her face.

"How do you feel now?"

"You think Shai'll come back to you?"

"Didja figure on guilty?"

"What about custody, Hana?"

"Ya gonna go out tonight and *celebrate?*"

*Celebrate?*

Her voice is shaking. "I lost my son because of Rabbi Helbrans. I waited two and a half years for justice. He gets what he deserves. He has to pay for what he did, taking my boy and turning him away from his family."

*Celebrate?* I still don't have Shai back. The guilty verdict don't wash away I lost him. He hates me.

A reporter spies Vecchione and Vinegrad emerging from the courtroom and dashes for them. Helluva pair of D.A.s. Feathers in their caps. "Would you comment on the verdict?" he asks Vecchione. "Did you expect it?"

"The evidence was there of a kidnapping. As unusual as it was." Short and snappy. No strutting.

Judge Owens has remanded Helbrans, responding to the prosecutors' arguments that he's a flight risk, an Israeli citizen who overstayed his visa by three years. Other hasidic witnesses have vanished. Helbrans could skip out, too.

Reporters churn out possible sentences. Helbrans could face a minimum of two to six years. Or a maximum of eight to twenty-five. Which way will it go? Sentencing is slated for November 22, Thanksgiving week, a favorite holiday for Americans. Malka Helbrans will be sentenced December 15, ten days before Christmas. Will the holiday spirit soften the judge? Twenty-five years? Whew.

On November 14, a week before sentencing, *Newsday*'s Monday edition breaks the Heyman story.

Unobserved in the gallery, Patsy Heyman has been sitting quietly, watching and waiting. She has come to the trial to give Hana moral support. Now, with the guilty verdict delivered, she feels free to speak out. She says that Shai Fhima's eery journey among the hasidim is a familiar story.

"My three children were abducted from school when we lived

in Belgium." She tells how her ex-husband took them in a custody battle dispute in December 1986, and hid them in a hasidic community for over six years. After their divorce, he appealed to the hasids to help him kidnap and conceal the children. She looked for them in Brussels, in Antwerp, in London, and in Mexico. Then in Monsey and Monroe and in Brooklyn's Williamsburg section.

Why is she telling her story now? For Hana's sake. To publicize the shared agony of the two mothers.

"Shai was not the first time that something like this happened," she speaks to a reporter from a friend's house in Virginia. "And it may not be the last," she warns. Patsy Heyman is careful to say she's not blaming all hasidim. But the people who helped her husband? *"They believed they were above the law."*

For six years, she hounded hasidic communities around the world. She handed out fliers on the streets and begged officials to take action.

"Sometimes I spoke to people who knew where my children were, but they still would never tell me."

A tipster told her her children were in Monsey. But when she got there they were gone because the tipster warned the children's caretaker.

How did she meet Hana Fhima?

After six years, U.S. authorities, *searching for Shai in early 1993*, found her three children. They were hidden in Kasho.

On May 7, 1993, she was reunited with the children by the FBI. That evening, they all boarded a flight back to Belgium.

"I want to help Hana," she says. "Maybe people should know that Shai is not the first time it happened. I had a happy ending with my children. But Hana—she still got a nightmare to live with."

# 41.  THE SENTENCE

"**I**'m ready to walk the hell out," Larry huffs at Steve. "You?"

"Give 'em ten more minutes. Then we're outa here."

They've been sitting, standing, pacing. Kept waiting almost an hour in the D.A.'s reception room. Vecchione doesn't come out. Vinegrad doesn't come out.

"What kinda deal is Hynes working out with them?" They can talk freely, no one else is there.

Steve shrugs. "You think Vecchione's gonna ask for the max? Send him to the slammer for twenty-five years?"

Larry won't speculate. He wants to hear it from the D.A.'s mouth. That's why they drove in from Oakland, hit gridlock at the tunnel and got every red light crosstown. And this is what they get. "Beautiful. I'm on the phone almost every day for five weeks. 'Hey, Alan, what happened today, how's it going?' " And today they can't even get past the glazed-eyed black guard in the glass booth.

Steve scoops a newspaper off a table. Scans the weather report, then whacks it back, almost knocking over the lamp.

Steaming, Larry stares at the impressive letters marching across the wall. OFFICE OF THE UNITED STATES ATTORNEY, EASTERN DIVISION OF NEW YORK. He paces, stops at the photos on the walls, artsy shots of Manhattan skylines.

The guard is tapping on the glass. "You can go in now."

A buzzer releases the door and they stride down the hall.

Vecchione's office is smaller than they expected. Alan Vinegrad is there, too. No Hynes. Obligatory handshakes, everyone seated, then down to business.

"So watta we got?" Larry asks. No pussyfooting around, no lawyer banter. Let 'em know he's pissed.

The two district attorneys seem embarrassed.

Vecchione clears his throat. "I've received instructions to take no position on the sentencing." He's fiddling with his pen.

*"What?"* Larry can feel his neck muscles tighten. They're gonna soft-pedal it. Take the least offensive course.

Alan Vinegrad says nothing.

The message is clear. Orders from the top.

All the way down in the elevator, Larry is fuming. *"No position? No position?* Hynes did it to save face. To keep his connections with the hasidic community."

"Yup." Steve grumbles. "Convict the criminal. But don't seem too harsh. *Don't* offend the hasids. You know, he attends their fund raising campaigns? He shleps all the way up to Monsey for them, Lar."

The elevator door opens and they step out.

It's Tuesday, November 22.

Today Judge Owens will sentence the rabbi.

The Brooklyn courthouse is packed with hasids. In the hallways, hundreds of supporters who couldn't get a seat in the courtroom are lined up behind police barricades, rumbling like dark clouds bumping into each other.

Court officers, on red alert, are everywhere, positioned to restrain any outbreaks, their watchful eyes swarming over the crowd. Arms folded across their chests, feet spread apart, their stance is a warning: Stay behind the barricades. Don't make trouble.

In the courtroom, Hana, Larry, Elaine, and Steve sit huddled together, a small white dot in the black playing field.

Before sentencing, Judge Owens allows the parties to speak.

Hana first.

"Your Honor. I lost my son to people who control his mind." Her voice is shaking. "Your Honor, Rabbi Helbrans started this kidnapping. It is because of him I lost my son. Maybe forever."

She asks the judge for a stiff sentence, citing her continued estrangement from Shai. "Please, your honor," she pleads.

"Thank you." The judge calls for the rabbi to speak.

Every eye fastens on him.

For five weeks his beatific smile has been beaming pleasantly at the judge and jury. But he has not spoken. Has not testified. Not a word. Nothing on the record. What will he say?

The burly rabbi stands up. His smile gone.

He rambles, he stutters, his voice is highly emotional. He makes an appeal that drags on and on. Ten minutes. Fifteen minutes. Twenty minutes of unconnected remarks. He reviews two thousand years of Jewish oppression. He compares his plight to other Jews falsely accused by anti-Semites. He slips back and forth from broken English to Hebrew to Yiddish, amid shouting matches and angry outbursts from the hasids in the gallery, a Greek chorus offering commentary and opinions.

Judge Owens listens. He allows him to continue.

A translator, a scruffy old man who could be mistaken for a homeless person, stands next to him giving the court interpretations each time he lapses into rancorous Hebrew and Yiddish.

Two court artists, a man and a woman, are sketching on brown paper. The woman starts out with a few lines, rapidly fills in more, then more, until a Rabbi Helbrans emerges out of nothing. She has captured his face. Blustering. Angry.

For thirty minutes he rants that the charges against him are a blood libel. A new Jewish lie that Jews used blood to make matzohs. Hana Fhima and Michael Reuven are *spiritually low-life people*. Liars who made up the whole story.

"I have passed through the seventh partition of hell," he cries, ". . . all because a j-j-jury believed them." He tells the judge that stories of blood libel cost the lives of millions of Jews who burned at the stake. He starts, he stops, he drops one thread and picks up another.

It is astonishing to see the amiable man who has sat quietly for weeks, erupt into forty minutes of unconnected remarks about Jewish persecution. "The same thing happened to this case. We are not people who kidnap children," he snaps at the judge.

Thaddeus Owens has had enough.

"I understand persecution, my people have suffered, too," the black judge replies with firmness. "But religion is not on trial here. I have suffered as much as any Jew or Rabbi Helbrans has suffered. As have my ancestors."

A hasid leaps to his feet and shouts back at him, "I'm not sure about that!"

Immediately, proceedings are disrupted. Court officers move in to eject him and additional police fill the aisles to assure order among the men sitting on one side and the women sitting on the other side, many exchanging bitter feelings over the rabbi's modern-day persecution.

Then order is restored.

Both sides have now addressed the court.

Judge Owens turns to Vecchione. His turn.

He rises. He does not speak directly to the judge. Instead he holds a prepared statement from Brooklyn D.A. Hynes and he reads Hynes's words.

"An ordained rabbi is convicted of a felony and must go to jail. A family—mother, father, and child—are in total disarray . . . distrust and antipathy abound in their lives." Hynes's statement asks not for the *maximum* sentence. Only for a *fair* sentence.

Larry jabs Steve. *"Fair? A fair* sentence?"

Vecchione looks up from his paper. "I take no position on the sentencing of the rabbi."

Hana stiffens.

Steve and Larry exchange looks of contempt.

Steve lays a comforting hand on Hana's arm.

Now it's up to the judge. All eyes on him.

Thaddeus Owens has listened patiently to all sides. He has let the rabbi speak his mind for forty minutes. The mother has spoken. Hynes has spoken. Vecchione has spoken. Everyone heard from.

He imposes sentence.

*Four to twelve years for the first charge of kidnapping. One to three years for the second charge of conspiracy. To run concurrently.*

They scream, they curse, they cry. They jump to their feet and shake their fists. Purple with rage, they turn the courtroom into mayhem as court officers snap handcuffs on the rabbi.

"Remain seated! Everyone remain seated!"

Malka Helbrans, a few rows behind Hana, erupts into wrenching sobs, hands flying in the air. "You!" she shrieks at Hana. "You ate in my house. Tell the truth. You're lying. You'll pay for this!"

"You kidnapped my son!" Hana whips around and shouts back.

Malka Helbrans's wrath turns on Owens. "Aren't you afraid of God? Putting an innocent, wonderful person in jail." She's screaming at him, she wants God's vengeance. "I want to talk to the judge. I want to say the truth."

"Quick! This way! Out!" officers call to Hana.

Swiftly, under protection, her group is hustled out the back way, up a flight of stairs to safety.

Out in the halls, court officers are trying to control the mob pushing against the police barricades. Some manage to break free. They make a beeline for Malka Helbrans, surrounding her as she leaves the courtroom, shielding her from the cameras with their wide brimmed black hats. Others take up chanting, "We want justice! We don't kidnap kids!" A few get into a shoving match with court officers and the noise level rises to the beat of "We want justice! We want justice!"

In the same Brooklyn courthouse where Lemrick Nelson, a black youth, was acquitted of murdering a Jew, Rabbi Schlomo Helbrans is taken away to serve four to twelve years in prison.

*Was justice served?*

Out on the front steps, reporters swarm around Hana as she tries to escape.

A plucky woman journalist with a red beret calls, "Hana, Hana. Aren't you overjoyed with the ruling?"

"Yes, of course," Hana replies as they crush in on her. "It was very hard to see my son testify against me and accuse me of things that never happened. But inside my heart I knew that this is not Shai talking. This is the Shai these people create."

A reporter with a gravelly voice pokes his mike in her face. "On the custody battle—think you'll get your son back?"

Steve jumps in protectively. "She's got a major uphill fight." He grabs her arm and pulls her along, Elaine and Larry shielding her.

"Ya gonna get Stanger to give you back your boy?" Another mike trails her. "Ya gonna let him be religious?"

Hana stops to answer this one. "I'll let Shai practice his faith. But I want psychiatric counseling for him. Shai never wanted to become an orthodox Jew. I don't really think that's what he wants. That's how they changed him and what they make him believe. Before we met Rabbi Helbrans, Shai never talked about being religious or being kosher."

"What about Judge Stanger? He awarded Rabbi Zaks custody."

"I don't know what's going to happen." She looks away and her eyes fill up. "Maybe . . . there's a chance of losing my son *forever.*"

Flashbulbs go off, catching the mother at this bittersweet moment.

"What's your chances?" a voice rings out.

"I think I still have a chance to get him back and save him. I know it's going to be hard and take a lot of time. But we got to do it. Even if there's just a one percent chance it's going to succeed."

With that, Larry and Steve yank her away.

✡   ✡   ✡

"Rabbi Helbrans's conviction is an obscene verdict," says Rabbi Zaks. "Shai was devastated by it. This child is not brainwashed. He is free to come and go as he pleases."

Waldman says, "We only want to help the child." To a blonde reporter with a winsome smile, he says: "Look, what can the mother do for him?" His palms turn up. "Nothing. A welfare mother with three other kids. Separated, no father. We want to help this boy."

Rabbi Zaks says he's sure Helbrans will win on appeal. "Hana Fhima is deluding herself if she thinks Stanger will give her son back to her."

Newspaper and magazines appear sympathetic to Hana. They describe a distraught mother who may have won the battle, but lost the war.

Not the Jewish press. *This is justice?*

# 42.  POST-TRIAL REPLAYS

"**G**arbage. I don't believe this garbage." Larry slaps the page back on the kitchen table. Rabbi Weinberg has faxed him a batch of articles from the Jewish press.

"Keep reading," Elaine says as she clears the chocolate pudding dishes. "It gets worse."

"What crap. Look at this." He reads a phrase. "Helbrans was victimized."

Clearly, Shai Fhima's kidnapping story has raised serious questions for rabbis and Jewish organizations. Issues of religious conversion and parental authority take top billing. Is this the tale of a secular boy's conversion? Or was it a cult using mind control? The Brooklyn Supreme Court ruled it a kidnapping. But for Jews, more compelling than the legal are the moral issues. What really happened to the kid studying for his bar mitzvah?

"Nothing on our side?" Larry is shuffling through the curling faxes with rising agitation.

"On our side? A few, you'll get to them."

He pushes his coffee cup aside and tosses a fax in the air like confetti. This one has him steaming. "Kidnapping is not immoral. How about murder? Will they *kill* in the name of religion? Is that coming next?"

"Shhh." She's glad the kids made a fast getaway and they're out of earshot. They don't need to hear their dad going bonkers.

"Listen to this one from the *Jewish Week*." He reads it to her. " 'The jury consisted of nine blacks and three others. By no stretch of the imagination could they be regarded as the rabbi's peers.' That's their argument. Listen to this. 'The jury deliberated only a few hours.' Too short, they claim . . . 'to weigh the sharply conflicting evidence that ran to 2,500 pages. The verdict was wrong.' " He looks up and grabs another fax. "This one says that Vecchione's summation was inflammatory and abusive to the hasidic community."

"Vecchione was abusive?" She raises an eyebrow.

"Listen. 'The prosecutors' prejudicial conduct played on turning Helbrans into a deviant. . . .

"So," she sums up, "they blame the jury, the judge and the prosecutors."

"Especially Owens," Larry says. " 'Owens issued a tidal wave of rulings that hamstrung the defense and his overall attitude was questionable.' "

Actually, Judge Owens, in his private post-trial replay, feels satisfied as he looks back. It didn't take any special courage to reject the plea bargain; it was the right thing to do. What he looked at was the evidence and what's fair, and then he came to a conclusion. You never know what the jury is thinking. But on this one, they had to be impressed with the prosecutors and their preparation.

My job, Owens likes to say, is to see that people get a fair trial, that the constitution guarantees for *both* sides. I don't think about sending any message. Hey, the courts are the tail end of the problem. Society looks upon us to uphold the constitution. That's what I did in this trial.

Plackenmeyer's post-trial replay he shares on the phone with Larry.

"Right from the start, they were ignoring clear evidence of crime and it was a monumental effort to get action. It was a roller coaster ride. Every time you thought you were there, a new monkey wrench was thrown in. It was a kidnapping, an ongoing crime, Larry. *This was the scariest trial I've ever been involved in.*"

Larry's post-trial replay sends him back to the faxes. Some in the Jewish press see it as a terrible miscarriage of justice. But they *do* kidnap kids. Helbrans did it, the three Belgium kids were kidnapped, and others. He reads the fax from the *Forward*.

"The rabbi was unfairly smeared and the youth was portrayed as the victim of a cult."

Rooney is quoted.

"Nothing less than an attack on the hasidim."

He picks up the *Jewish Standard*.

We got a good one? Someone on our side? He grins.

It's about *ba'alei teshuvah:* Jews who leave secular life to become religious. It's pretty good. An interview with a New York psychologist, Esther Perl. She has clients who are . . . sort of newly religious. And it's about when a kid wants to become religious and the rest of the family doesn't.

"An emotionally turbulent home," he reads, then lifts his head. "Boy, has she got that right," he says aloud.

She talks about the vulnerability factor and how zealots offer an alternative home, another family. They focus on the kid, make a big fuss over him.

The next fax also makes him brighten. "Kidnapping is kidnapping. I'm disappointed to hear that any individual within the Jewish community would justify that act as a humanitarian act." Hurrah! One more sane person.

Steve's right. All extremists are alike. It's gotta be their religion, their way. And as long as they get away with it, murder could be right down the pike.

Collecting the faxes, his eyes fall on the homefront section of the *Jewish Standard*. "Tai Ellin-Byrd. She was on the jury."

"Justice was served," he reads out loud. "The sentence is morally appropriate. The jury was pretty much unanimous." Terrific. He heads for the sofa, to enjoy it.

"Helbrans had no sense that what he did was kidnapping. He didn't feel anything he did was wrong. There's a different moral code."

The article calms him. Maybe the world hasn't gone berserk. If one juror understands it . . . and it was *unanimous*, hey.

"Listen to this," he yells over the noise. " 'He wanted Shai to be religious and the family to be religious. That's why he took Shai. There was absolutely no evidence that Shai was abused or beaten. Shai didn't like the rules in his mother's house, so he ran away.' "

He looks up, pleased. "This juror really got it."

He keeps reading.

"He seemed like a sullen, selfish boy with a bad attitude. He was rude to the judge and the prosecutor and the defense attorney. He slouched and rolled his eyes at the jury. This is not a small helpless child who has been beaten. This is a healthy, angry teenager who got caught. Still, I don't know if the damage between the two can be repaired."

Can Shai and Hana become a family again? Larry wonders.

The answer comes from Hana.

She tells reporters who swamp her with phone calls that she's no longer a victim and she's going to try to get Shai back and be a family again. "I can't give up. If I do, what's left?

"If somebody back then told me what I would have to go through—that my son would be kidnapped by a rabbi and I'd still be fighting to get him back—I would have told you, I'd be a crazy woman by now. But when it happens, you find a strength you didn't know you had. Because this is your son."

Maybe the blackest days are over.

With the trial behind her, Hana becomes fixated on the custody battle. Getting Shai back is all that matters.

In her second-floor apartment in Maywood, New Jersey, she keeps his pictures everywhere. In the living room, on the window sill and on the bookcase. She puts his baby pictures in the bedroom she shares with Shiran, where the drawing from Paris hangs on the wall with the cat posters. Her favorite shot is a little boy, about two, with a wide toothy smile and silky blonde hair.

"For Helbrans, maybe this ends in jail," she tells Steve. "But for me and Shai." She shakes her head sadly.

"It's going to be tough," Steve agrees, "all uphill."

"What's happening in Rockland County with Stanger . . . ," she can't find the right words. "To me it feels like a *second kidnapping.*"

# 43. THE END OF 1994

"Maybe I'll look for a deprogrammer," she tells Steve as she signs papers and hands him back the pen. "I'll call back the guy in Boston, I'll find his number." It's been on her mind all week.

"A deprogrammer?" From behind his desk, he scowls. "They're expensive. Illegal. You're talking all kinds of problems. Not now, Hana." Judge Stanger won't budge and Shai's still in the hands of Waldman and Zaks. Which is why it feels like a *second* kidnapping to her.

"The trouble is the deprogrammer, he wanted up front money. They all want money," she sighs. "I have to think about it."

"Let's concentrate on getting custody. We're not up to deprogramming, we haven't got him. One step at a time."

She nods. Concentrate on making Judge Stanger change his mind. But how?

*Dear God, please, please take him off the case, with him we don't stand a chance*, she prays at night.

What takes her breath away is the swiftness of God's answer.

Only days after Helbrans is sentenced, Judge Bernard Stanger suffers a massive stroke. He dies a week later.

She's at the stove, about to spoon macaroni and cheese on the kids' plates when the phone rings. "Okay, okay, I'm coming." She puts the pot back on the burner and turns the flame down.

It's Steve, his voice strangely excited. "Stanger died. This changes everything."

"He died?" A flash of heat smacks the back of her neck. "When?"

He fills her in. "We stand a chance now. They'll appoint a new judge, Hana, we're gonna get a new judge." The words come fast, he's making plans.

"He died? Stanger died?" She tastes guilt. I didn't ask God he should die. I only prayed he shouldn't be the judge for me and Shai. An exhale of breath. "God sees everything."

"A new judge means a new slate. It changes our odds." He's all fired up.

"So who's gonna be for us the new judge?"

"We don't know yet. Sit tight."

She hangs up, dazed.

Outside it is pitch black. Though it's only five-thirty, she can see her refection in the window. "Stanger's gone," she murmurs, "off the case. Thank you, God." My luck is changing.

She plunges the serving spoon back into the pot, stirring the macaroni vigorously so it doesn't stick. And she breaks into a smile. For the first time since Shai was kidnapped, Hana feels the smile right down to her toes. Wide and toothy like Shai's smile on his blonde baby picture.

She turns off the flame and goes to the framed snapshot. Picks it up and studies it tenderly. "You got that smile from me, Shai. From your mother. You know?"

She puts it back on the table.

"Okay, kids, dinner's ready."


More good news comes tumbling in.

This time from the Brooklyn Supreme Court. On Friday, December 9, Mordecai Weiss enters a plea of guilty to fourth degree conspiracy.

"He admitted?" she asks Steve when he phones. "I can't believe it. Weiss squealed on Helbrans? He testified against another Jew in court?" *Msira.*

"Yup. He admitted guilt."

"What did he say?"

"That he took Shai that weekend and turned him over to Rabbi Helbrans."

"See? See? For two years he said he was innocent, he

swore he put Shai on a bus. A pack of lies. Now comes out the truth."

"Yup."

"He goes to jail?" She wants to hear the sentence. "How long?"

Steve hesitates. "The judge ordered him to pay a fine of $10,000 and serve a term of five years probation."

"Probation?" she cries indignantly. "Not jail?"

Steve predicted her reaction before he picked up the phone. "Let's look on the bright side. Things are going our way. I'll send you the clip, it was in *Newsday*. Gotta go, my other line is ringing."

It arrives the next day. She reads the clipping once, twice, then reads it again.

"I took Shai with the understanding I would return him to his mother. But while in my custody, Shai told me he did not want to go home and I took Shai to Rabbi Schlomo Helbrans's home so Shai's mother would not be able to find him."

Asked by Judge Owens why he lied, he replied, "I lied to the police so I would not get me and rabbi in trouble."

For Hana, it comes two years too late, this admission of guilt. They're liars, all liars.

She reads that Owens agreed to drop the charge of second degree kidnapping. But he ordered Weiss to pay a $10,000 fine and serve a term of five years probation. Exactly what Steve told her. It makes her even more furious to read it.

She puts down the article and calls his office.

"Weiss doesn't go to jail—this is justice?" she snaps at him. "I can't believe Owens did that."

"He made Weiss pay the money to a nondenominational charity." It infuriates Steve that again the prosecutors took no position on the sentence. Could have gone to four years.

"He pays to a charity and that's all? Finished?"

To a reporter who phones asking for her reaction, she says she's very disappointed. "Weiss should serve some jail time for taking my son."

✡   ✡   ✡

This time it's Larry who calls.

"Got good news, Hana."

"What?"

"A Brooklyn appeals judge ruled on Helbrans's request to stay the execution of his sentence pending an appeal."

"What does it mean?" Lawyers—they talk like that.

"Helbrans's appeal was denied," he reports.

"Denied? Good. And Malka Helbrans?"

"She comes up for sentencing next week, Hana."

Steve reaches for the phone. His call is not going to make Hana happy. On Thursday, December 15, Judge Owens set aside the conviction of Malka Helbrans. Better schmoose a little.

"Yeah, yeah, the kids are fine," she replies. "Something happened?"

"Malka Helbrans . . ." His voice sends the message.

She can guess. "She's free?"

"Owens said the evidence was not legally sufficient."

"What?" Judge Owens was her angel. "What does it mean?"

"He said he really thought she was part of it, but he didn't think they legally proved it."

"So Malka Helbrans and Mordecai Weiss, they both get off." Bitter disappointment. "They don't go to jail. Nothing."

"No."

"This is justice? She gave money to charity like Weiss?"

"No, no, only Weiss. He handed over a $10,000 check to the prosecutors." Why tell her the check was written to the Police Athletic League?

What closes the grueling days of 1994 is a short paragraph in the newspaper that catches Hana's eye. *During a radio program, Governor Mario Cuomo says that he'll take a look at the Helbrans case.* Oh my God.

"He'll take a look at the Helbrans case? What does it mean?" she phones Larry at the office. "The governor, he'll get Helbrans off?"

"Forget it, Hana, it's political talk. Concentrate on the custody. The news is good. We appear before a new judge. Maybe not the best we could hope for, but good, very good."

What he doesn't say is that with Shai turning sixteen in early February, only weeks away, their reconciliation seems unlikely. Sixteen is willful. And Shai is in Zaks's pocket.

He walks into Steve's office.

Steve looks up from his desk. "What?"

"She saw the Cuomo article and she's bent outta shape, really scared."

"It's nothing." He brushes it aside.

"I told her that, but you know Hana. She still thinks Shai's gonna come back to her and she'll turn him into the sweet little kid he was at thirteen."

"Not by a longshot." Steve sighs. "You know why?"

"Why?"

"Because Helbrans stole his soul, Lar."

A thoughtful pause. "True. True."

*Getting Shai back* is the legal challenge. With a new judge, it could be won.

*Restoring Shai's soul*—that's another question.

"Yup," Larry nods sadly. "Helbrans stole his soul."

PART VII

1995

# 44. SHAI DISAPPEARS

Since the new year began, Hana has been searching for a sign that 1995 would restore Shai to her. That the new judge—a woman—would reverse Stanger's stranglehold on the justice system. With Stanger out of the way—*thank you, God, thank you*—maybe this new judge will put an end to the second kidnapping, a legal kidnapping arranged by Stanger and the rabbis.

"You think she'll be on our side?" she asks Steve over and over.

On February 15 in Rockland County family court, Judge Elaine Slobad turns the bleak winter Wednesday into pure sunshine for Hana. She throws out almost all the legal issues surrounding the custody fight and she orders Shai to be returned to his mother.

Thorsen scowls. "There's no court in New York State who can tell Shai who he can live with."

For Hana, it is a day of triumph. Bittersweet. Because last week was Shai's birthday, he turned sixteen. She hears that he's driving a car now, provided by Zaks and Waldman. And though Helbrans is serving time in jail, there is less comfort in that than she had imagined. After three torturous years, Shai is still in the grip of the Monsey rabbis: Aryeh Zaks and Lieb Waldman. His mind is controlled by them. His soul belongs to them. It has eaten a hole in her heart.

She trembles as Judge Slobad's orders: "Custody of Shai Reuven is returned to his mother Hana Fhima. This case is remanded to New Jersey. He is a New Jersey boy, he lived in New Jersey, the case does not belong here."

Despite Shai's writ of emancipation from his parents, the judge orders Zaks to produce the boy within sixty days. The parties must

appear in Bergen County family court before April 4 to deal with
the one legal issue Judge Slobad leaves standing. An order by Judge
Sween last spring saying the custody matter should be decided in
New Jersey because Shai was a runaway from that state.

Hana and Steve come down the snowy steps of the New City
courthouse glowing.

"Sixty days," Hana chirps. This judge has restored her faith in
the system. "In sixty days Zaks has to give Shai back to me."

"And we're done with Rockland County. It's back to New
Jersey." Steve leads her into the winter chill and they head for the
parking lot.

"First thing, I'll call Rabbi Weinberg." The sharp wind on her
back feels exhilarating. She feels light headed, the snow shim-
mering under a brilliant sun is the sign she has been waiting for.
Shai will return to her in 1995.

Steve slams her car door shut with solid satisfaction. "We
finally got a fair shake."

"He was good to me for three years," she continues her
thoughts about Rabbi Weinberg as they head back to New Jersey.

The reform rabbi of Beth Haverim lives in Monsey. His son
and his wife have both reported sightings of Shai. Smoking off the
back porch of Rabbi Zaks's house. Driving a car. Hanging out in
town with other boys, and making a nuisance of himself. But any
news he brings about Shai makes her happy and she gobbles it up.
Rabbi Weinberg has comforted her for three years. Next year he
will bar mitzvah Osheri.

"He was smoking?" she asked him.

"He's a rebellious kid." He made light of it. "He's confused.
They manipulate him with money and clothes and computers.
He's angry, he's acting out," he told her.

Steve said the same thing. "He's a kid with power now. Understand? Enjoying the limelight. He's a rock star. He's got media
attention. Microphones in his face. Video cameras. It's an ego
thing. The rabbis play to that."

"Sure." Her consistency and ferocity about Shai have not wavered. "It's not the real Shai. Not my son."

Driving back to New Jersey—*we're done with Rockland County*—she is full of plans.

"First, my mother, I gotta call Israel. You know what, Steve?" There is a happy urgency in her voice.

"What?"

"Once I get Shai back, maybe . . . maybe me and the kids we'll all go back to Israel. This summer maybe. My mother will help me, we'll be a family again. It will be okay."

Steve pats her gloved hand. Nice to see her smile for a change.

"The judge, she said sixty days." She turns her face to him for a confirmation. "Right?"

"Yup, they got sixty days to produce him."


A small article in the *Patriot News*, a Harrisburg, Pennsylvania, paper, adds to their exhilaration.

"Listen to this, Hana," Larry phones her. "You listening?"

"What?"

*"New York man pleads guilty to embezzling funds. Faces possible twenty-month sentence.* It's Waldman, Hana. They got him on embezzling in Federal court in Harrisburg."

"Embezzling? What it means?"

"I'll read you the highlights. 'With his full graying beard and dark business suit and yarmulke, Lieb Waldman looked every bit the rabbi he was trained to be. . . .' He reads parts of it. " 'The forty-six-year-old New York resident pleaded guilty to embezzling approximately $900,000 from a bankrupt company which had owned two office buildings known as Ararot One Plaza. Instead of properly maintaining the accounts, Waldman, the Romanian immigrant and father of six, shipped most of the money out. . . . He combined stolen funds. . . .' Well you get the picture. He's a crook. Wait, here's more. 'Regarding restitution, Waldman does not plan to use his $800,000 Monsey, NY home but will instead either sell a Florida property or refinance a major construction project he is involved with in Jerusalem.' Nice, huh?'"

"See? All the pieces are coming together," she observes with satisfaction. "Helbrans is in jail. Freund is convicted. Weiss is convicted."

"And now Waldman." Larry's voice is gleeful. "Convicted of embezzlement."

"He was in the conspiracy, he was the one—they don't say it in the paper?" she asks.

"No. This is about him laundering money. Fraud. Not about the kidnapping. One of his shady real estate deals."

"And all the families who hid Shai, all of them, they should go to jail. Their names should go in the paper, like Waldman."

"Well . . . I thought you'd enjoy this. Gotta go."


Sixty days pass. Rabbi Zaks does not produce Shai. His lawyers claim they can't find him. Has the boy disappeared again? For a *third* time?

Hana's apprehensions return, flooding her with fears.

Despite Judge Slobad's court order, she doesn't have Shai. The rabbis and the lawyers are stonewalling her. New nightmares fly into her head. Did they send him back to France? To Canada? At night, she paces around the apartment and stares out the window at the deserted streets. Where is he now?

"What good it does I have custody? What good?" she complains to Steve. Frustration releases her Israeli rudeness. "You gotta *do* something."

Steve has phoned the attorneys. Phoned Eric Thorsen. Phoned and phoned. They ask for postponements. They reschedule court days. But no Shai. "We'll hit them with a contempt charge," he concludes.

He takes a harder tack with Thorsen.

"Where's Shai? You have to produce him."

"We don't know." Thorsen claims he hasn't got a clue. Zaks has no information. Waldman has no information.

"Sure, sure." Larry's opinion of Thorsen was never as sanguine as Steve's. "Like he didn't know the kid was stashed away in France last summer. It's another cover-up. Thorsen knew about France. He knows where Shai is now. Thorsen is protecting his client."

Hana agrees with Larry. "Thorsen knows. He's a snake like the rest of them. He's covering-up, they're hiding him."

She phones Steve over and over. "You think he's in France? In Canada?"

"Who knows? Canada, France, it's all conjecture. As long as they refuse to produce him, they're defying a court order."

Now it is May. Five months into 1995.

Hana and Steve drive to Hackensack to appear before Judge Sween in Bergen County family court. Flowers are blooming in the courtyard at the main entrance. Flags are flying over the war memorial and people sit on the stone benches taking in the sun.

"Your Honor," Steve addresses the New Jersey judge. "Shai's lawyers have not produced him. In defiance of a court order."

Judge Sween wets his finger to turn a page, then looks up and passes his hand over his thinning gray hair. He frowns. Clearly, he is annoyed. "Where is the boy?"

Hana's eyes fill with tears and she presses a hand to her forehead. *Where's Shai?* It goes on already three years.

"Your Honor," she stands up and faces the judge. "No one will tell. They say they don't know, they say he's gone."

"Gone?" Sween's neck reddens.

"Your Honor," she implores him, "what good it does, I have custody? What good?" All the court orders in the world cannot produce Shai.

May. No Shai.

June. No Shai.

He has disappeared for the *third* time.

# 45. SHAI IS PICKED UP

School's out and the kids are home.

July gives way to August. A summer more punishing than last year's winter blizzards. A heatwave sits on the metropolitan area like a blanket of fire. Temperatures in the high nineties, the humidity so oppressive it's difficult to breathe.

Hana's fans buzz at full tilt day and night. She takes the kids to the community pool to cool off. Or they escape to the mall for air conditioning. Everyone's hoping for a thundershower. Maybe Hurricane Erin, out of Florida, will bring relief.

On Thursday, August third, the eleventh day of the heatwave, it reaches a searing 97 degrees. Larry decides to take Elaine and the kids to Spring Lake for a long weekend at the Jersey shore. Leave Friday, be back in the office Tuesday.

On Friday morning, his secretary buzzes him. "Sheriff James Kralick from Rockland County."

"Put him through." Kralick is a nice guy. "Hey, Jim, what's up?"

"We picked Shai Reuven up."

"When? Where?" He grabs a pen.

"Last night. In Monsey."

He makes a beeline for Steve's office. "Kralick just called. They got Shai, he's back in Monsey."

"What? He's back?" Steve springs to his feet.

Larry fills him in. It'll be on the wire and hit the morning papers. "We got a court appearance Monday morning in Bergen County. Judge Sween."

"It's okay. I'll take care of it," Steve says. "You go to Spring Lake, get out of here."

Larry looks doubtful.

"It's okay. Go. Get outa here." Why should his weekend go up in smoke?

Steve phones Hana. "They picked Shai up. He's in Monsey."

"What? What?"

He tells her what he knows, trying to keep his voice calm.

"Last night, the Sheriff responded to a tip that he was back . . ."

"He was with Zaks?" She has to know.

"They found him on a playground in Monsey. Late, almost ten o'clock at night. They pulled him in on an arrest warrant."

"Where was he? Where was he?" She presses her fingers to her lips.

"He won't tell. But you'll see him in court. We have an appearance Monday morning. You'll talk to him then."

"He'll be in court Monday?"

"Yup. Judge Sween. You need a ride?""

"Monday. Monday." *Thank you God*. Shai's back.


A New Jersey reporter picks it up on the wire. The missing kid is back? A break in the case? Saturday morning, she drives out to Monsey to look around. Not a car is moving: it's sabbath. And the temperature is ninety-five.

On the streets, hasidic men are wearing hats and long black silk coats tied with a sash, their hands clasped behind their back. Women are strolling in pairs wearing long dresses to their ankles and long sleeves to their wrists.

She drives past the Chofetz Chaim Heritage Foundation on the corner of Route 306 and Maple Avenue. Is this the yeshiva playground where Shai was picked up? A few straggly shrubs, a lawn of crabgrass and a cyclone fence with a sign *absolutely no thru traffic, violators will be prosecuted*. She drives past small split level homes on Phyllis Street, past yeshivas, past yellow school buses with Hebrew letters, parked outside. Past a seedy strip mall.

Monsey has no police station. So she pulls into the Ramapo Police on Route 58 East. She talks with Dispatcher Jean Iacono who sends her to the Rockland County Sheriff's Headquarters. "Talk to Sheriff Kralick," she advises pleasantly.

Kralick is not at the Correction Center, a modern one story brick building. But she finds Patrol Officer Ken Jonston, one of the officers on the night shift who transported Shai. He talks to her guardedly, doesn't want to say too much.

"You picked him up, officer. Where was he all these months?" she asks.

"He won't say where he stayed," the tall, good-looking officer replies. "But he was spotted in Rockland County in recent weeks."

The Saturday edition of the *Rockland Journal-News* runs with a headliner in the B section. Steve Lieberman, the reporter who has been covering the case, has the byline. Under *SHAI FHIMA REAPPEARS, AGAIN*, he writes that Rockland Judge Elaine Slobad has ordered the teen to attend a New Jersey custody hearing. That sheriff's deputies caught Shai on a Route 306 playground in Monsey. Shai told them he returned three weeks ago, but he wouldn't tell where he was.

The Newark *Star Ledger* runs an Associated Press wire release under the headline *MISSING FOR THE THIRD TIME, RAMSEY TEEN TURNS UP IN N.Y.*

Ben Ostrer, Zaks's attorney, says Shai will spend the weekend with a Monsey rabbi, not Zaks. And he'll produce the boy on Monday in Judge Sween's courtroom. Unidentified sources say the boy was in Canada.

"In Canada?" Hana squeals to Steve. "He was in Canada?" She has a million questions. "You talked to Thorsen? What did he say? Shai will be there Monday?"

"He'll be there, Hana." He doesn't embellish.

To Larry, he reports a modified version. He calls Larry at his hotel. "What Thorsen actually said . . ."

"What?" Larry asks.

"He said he's been paving the way for him to return for weeks. He said Shai called him during his five-month hiatus. But he never asked him or Zaks where he was staying."

"*That's* what Thorsen said?"

"Yup. He said, 'All I know is that he was safe and he wanted to return and get his life together.' "

"Bullshit! Waldman's behind it. He probably fixed another phony passport."

"Listen, Lar. I'll be in Sween's courtroom on Monday. You'll be back Tuesday, right?"

"I'll call you Monday night, I gotta hear it."

Sheriff Kralik, interviewed by the press, gives his view in no uncertain terms. Keeping track of Shai Reuven has become tiresome. Expensive, too. His office spent over $13,000 guarding the boy in February and March 1994. Translation: the kid's a pain in the ass and we're glad to get rid of him.

"I hope the judge sticks to her guns and sends him to Bergen County. I've had enough of this."

All weekend Hana is jumpy. Her neck and shoulders ache, she can't sleep and she yells at the kids over nothing. Let it be Monday already. She has told them Shai is back.

"I have to be in court Monday morning." It's a message her children are used to, words they know. Court appearance. Judge's orders. Lawyer's motions.

"Osheri," she turns to him. "Don't let them watch television all day. Okay?"

He nods and adjusts his glasses. He understands. He's the oldest so he has to mind his brother and sister. A neighbor will look in. They've done it before. "You think Shai'll come home Monday?" he asks. It would be a wonderful birthday present. His birthday is Wednesday, August 9.

"We gotta see what the judge says."

She phones Steve again at home. "Any news?"

"No."

"Maybe he wants to come home," she tells Steve. "Maybe he got a change of heart and he's done with the craziness." She has read an article about cults in a magazine. How a person after years can snap out of it. How the mind control can backfire and you can wake up from it. Maybe the same will be with Shai and now he's ready to come home.

"I'll pick you up ten-thirty sharp," Steve says. "Gotta be there at eleven."

"You think he'll show up, he'll be there?"

A long sigh. "Maybe you're right. He's tired of running. Tired of being on the lam. Maybe he's getting some sense, he's past sixteen."

"That's what I was thinking." Yes, he'll be there. He's done with them, he wants to come back and be a normal boy.

"Ben Ostrer's bringing him in, Zaks's attorney," he reminds her. "Anyhow, that's what they're saying. So let's be there early, I'll pick you up." He knows her car is on the fritz again and the buses are unreliable.

"No, it's okay. Rabbi Weinberg, he's gonna come for me. We'll be there ten-thirty, we'll come early."

By Monday, a respite from the twelve-day heatwave drops temperatures from the nineties to the sixties. As Hana and Rabbi Weinberg cross the huge parking lot, people are smiling with relief.

The Bergen County courthouse is an impressive edifice. Hana notices it today. Nicknamed the Little Whitehouse, its golden American Eagle is perched majestically on the rooftop, resplendent in the brilliant sunshine. Attorneys, swinging briefcases, and clients, in all manner of dress from sneakers to stiletto heels, pour into the main entrance. The courtyard is filled with bright flowers.

*Will he show up?*

Upstairs, at the second-floor courtroom of Judge Sween, a uniformed officer stands guard at the double door entrance to Number 226. Attorneys fly by, greeting him with "Hi, Ralph." And the doors bang shut.

"Only lawyers may enter," he announces sternly.

Hana and Rabbi Weinberg wait nervously on a bench under the eight arches that form the rotunda. They watch other people draped against a wall sipping coffee from styrofoam cups. A few glance upward at the marble columns that soar to the stained glass globe two stories above them. As their attorneys appear, they jump up, shake hands, and immediately discuss their case. Anxiety floats in the air.

Steve arrives, briefcase bulging, and heads for their bench.

Rabbi Weinberg stands up and they shake hands. His white hair is flattened by the fisherman's cap in his hand and his light gray seersucker suit and pale pink face turn him into a pastel drawing. He has come to support Hana. Also to see Shai, though the boy hasn't spoken to him in years. Probably he's heard Zaks and Waldman refer to him openly as the *deformed* rabbi. But this morning, in his jacket pocket he has something he dearly wants the boy to see. Maybe it will warm him up. Make the day go smoother. Even foster a reconciliation.

He pulls it out and hands it to Hana. "Look. I want to show this to Shai." It's a photo he took of Shai's grandparents and Uncle David, Hana's brother, when he visited Jerusalem some months ago. "Maybe it'll soften him up." Maybe Shai Fhima wasn't the smartest twelve-year-old kid in his bar mitzvah class back in 1992, but he had a sweetness then. He wasn't *farbisen*. Maybe this photo will touch him.

At ten past eleven, the other side arrives.

First, Eric Thorsen. Nattily turned out in a well-cut business suit and silk tie, he nods to Hana and Steve.

Then Mitchel Ostrer, a young man from the prestigious law firm of Sills, Cummis, Zuckerman, Radin, Tischman, Epstein, and Gross. Here to represent Rabbi Zaks.

Next, out of the shadows steps a heavyset, unkempt bearded man in a black yarmulke and wrinkled suit.

"It's Waldman," Hana whispers to Rabbi Weinberg. The sight of him frightens her. He's here again.

A lone woman reporter appears out of nowhere and approaches Waldman. Hana bends forward to hear their conversation.

"Excuse me. Are you one of Shai Reuven's attorneys?" the reporter asks him pleasantly.

"I'm a businessman," he replies curtly.

"And what business is that, sir?"

"Real estate."

"Here in New Jersey? Your holdings are in New Jersey . . . ?"

"Privileged information," he snaps, cutting her off. Then turns away and pulls out a cellular phone.

"Excuse me, sir, aren't you Lieb Waldman?"

"Yes."

"Then you're Rabbi Zaks's father-in-law and . . ."

"What do you want to know? Why I care about the boy? Why we want to help him? I'll tell you. He's a lovely boy, there's nothing wrong with him, you'll see for yourself. He wants to be an orthodox boy. We want to help him. His mother can't support him, she's on welfare, no father. We can give him what he needs." Interview over. He turns away, he has calls to make.

She can hear him. His voice, even in Hebrew, is demanding. He turns to the wall and barks orders into his hand.

"You think he'll show up?" Hana asks Steve a third time.

"That's what they're telling us. Ben Ostrer, that's Mitchel's brother, is supposed to be driving Shai."

Twenty minutes go by.

Hana tries to be calm. Her eyes on the staircase. On the elevator door.

Will he show up?

She has so much to say to him.

# 46. MOTHER AND SON TALK

Hana sits stiffly, her shoulders hunched like someone out in the cold. Will Shai come? Is he all right? Where was he so many months? Canada? If it goes good with Judge Sween, I'll find him a deprogrammer. She reaches back for a name.

Goldberg. Bill Goldberg was the therapist from Rockland County, a nice man. He understood cults and brainwashing. How a rebellious kid, an immigrant dropped into a new country, could be taken in. How they reach into you and give you reasons to follow them. How their faces smile and they make you the center of attention. Goldberg tried to make a bridge between me and Shai, me crying the whole session. Because with my own eyes I saw how Shai was mixed up. So angry he wouldn't even look me in the eye. Maybe I'll call Goldberg, he'll find me somebody.

She looks around the rotunda. Still no Shai. Even the lawyers are getting edgy, their eyes darting.

How will he act to me when he walks in? A boy without his family and a normal life since thirteen, there could be plenty damage. Whatever he did, whatever he said, it was not my Shai, it was what the mind control made him do. Can a deprogrammer turn him back?

She glances at her watch. Almost eleven-thirty.

Maybe what happened he was looking for a father. His real father lives in Israel with another wife and other children. And with Jacky he had a stepfather who beat up his mother. Then comes along Helbrans, to be a father to him. He's confused. Helbrans, saw it and took advantage.

She glances up. Thorsen, Ostrer, and Waldman are standing together, joking and laughing. Ostrer she doesn't know, but what she sees is three conspirators keeping Shai away from her.

With Helbrans in jail, why are they still fighting for Shai's custody? Why another lawyer on Waldman's payroll? Steve showed her Ostrer's card. *Mitchel E. Ostrer. Of Counsel.* He pointed to the law firm's name SILLS CUMMIS ZUCKERMAN RADIN TISHMAN EPSTEIN & GROSS, P.A. "Big firm."

"You think they're afraid Shai knows too much? He'll tell who hid him?" She had put the same question to Larry.

"Of course," he snapped back. "The kid knows where all the skeletons are buried, he could blow the whistle. Name names. Name the families that harbor kidnapped kids. Name the kids they kidnapped. Shai wasn't the first boy, we know that."

She shook her head. "No Jewish boy is safe from them."

Then Larry delivered his all time one-liner. *"They weren't trying to save Shai's soul. They were trying to save the rabbi's ass."* And he had the guts to repeat it to reporters.

She turns to Steve now and repeats the same question.

"You think they're afraid Shai knows too much? That's why Waldman got another big lawyer?" It is a device that gives her comfort. If Larry and Steve disagree, she has two opinions to play with. If they agree, she counts it as double proof.

She likes Steve's habit of repeating the question. His thoughtfulness. No snap judgments.

"Why did Waldman hire another big lawyer?" Steve's eyes crinkle and Rabbi Weinberg leans in to hear his answer. "Because it discourages others from suing them. It establishes their power. It sends a message: Don't mess with the hasidic and orthodox community. You can't win against us."

"That's right," Rabbi Weinberg chimes in.

"If they can shut us up," Steve continues, "they get away with it. Look, Hana. Until you came along, no one stood up to them. They were above the law. Free to abduct kids, ship them to yeshivas and hide them. They had no interference."

"I know, I know." Talking to Steve makes her feel better.

"All that talk about how you violated Shai's First Amendment rights, how you wouldn't let him be religious, it was . . ." Steve is not a man who says shit easily, "baloney."

She nods. "They let him run around, no discipline. He doesn't have to go to school, just sit and study Torah. He travels to Europe, to Canada. They give him a car to drive, plenty of money. With me he rebels against the rules. With them, he's free. I remember how he bragged to Osheri, '*If you ever need money, I have a lot of money. Money is no problem with me.'* He needs psychiatric help."

She brushes a thread off her white jeans and checks her watch. Eleven-forty. Is he gonna show up?

Rabbi Weinberg pats her hand. "He'll come, he'll come."

They wait.


"*There he is!*" A shout rings out.

Hana jumps to her feet.

Thorsen, Ostrer, and Waldman rush toward Shai as he's led in by Ben Ostrer and the four men encircle him, cutting him off from Hana who is charging in, calling, *Shai, Shai.*

"Leave him alone." Thorsen blocks her way and waves her off. "Leave him alone." A move so unnecessary, it brings tears to her eyes. Because Shai won't even look at her. He turns away, recoiling at her voice.

She backs off and plants herself a few feet away. Tries to catch a glimpse of him. She can see his black Fedora bobbing to their instructions. His shiny black shoes and white shirt, no tie. With his black suit and sidecurls, he looks every bit the hasid. *Dear God, is he theirs?* A convulsive gurgle rips from her throat. Will the poison they fed him be a virus in his blood forever?

Rabbi Weinberg tries to penetrate the circle.

"Shai, Shai," he calls, thrusting the photo at him. "Look, I saw your grandparents in Jerusalem and your Uncle David. I got a picture for you. See?"

But sleek, pencil thin Thorsen and beefy, unkempt Waldman block his way. "Leave him alone. Get away."

"They love you," he coos, trying to shove the picture at him. "Look, it's your grandmother."

*"Please."* Thorsen yanks Shai away. Leads him into the courtroom to a bench and plants himself on the aisle to protect against further intrusions. The two Ostrer lawyers, like bodyguards, sit directly behind Shai.

Waldman and Rabbi Weinberg must remain outside.

Hana and Steve enter the courtroom and take a bench on the opposite side of the aisle and two rows back. Hana fastens her eyes on Shai, any sliver of him will do.

He sits slumped over, head down, eyes on his white socks and black shoes, his feet shuffling under the bench. His beautiful dark eyelashes flutter. He yawns. He replies to something Thorsen says. He rewraps a sidelock that got loose from around his ear. But look at her? The enemy? No.

The boy is sour. *Farbisen,* is Rabbi Weinberg's word. Look what they did to him.

The hum of the air conditioner is the loudest sound in the courtroom.

Steve's head is bent over his papers, focused on hammering out a new custody agreement. With Rabbi Helbrans stashed away in Woodbourne Correctional Facility, his primary concern is to establish that Hana has custody. Not *shared* custody. Not *provisional* custody. *Full* custody.

He remembers the day Larry stood there asking him would he do it? *A custody battle. Your bailiwick,* he'd said. How it took him only a nanosecond and he jumped right in. "Okay, okay. We go in *pro hace vice*. We do it."

And today, waiting for another judge, in yet another courtroom, in another state, he doesn't regret it. Not his style to brag, but he takes pride in the fact that they never gave up. Not Hana. Not Larry. Not him. Stayed on it since the day the kid was kidnapped three years ago. A matter of principle.

Sure Hana is exasperating at times. Demanding. Annoying.

Her *please* and *thank-yous* barely exist. Doesn't matter. Once you go in, you do it right, you do it graciously. The decent thing. Steve Rubenstein believed in decency.

So it's August 1995, and he's facing the same custody battle. Stanger has died. Slobad has sent it to New Jersey. Okay. It's up to you, Judge Sween.

After this *third* disappearing act, Judge Sween ain't gonna sit on it. He has insisted all along they have to produce the boy. Well, he's here. All the pieces are in place. Let it roll.

At a little past noon, the court officer motions to Steve.

"Judge Sween will see you. In chambers."

Everyone rises and files in.

Half an hour later, all parties exit. Stonefaced, they pass through the courtroom, through the double doors that bang shut behind them, and they spill out to the rotunda.

One look at Hana tells Rabbi Weinberg to keep quiet. He stands beside her. Steve flanks her on the other side.

"I don't understand," she turns to Steve with a tight look in her eyes. "What does it mean, the judge says *I* have to decide?"

"You have to make a decision, Hana." His voice tells her to get it straight. "Sween gave us *two* options."

"Explain me. Say it again." She can't afford to make another mistake. She's so close now, she has to do what's best for Shai. Because the judge is calling them back after a lunch break.

"Okay," he explains. "What it comes down to is this. The judge says: *One.* He can send Shai to the Children's Shelter. But if he runs away," he wags a warning finger, "he'll be picked up and held in a Correction Facility."

"Jail?" A tiny sob rips from her throat. "No, no," her hand shoves it aside. "I don't want no juvenile facility, no, no." She pulls herself together. "What's the *second* one?"

"It comes down to this. Shai has to agree to visit you on a regular basis. He'll stay in Rockland County, the judge will assign a place. But he has to come to see you on a regular basis. You have to start talking. And he wants a psychiatric evaluation."

"Okay. Okay." She snaps back. "I want us to start talking. As long as he's not with Zaks and those people. And he'll come to me every day?"

Steve raises his eyebrows. "We'll see."

Rabbi Weinberg looks doubtful. He doesn't want to see Hana hurt again.

He leans in to say a few gentle words.

"Hana. There are things in the Jewish tradition for mending poor relations between kids and parents." He wants to encourage her. "Go over to him," he motions to Shai sitting on a bench with the lawyers and Waldman. "Try to talk to him. Say a few words. Go on. He's right there."

Her eyes fall on Shai. She is hungry to talk to him, to be near him. But they're crowded around him. What chance does she have?

She looks back at the rabbi. At Steve. I should try?

"Go on," Steve urges her.

She stands up. Squares her shoulders. Clears her throat.

"You two . . . go eat lunch. I'm not hungry." Which means she's going to try.

Steve gives her the thumbs-up sign. And the two men exit down the hall.

When they return from the cafeteria, they see a miracle.

Hana and Shai are sitting on the same bench. No lawyers. Just the two of them. They are deep in conversation. A nod from him. A gesture from her. In a world of their own, they are speaking in Hebrew, in low calm tones.

Both men stop. Hang back. Quickly, veer off to one side.

Something wonderful is happening.

At two, Hana rises from the bench. She crosses the rotunda and comes toward Steve.

"It's settled. We talked. He'll stay in Rockland County and come to visit me. He drives. He'll come every afternoon."

"He agrees?" Rabbi Weinberg asks.

"Yes."

"Great," says Steve. "Let the healing begin."

In Judge Sween's private chamber, Steve stands before the judge. "The mother and son have worked it out, Your Honor. Both parties agree to be reasonable. Shai will visit her and they will begin talking."

"Good." Judge Sween brushes a thin wisp of gray hair back off his forehead and outlines his decision. For the next two weeks, Shai will stay with a rabbi he will appoint, not Zaks. He must visit his mother daily. And he wants a psychiatric evaluation. "On Monday August 21, all parties will reappear in this courtroom at eleven."

Hana exhales. It's a start. They talked already forty minutes. First angry. Mostly grunts. Then he glanced at her and she looked back at him. It got easier. And she said to him, "Shai. You'll stay in Rockland and practice your religion. And you'll come to me?" She held her breath.

He tilted his head. "If I'll have a car, I'll drive."

"He's going to call me tonight," she tells Steve, "before eleven."

As they leave the courtroom, Hana feels satisfied. "It went good," she says to Steve as they exit through the lobby. "He's gonna go for counseling. Get a psychiatric evaluation." A cautious hopefulness colors her voice.

Steve nods. Hey, maybe the kid's getting sick of hiding and tired of running. Sixteen's gotta be smarter than thirteen.

He senses something else.

Maybe the rabbis and the lawyers are getting tired of Shai. Thorsen seems to have lost his enthusiasm for the fight. Ben Ostrer ducked out fast. And Zaks is out of the picture.

Who's left?

Lieb Waldman.

# 47. SHAI DEFIES
# THE COURT ORDER

Last night she got up twice. Worried. Anxious. He's coming tomorrow. Talk only nice things. Ask him: You still play basketball? Like that. No arguments. The children will be with friends, she arranged it; they need private time.

"Shai, Shai, come in." She flings the door open wide.

He seems nervous, so she walks him through the apartment, shows him the kids' rooms, their posters and things.

He picks up a Giants T-shirt. "It's nice. Osheri made a nice room."

"Come on." She takes his arm, so thin she can feel the bone, and pulls him toward the kitchen table. "I bought you brownies." He sits down and she places a paper plate in front of him; her dishes aren't kosher.

"Enough!" he grins as she squirts a mountain of Cool Whip on top. She puts out a Coke for him, a Diet Pepsi for herself and sits down.

He pops open the can and guzzles. She steers the conversation to happy times. To her sister Shlomit, a teenager like him, only a year and a half older. And his grandmother. And sweet memories of Jerusalem. Soon his shoulders relax and what began with a shrug and a grunt ends pleasantly.

They hug each other goodbye and she smiles reaching up to him. "Look how tall you got."

"For a first visit, it went okay," she tells Steve.

On August 8, he visits her a second time.

He seems antsy. "I got a ride," he tells her, "I gotta leave early."

"You can't stay till the kids come home? I got ice cream."

He shrugs. He takes the sofa.

"It's okay."

She pulls up a chair. She cannot revive the conversation. She has exhausted family ties.

She tells a silly anecdote about Shiran getting lost in the supermarket aisle. It goes nowhere. The conversation chugs along with embarrassed starts and dead stops.

"So tell me. What do you study in school?" she asks. "Come on," she summons him to sit down with her at the kitchen table. It will go easier there.

He stands with both hands on the back of a kitchen chair. "Study?" A tinge of contempt for a stupid question. "I study Torah."

"I mean other subjects."

"*I study Torah.*"

He sits down, gawky, all arms and legs. He doesn't want to be here.

"You want a cupcake?" she smiles.

"Okay."

She takes an open box of Entenmann's cupcakes from the counter and puts it next to him. Two more cans of soda. "You drink coffee?"

"Not now." He's in a hurry, he wants to go.

He takes a bite of the brownie, head down. A listless sip of soda. Bored.

"You still like Steven Seagal?"

"Yeah."

"You saw his new movie?"

"Yeah."

She is working hard to keep the conversation alive and he's looking around to make an exit.

"Well . . . I gotta go." He pushes his chair back and stands up, his eyes avoiding her.

"When I'll see you?" She wants to pin it down.

"I'll call you."

A sinking feeling comes over her. He's here only because the judge made a court order. He's still connected *to them*. The visit feels like a message from them: *You'll never have him, he's ours.*

"You'll come tomorrow?" she yells down to him from the top of the stairs.

"Yeah." The front door slams.

She falls into his chair. It's still warm from him. She closes her eyes to sniff his scent.

He doesn't call the next day. Nor the day after.

What did I do? What did I say?

She waits. A couple of days pass.

She phones Steve.

"Shai came to me twice," she's babbling, "but he don't show up no more. If he'll run away, he'll go to jail."

"Twice? Only twice?" Trouble. He's defying a court order. "Wait one more day, let's see what happens."

"No, no," she protests. "I need someone experienced with cults." Her voice is rising. "You gotta phone Thorsen," she insists. "Find out why he don't come."

"Okay, I'll call him." He's got another client on hold.

"You gotta *do* something." A little gurgle comes up from her throat. Helplessness. Panic. "Steve?"

"What?"

"He needs therapy. A deprogrammer."

He can't get into it now. "We'll see."

He phones Thorsen. Gets through on the third try.

"We got a problem, Eric. Shai visited Hana twice. But he hasn't been back." He lets it sound like he's puzzled, it's not an accusation.

"Hmmm," is all Thorsen will say.

"Look. We agreed to a psychiatric evaluation and visits. What's happening?"

"Hmmm."

*"Where is he?"* This requires an answer.

Thorsen sighs, a long expulsion of air. "I don't know. He's out of control, Steve. He was supposed to stay with the rabbi that Sween appointed, but . . ." he trails off.

"But?" Sounds like Shai is sandbagging everything. His lawyers included.

Thorsen hesitates. "I don't know. Give me a little time, Steve, I'll get back to you." A pause. "Can we postpone til the thirtieth?"

Steve flicks the pages of his calendar. "I suppose so." He hangs up growling.

Dammit.

A kid defying a court order. Street smart and savvy. An experienced traveler with the wherewithal to slip in and out of airports, use false passports and get all the help he needs. What we got is a defiant adolescent with wings.

Wednesday, August 30, is another blistering hot day. A drought has overtaken the northeast and the earth is parched. The flowers in the plaza have flopped over. Reservoirs are dangerously low. Towns have restricted water: no car washing, no watering lawns. The air conditioning of the courthouse is a welcome relief to Steve and Hana.

This morning Mitchel Ostrer is the lone attorney present. He sits in the last row of the Bergen County courtroom. Thorsen is not here. Ben Ostrer is not here. Even Lieb Waldman has not bothered to come.

Judge Sween adjusts his metal rimmed eyeglasses and leafs through his papers. It's close to noon, he's tired, he's heard a flood of family problems. Now the Shai Reuven case. He wets a finger to turn a page. He's a lefty, and with a ballpoint pen, he scribbles notes before looking up.

He allows Steve to speak first.

"Your Honor." Steve steps forward. "Regarding your order providing for Shai Reuven to visit Hana Fhima, the mother hasn't seen her son for weeks. He visited her only twice."

Judge Sween's jaw tightens. "Where is he?"

"Your Honor," Steve continues, "we don't know. You ordered the boy to stay with a rabbi in Monsey. The best we know is he was living in an apartment with some other boys, but his telephone is disconnected."

The judge frowns and taps his pen. "Go on."

"When he failed to visit his mother after two visits, I contacted his attorney. Mr. Thorsen told me he doesn't know where he is."

"I see." He lays down his pen.

Steve clears his throat and steps closer. "Your Honor? What remedies do we have?"

"Remedies?" It is a question that defies an easy answer. He turns to the mother. "Your boy did not visit since when?" he asks. "What's the date?"

"August eighth, Your Honor. He came two times to me."

He looks at the mother. He sees a woman at the end of her rope, her hand covering her mouth to hold back the pain, a gesture he's seen many times in his courtroom when they're beaten and defeated. Remedies? They want remedies?

*"Some cases don't have solutions,"* he declares with resignation. Don't they understand?

But Shai Reuven has violated his order.

Without hesitation, he issues a warrant to pick him up: he's a runaway. He signs the order. "Next case."

Hana turns to Steve. "That's all?"

He nods and stands up to leave.

"Steve?" It's Mitchel Ostrer calling, motioning for him to meet him outside.

Steve nods and snaps his portfolio closed. "C'mon, Hana."

Out in the rotunda, an embarrassed Mitchel Ostrer approaches them. "I'm out of it," he says, head down, fumbling to shove papers into his portfolio. Then he looks Steve in the eye. "The minute I get back to the office, I'm off this case. *Out of it.*" He strides off.

Hana is bewildered. "Out of it? This is how it ends?"

No lawyers.

No Shai.

Steve shakes his head. Sween said it: *Some cases don't have solutions.*

Steve reads it to Hana over the phone.

The *Patriot News* carries the story with the title *Rabbi given jail time in $900,000 theft.* It says that Lieb Waldman, forty-six, a New York rabbi, was sentenced to one year plus a day in federal prison for stealing close to a million dollars in a real estate deal. On the ninth floor of the Federal Building in Harrisburg, Pennsylvania, Waldman's attorney, Joshua D. Lock, convinces Judge Caldwell to allow Waldman to surrender on October 17, after the Jewish holidays, to begin serving his federal sentence of twenty-seven to thirty-six months.

"He'll never show up, he'll never go to jail," Hana says, "I bet he left the country."

With Shai gone, there's no consoling her.

"Listen, Steve. You got one thing left."

"What's that?"

"I want from Jacky the divorce."

"You have the *gett* Hana," he reminds her.

"That's the religious divorce. I want now it should be legal." She takes a breath. "I want the papers to say it."

"Sure. I'll take care of it," he promises.

It won't be difficult to get custody from the thug who beat her up and sent her to a battered women's shelter. Thug: he read somewhere it's a word that comes from the Hindu *thugee.* A professional roadside assassin who kills by strangulation.

Hana Fhima will not be strangled.

She is determined. Resilient. Look how she stood up to the hasids. And screamed kidnappers to Bill Plackenmeyer. Cried *conspiracy* about Mordecai Weiss and Tobias Freund. Went toe to toe against Hynes. Organized that rally in the park in Brooklyn. Fended the cross-examinations of Joyce David and Paul Rooney. Gave hours of testimony to Vinegrad and Vecchione. Fought it out in the courtrooms of Stanger and Slobad and Sween. Defied Zaks and smacked Waldman with her folded newspaper. Held tight against a string of their lawyers. Eric Thorsen. Nat Lewin. Eleanor Alter.

A long list. A long road.

She never gave up.

# 48. WOODBOURNE CORRECTIONAL FACILITY

"**G**uess who's handling Rabbi Helbrans's appeal?" Steve plops down in the chair facing Larry's desk. "Gerald L. Shargel. Name strike a bell?" he asks with amusement.

"Shargel? Sure. He defended John Gotti, the Mafia kingpin." Larry does his Groucho Marx eyebrow jiggle.

"Wanna hear a coincidence? I knew Shargel's sister in school. He's one helluva attorney." Nothing about an appeal on the wire. No interviews of Helbrans in the slammer. Though a woman journalist, who called him for an update, told him she almost talked her way past the lobby guards.

"I told them, 'This is my *second* Sunday visit to Woodbourne Correctional Facility. C'mon guys, you gotta let me see him, I traveled two hours.' Three officers are on duty: Skordinski, Caruso, and Rosen, eating a late lunch outta styrofoam take-outs. Skordinski offers the opinion that Helbrans took the weight for someone else. Caruso jokes about his name, says he sings like a frog. And Rosen confides that he's Jewish and the rabbi's list of approved names is mostly rabbis, but Helbrans's mother came from Israel to visit him.

"They told me that one day forty or fifty hasids piled up in the parking lot saying: 'I just want to shake his hand. He's such a good man, it's an honor.' "

Steve listened: information is power. "What happened?"

"I kept asking questions. 'Does he get a lot of visitors?' They said maybe four at a time come, plus his spiritual advisor. They told me he's not double bunked, he's got his own cell, and his kosher meals are checked with each delivery."

"Glad to hear it," Steve joked.

"I begged them: 'C'mon guys, give me five minutes. I wrote the rabbi two letters. Don't send me back empty-handed.' "

"You get in?" He wanted the bottom line.

"No. They said the inmate's gotta approve his list of visitors, I'm not on the list."

Her second call, a week later, was even more interesting.

"Steve? The hasids from Monsey are leaving messages all over my machine. One woman woke my husband up close to midnight, a Mrs. Teller, asking if I'm Jewish and I shouldn't bother writing again to the rabbi. Then a Mr. Goldman calls me: *Leave the rabbi alone.* And he won't give me his number." She took a breath. "The effort they're making to keep me away. . . ."

"Hmmm."

"See, I really *do* want to hear the rabbi's side, it's what a responsible journalist does." A pause. "It gets better."

"Better?"

"Two more phone calls. Not from Monsey. From New York. Helbrans's appeal lawyers are calling me. First Gerald Shargel. Then a Stanley Neustadter."

"What'd they say?" His ears perked up.

"Shargel was charming. Told me to watch the the U.S. Open. But the message was back off. Stay away from my client."

"And the other lawyer? Neu . . . ?"

"Neustadter. He talked longer than Shargel. He said there's no way under God's sun he's going to change his recommendation to the rabbi. 'I told him not to speak to anyone until all his appeals lose or we reverse the conviction or all appeals are made and the final determination is made.' Neustadter told me straight out: 'You can't talk to him.' " She laughs. "I struck out."

Rosh Hashana and Yom Kipper arrive. The sound of the shofar ushers in the New Year. New beginnings.

Hana cannot sleep. She gets out of bed. Barefoot, she pads into the living room. Stands at the window contemplating the darkness and the starry night.

In the silence, she recites a Rosh Hashana prayer in Hebrew:

*Happy are we that God has granted us another year of life. And may it be His will to inscribe us for happiness and peace in the Book of Life for the coming year.*

At the beginning of the new year, God writes down who will live and who will die. Her mother told her that.

"Take care of Shai," she whispers. Then she bows her head and recites the shema in Hebrew.

*Hear O Israel. The Lord Our God, the Lord is One.*

She raises her head and fixes her gaze on a bright star.

"Please God. Please. Give him back to me."

In the morning, she calls her parents in Israel to wish them *La Shana Tovah*. She tells them the children are back in school. New shoes. New backpacks. She laughs, she jokes, she wants to appear upbeat to her mother and father.

But at night, alone in bed, she makes the same prayer she recites every night, her mouth pressed against the pillow.

*Dear God. Please God. Help me find Shai. It's almost four years. Please, God. Give me back my son.*

In late September, the journalist tells Steve she visited the border guards at the Niagara Falls entrance to Ontario, Canada. They showed her pictures on the bulletin board of lost and stolen children. She learned about *Project Return* from Bernice Devooght, the international coordinator.

"It's part of a partnership with the Royal Canadian Mounted Police to help find missing children. They keep a registry and they do computer age progression to update what a missing child would look like today. But not a clue about Shai Reuven."

The assassination of Israel's Prime Minister Yitzhak Rabin stuns the world on November fourth.

"What? What?" For Hana it is a tragedy that tears opens her own wound as she watches scenes of shocked and sobbing Israelis on television. "It was a Jew? A Jew killed him? A yeshiva boy?" She claps a hand over her mouth.

Everywhere you go, Jews are shaking their heads. Stunned. Silent. Confounded by a world gone mad. Reviled by the shame of it. A religious Jew assassinated Rabin.

Only a week ago, David was bar mitzvahed in a joyous celebration. Larry and Elaine watched as their son chanted from the bima the Hebrew words that unite Jews everywhere. Such pride to be a Jew.

Now this. Larry is plunged into sadness.

"It's happening all over, Steve. Extremism. Fundamentalism. Crazies. Look at the ultraorthodox."

"So you murder the prime minister?"

"Look at the Hare Krishnas. Look what happened to Shai."

*It always come down to Shai.* Hana's loss, unresolved over four years, sits on their chests like a boulder. But today, the assassination has their blood boiling.

Larry can't stop talking about it. "And what about the Branch Davidians? You read about that teenage girl inside their compound? Kiri Jewell." He takes a breath. "Hey, look at the Moonies. Sun Myung Moon married four hundred couples via satellite from South Korea. The poor bastards are brainwashed."

Steve nods.

"And what about that Japanese sect with the poison gas in the subway attack? Hey, all cults are the same."

"It scares the shit out of me. Holiness now includes murder. Murder is holy."

The intercom buzzes.

"Hana Fhima on line one."

Larry holds the phone out to Steve. "It's Hana. You take it."

"No, you take it."

They can hear her sobbing.

"Hello, Hana," Steve says as kindly as possible.

# PART VIII

## 1996

# 49. MICHAEL'S STORY

By January 1996, the heavy snowfalls that began in early December are threatening to break all records. Hana stays tuned to the radio for school cancellations and early dismissals. Watches road closings and traffic snarls on television. One blizzard on top of another is keeping everyone housebound.

*Does he have a warm winter coat?*

With the days darkening by four-thirty and the nights long, she has time to brood about Shai. If I did this instead of that . . . if I didn't say this . . . would I have him back with me now? For four years she has oscillated between hope and despair, believing firmly in God's justice. Believing deeply that He sees everything and He will make it come out right. But sometimes, alone at the kitchen table, the kids asleep and the apartment silent, she asks herself questions.

Where was God when Shai was kidnapped? Why was He silent? Why did this happen to me? Is it a punishment I did something terrible? What? What did I do? It wasn't God did it to Shai, it was *me.* My life did it. Something I did, it made him hungry for Helbrans.

Will I ever see him again?

She remembers a psalm, it flies into her mind. *Out of the depths I have cried to thee, O Lord . . . I wait for the Lord, my soul waits, and in His word I hope.*

I am waiting, hoping. When will it end?

Should I return to Israel?

The kids are happy here. Doing good in school. Why start with moving? Maybe I'll take classes to improve my English. America is still the land of opportunity. Life will get better. God will give me a sign. She folds her arms across her chest, vexed by her indecision.

Why is my life so full of battles? Maybe I sabotage myself, maybe I miss something that other people have. Two marriages I made. Two divorces. Not a good record. But I *am* a good mother. For my children, I would do anything. Because if you can't be a good mother, what else matters? Mistakes, yes. Perfect, no. Maybe I was stupid what I did with my life. Bad luck with men. Steve will soon finish me up the divorce, it will be over.

What Hana can't live with—her throat tightens as the words form in her mind—is: *Shai don't want me for his mother.* A man don't want you, you can live with it. Not your child.

She stands up and goes to the living room window. Gusts of snow and howling winds rattle the glass and she steps back.

*Does he have a warm winter coat?*

Sometimes it is too much.

At night, Shai visits her. He stares at her. She feels unspoken grief passing between them. A concrete wall presses on her chest, making her cough. She can't breathe. She bolts up. Awake. Panting. All day, she carries his stare inside her, wild with helplessness.

Yesterday, in the mirror, four gray hairs. Leave them there, one for each year I am without my son.

In the end, what good it all did? The attorneys, they made brilliant summations in court. Hana has her own summation. Two sentences. *They stole his soul. Shai is theirs.*

On Thursday, January 18, Steve concludes Hana's divorce from Jacky. "Okay. It's official. You have the papers now." They are walking out of the building, heading toward the parking lot.

"Thank you, thank you. Thanks for everything you did. Larry, too," she says, gushing a rare expression of gratitude, a bounce to her step.

All this for divorce papers? "Yup, we're finished. This dots the last i. We're done."

There is satisfaction to a proper closure, he thinks. We fought the good fight. Of all our pro bonos, this was the most costly, the longest, and the most emotionally draining and we accomplished what we set out to do. Saw that the criminal justice system punished the kidnappers. "Yup, it's over."

They arrive at his car. At that moment, as his key slides in the door, the sun emerges from under a dark cloud, dousing them in a halo of brightness.

He looks up at the enamel blue sky, blinking. Against the glare of the snow, Hana seems to be glowing. Something in her eyes, in her posture. *She wants to tell him something.* You don't work for a client for years and not register their emotional state.

He lets her get into the passenger seat. Turns on the ignition, then the heater. Should he buy her lunch to celebrate?

"Steve." She lays a hand on his coatsleeve.

He lets the motor run, doesn't back out. "What?"

"Shai is with Michael," she says softly without blinking.

*"What?"* His hands tighten around the steering wheel.

"Shai is back in Israel. In Arad with Michael."

"How did he get there? What happened?"

"I'll tell you in the car. Go." She wants him to drive. It will be easier to explain with his eyes on the road.

He buckles his seat belt and pulls out. "Okay. How did he get to Israel? Where was he? How did you find out?"

"My mother called me. Shai called her after he got to Michael. I already talked to him on the phone."

He is flabbergasted. "You talked to Shai?"

"It was already in the paper, *Maariv.* My sister's sending it to me." She's spilling it out. "How it went. . . . He was in France, in the yeshiva, the same from before. But now he don't like it. No money. No friends. No place to go. So he went to Paris to the Israeli Embassy."

"The Israeli Embassy? He went there?" He is astonished.

"They said, you're Israeli, go back to Israel."

"Whew." A low whistle.

"He's not religious no more." She says this with pride.

"No?" He shakes his head. "Really?"

"He goes to a public high school. A regular school." Her eyes fall into her lap. "He lives with Michael."

"With Michael." This must hurt. After four years of anguish, a custody battle, a kidnapping trial, stalking yeshivas. . . . And the kid returns, not to her, but *to Michael*. He's not religious anymore. Like it never happened. Like Gilda Radner: *Never mind.*

He turns to her, measuring the pain.

She gives him a sad little smile. "I'm happy for him."

"Sure."

"I mean, I'm not happy he went to Michael. But I'm happy he's away from them. He's secular. A regular boy. Normal. He talks to my mother and father. He got a family. So I have to be thankful. The religious part is over."

"It is? It's really over? Just like that?" He snaps his finger. He's heard about kids who leave cults and have a reawakening after trying on different coats. While the hasidic community was bombarding him with gifts and attention, he was theirs. But in France, he was alone, on his own. Maybe he saw their scheming, their deviousness. Maybe he couldn't take it anymore. When they kidnapped him, he was thirteen and impressionable. At seventeen, a different person.

"Is he happy, Hana?" They are waiting at a red light and he studies her face.

She considers the question. "He sounds good on the phone. He has already friends. He's studying hard, he was out of school four years so they put him in tenth grade." She sighs. "He's smart, he'll catch up."

"So you talked to him."

"I talked to him. Yes."

Larry goes bananas.

"You're telling me the kid went to the Israeli Embassy in Paris and they put him on the next plane back to Israel?"

"Right."

They are in Steve's office. Larry is wide-eyed with disbelief. "Shai called Hana's parents. And they called her."

"Yup."

Larry smacks his thighs and stands up. "Phew! This," he declares, "is vindication. Proves everything we said. He's back in public school, he's not religious. Don't you see? He was *never* a hasid. It was *never* about religion. All that crap was a smoke screen. It was always about kidnapping. Which is what we said all along." Excitement has pushed his voice up. Vindication tastes sweet.

"Absolutely." He knows Larry is about to conduct an autopsy, a postmortem examination.

"This was about a boy who they wanted to be this great religious person: a zaddik. It was about saving the ass of a rabbi who did a stupid thing and kidnapped a kid. The *wrong* kid. Helbrans is probably guilty of several kidnappings. Only this time he picked the wrong kid."

"Exactly. He didn't know what he was getting into." Steve is enjoying his running commentary.

"He never realized he was up against someone like Hana. And you and me, Steve. We had the balls. And we weren't going to let it rest. Hana wasn't scared off. Ultimately, the D.A. was forced to do what he had to do." Larry is positively gleeful.

"Right. Absolutely right. Total vindication." Steve is gobbling it up. A happy ending after four years of hell.

"Helbrans's biggest mistake was kidnapping *this* kid. And then they all tried to cover it up. To argue he was never kidnapped. And the joke is saying he's a hasid and he really wanted to be a hasid. Bullshit!"

"Right. Right. This is the ultimate vindication."

"True." Larry can't stop chewing on it. He's pacing up and down, wagging his finger to make each point. "Eventually this had to happen. We knew from the beginning this kid never wanted to be religious. C'mon. He lands in Israel, he's there a couple of weeks and he's *secular*? Going to *public* school?"

"I'm happy for her," Steve adds, "really happy. She'll come to grips with it."

"She feel bad he's with Michael?"

"She can live with it, Lar."

"Boy what he put her through. Whew!"

"It was in the papers, Lar. Michael gave the interview to a reporter. Made himself the big hero."

"Of course. Now it's Michael's story." Larry lets out one hefty guffaw.

From the *Patriot News* comes another vindication.

Steve reports it to Larry. "Listen to this. We got a cherry on our whipped cream."

"What?"

"Waldman's date to surrender was extended so he could observe the Jewish holidays. But, he doesn't show up. A fax comes from London. He's being treated for a heart condition, he can't travel."

Larry roars. "Sure. Sure."

"There's more. He was arrested December 31 trying to get out of Canada and back into the United States."

"No shit."

"You'll love this, Lar. He was caught carrying a phony passport in the name of Stephen J. Fosterman. Picked up by the Canadian Royal Mounted Police."

"Stephen J.Fosterman?" Larry is howling.

"He pleaded guilty and did thirty days in Toronto."

"Wait till Hana hears this."

"He's out on $600,000 bail awaiting extradition. He comes back, he goes to prison. Like his buddy Helbrans."

Larry punches his palm. "Hey," he reminds Steve. "Remember the day Hana chased Waldman down the hall and whacked him with the newspaper?"

"I gotta call her. She's gonna love this."

# 50. SHAI RETURNS TO ISRAEL

The *Maariv* article her sister mails from Israel arrives. With trembling hands, Hana unfolds the pages. She spreads it out on the kitchen table. *Oh my God. Look.*

Across page twelve and thirteen, is a blowup of Shai and Michael lighting each other's cigarettes like army buddies. Shai's sidelocks are still wound around his ears because it is the day he arrived in Israel in late December, and she can see immediately the story is Michael's: how Shai returned to *him*. Father and son are reunited.

This interview is weeks old. And she spoke to Shai only a few days ago. So why do the words still sting? The photos, too. It feels like a cruel joke.

She hunches over to study the picture. A boy, not yet seventeen, with his father lighting his cigarette. She rubs her forehead. A headache is nailing a path across her temples.

Another photograph. This one shows *the family:* Michael, Lilit, and their two boys. Shai's arm is draped around Michael's shoulder. In front, a cake to celebrate the father-son reunion.

*That's not your family, Shai. We are your family.*

She reads it. The Hebrew words slap her in the face. Three pages screaming Michael and Shai.

*About the mother? Nothing. Me? I am erased.*

Bile churns up from her stomach, coating her tongue.

"Look at that," Michael says. "He left a little boy and look how tall he is now."

"I missed you, Father, I'm happy to be back home."

"This is the happiest day of my life," Michael responds. Then Michael recounts how he ran all over the world to trace Shai.

*All over the world?* Her fists clench.

He says he paid a lot of money to lawyers. Made friends with the FBI and with street gangs. Followed hasidic students and rabbis. He tells how he was wired in Lev Tahor. How Shai disappeared again and he returned to Israel defeated. "He felt like a loser returning without his son, but he had to make a living."

It's all there. Photos. Quotes.

He tells how Shai fell under the spell of Helbrans and how the hasidic community transferred him from one yeshiva to another. How he flew to France in September when Shai was arrested at Orly Airport traveling with a false passport. He explains how it's not a problem to get a "kosher" passport. It's common, it's easy to get away with it because to the police all hasidim look alike.

*I went to Paris, too. I screamed at them: Where is my son? I want my son. I am the mother.*

But just before Michael arrived, Shai befriended a French police officer and asked to go out for a cigarette.

"Your son went out for a smoke, he'll come back," the Frenchman said. "He left here his money and clothes."

Michael, with a tired smile, knew his son had disappeared again.

Now Shai picks up the story. He claims he would have stayed if he knew Michael was arriving.

"I was wanted all over the world. I didn't know how to get out of it . . . so I ran away."

*Yes, my son, you ran and ran. Four years you ran.*

He knew he was needed in the United States to appear in Helbrans's kidnapping trial. But he was afraid to get into the States through New York. So he rented a car.

Now Shai steals the spotlight from Michael.

"I drove to Belgium through Luxemburg. From there I drove to Holland and from Holland I took a ferry to London. Then I took a plane to Canada. Then to the United States."

Hana's hand flies to her chest. *Oh my God. A child sixteen. He was running from country to country.*

He had a driver's license provided by the haredim in New

York. He has been in planes, small hotels, airports, and yeshivas. Has lived under assumed identities.

*This is to brag from?* Hana pinches her nose to keep her emotions from exploding.

Now Michael picks it up.

"I knew that Shai must testify for Helbrans. So I came to the United States. We met on opposing sides. He believed Helbrans was innocent."

"Even today I am telling you he (Rabbi Helbrans) did not abduct me," Shai adds.

"You were too young then. Let us not argue about it," Michael replies.

Michael tells how in March 1995 he came to the United States to bring Shai back. But he was up against expensive and experienced lawyers paid for by the hasidim. How he appeared in courtrooms from New York to New Jersey. But he saw he couldn't handle his son. "At age sixteen, I understood I could not make him come to me. I decided to return to Israel and stop the chase."

Meanwhile, Shai was transferred back to France. He was hidden in Yeshiva Ma'or Yoseph in a little village Vziir.

But thoughts came to him. Longings.

"I missed my father," Shai tells the reporter. "Life in the yeshiva was boring. There were very few guys there and most of them left to go to Israel. Nobody watched us. I would get up at noon. Do nothing. I got fed up. I wanted to go home."

*Home? Home is with Michael?*

Though he sees himself as a religious person, he used to go occasionally to discos. "I would take my sidecurls and pull them back into a pony tail like Steven Seagal. I'd go to have fun." He went to action films, smoked, rented a car, and traveled all over Europe. Once or twice he went to a casino.

*You did this? All this, alone? A child?*

"I was in Luxemburg, Belgium, Holland, and back to France all in one night."

Then, two and a half weeks ago, the article continues, Shai's longing for his father increased.

*For your father? Your father? Nothing about your mother?* Hana counts back. Middle of December? I was looking out the window half the night. *Does he have a warm winter coat?*

Michael's phone rings in Arad. "Aba, come and take me away from here." But while making the arrangements to travel, Michael got word that Shai disappeared, this time to Geneva, Switzerland. A few days later, another phone call: "Aba, come and take me."

"This time you're coming on your own," Michael replies.

Shai hitchhikes to Paris and talks to Yaakov Ben Ami at the embassy. The Israeli consulate in Paris gets into the picture. Dedi Zucker, member of the Israeli Parliament who had been in touch with Michael, helps to provide money for the trip back and aids in securing a visa. Twenty-four hours after Shai walked into the Israeli Embassy in Paris, he was on an Air France plane back to Israel.

Michael came to the airport with his eleven-year-old son to welcome Shai. And he brought a few friends for security reasons. "I don't want to take chances."

"I'm sorry about these past years," Shai says to his father as they embrace.

In the car on the way, Michael tells Shai, "I want you to know you have a warm family. A loving father. And Lilit will be to you a mother."

*What?* The icepick in her chest doubles her over. *Lilit will be your mother? NO! NO!* What Michael puts in the paper, true or not true, it don't matter. But this rips her heart out. *I am your mother.* A silent scream. *Me. Me.* She pounds her chest. You got him now, Michael. But don't take away *I am his mother.*

She rubs her eyes, she cannot read anymore. Not another word. She stands up. But folding the paper, she is drawn to one more paragraph. How Shai is not sure if he wants to cut off his sidecurls and he says he wants to stay religious.

"We'll do what you want," replies Michael. "No pressure. You want to cut the sidecurls, we'll give you the scissors. You don't, no problem."

It pulls her back to reality.

This article—who cares what it says? Who cares Michael put his mark on it? It's old news. Shai is already in public school, his sidecurls gone, a normal boy. So Michael had his day. Let him.

She sits down again, calmer. Reads it to the end. How in the apartment, a balloon and a welcome home sign greeted him. How the cake was cut and the family posed for the photographer: father and son crossing arms to light each other's cigarette.

She turns back to that page. Looks closer. Studies her son's face. So handsome.

So Michael had the last word. "I closed a crazy circle. A small child left me and a young man came back. Now we are like friends. He was born when I was a young soldier in basic training."

*He was born when I was seventeen,* her heart screams back.

So he went to you Michael. It's okay, all I care is he's safe. They don't have him no more.

She reads a little more. How Shai shows off pictures of himself in every city, reconstructing his amazing adventures in the hasidic underground.

"Look. Here I am in England. Canada. Holland. Luxemburg. America. France."

Enough. Hana lays her head down on her arms and weeps. Soft blubbering sobs roll off the kitchen table.

*Michael got him, not me.*

*But he's safe.*


"I talk to him on the weekends," she tells Steve. "He sounds good, normal, so I think the spell Helbrans put on him is fading. He likes public school, he's studying hard."

"Great." Do mother and son speak about the unspoken? What Helbrans really did? Zaks? Waldman? Who hid him?

"When the phone rings early in the morning, I know it's Shai. He talks more and more what happened."

The *Maariv* article lies folded in her bottom drawer. Who cares? She and Michael talk on the phone when she calls. Better to make peace.

"What matters is Shai," she tells Steve. "He's out of their influence. He's safe. He's . . . how you say?" Her English is not good enough.

"You mean? . . . he's reclaiming his soul?" he offers.

"Yes."

What she longs for is to *see* him.

She aches to hold him.

She has lived too long and too deeply in the vortex of her sorrow. It is something only a mother understands. That love for your child—the flesh of your flesh—pushes all other loves aside.

"How can I see him?" she sighs to Steve.

The answer comes in a small package.

Shai has appeared on Israeli television.

Her sister sends her the tape.

# 51. SHAI IS ON TELEVISION

The three children are on the floor huddled around the television set, their eyes wide with excitement. Shai will be on TV? Like a movie star? Hana slips the video into the VCR and it begins. A woman interviewer is speaking in Hebrew, but it's hard to follow.

"What'd she say . . . ?" Shiran asks, bewildered by the rapid clip of Hebrew words. "Where's Shai?"

"Shh, shh," Hana warns, holding a finger to her lips.

The video is on the European system, not for American VCRs. But she picks up that the show is about the Satmars. How they kidnap kids and force them to be ultrareligious. The interviewer, bright and attractive, is saying they stabbed someone nine times in the stomach? It's not clear. But the camera is sweeping away to Shai.

"It's Shai, look, look," the kids scream.

"Look at him," she sings as Eliran and Osheri scramble closer. He looks wonderful, wonderful. She is concentrating on his words. Listening. Watching his facial expressions and his gestures, but the tape is too scrambled to understand.

Still they watch to the end, drinking in Shai.

She phones Rabbi Weinberg. "I got the tape. But I have to have it fixed for American VCR."

"Don't worry, near my house is a place," he replies.

"How much it will cost?"

"Maybe twenty-five dollars."

Next she phones Alan Vinegrad and describes what the tape appears to be. "It's about Satmars and Shai is telling the interviewer his experience."

He is extremely interested. "I'd like to see it. Would you mail it to me?"

349

"First I have to have it fixed for American VCR. And it's in Hebrew."

"Okay, send it to me, Hana. I'll have it translated into English and I'll send you a copy," he promises. "Would you like a copy?"

"Yes, yes." This way I'll have every word Shai says. It will be written down. No mistakes. Every word in English.

She talked to him February tenth. It was his birthday February eighth. Seventeen. And he told her on the phone, "Mom I made a lot of mistakes. I said every word they told me to say. *They* wrote the letters and they made me copy for the handwriting."

"I know. I know." He's starting to talk about it, it's coming out of him more and more. He admits now what really happened.

"I said to them *I want to go back with my mother*. And they showed me that book."

"The same book Helbrans made me read. I remember. How you'll burn in hell and be with the devils in the forest." To scare you, my son, to keep you in line.

She slides the transferred tape into the VCR. This time, with the kids in school, she can concentrate.

What a difference to understand the words. His smart eyes, his sweet face only two feet away. If only she could reach out and hold him. How good he looks, so neat. No more with the sidecurls and black fedora. He's wearing for television a normal shirt, blue and white stripped. And he speaks so nice. So grown up. Entranced, she watches it to the end. Rewinds it and watches it all over again.

The nightmare is over. The sleepless nights. The courtroom battles. Shai is free. He's not theirs anymore. He's starting to come back to himself, to realize what happened to him. The *Maariv* article, it was a joke. The videotape shows the real Shai, how he is now. She's talking to him regularly on the phone and he's warm to her. Like on the tape, smiling.

*"When are you coming back, Mom?"* he asked her.

Coming back? "I don't know."

Michael is cordial when she phones. And for Shai's sake, she wants good relations. She has to talk to Michael to get to Shai. What happened is over, what good to look back?

What matters is you know where Shai is. He is safe in Israel with Michael. And you can talk to him. He calls you and the children speak to him. So let Michael show off he's a good father.

Now I look back, I can admit I made a lot of mistakes. I didn't know how to be a mother and a parent. And Shai? He admits now he made mistakes. But he's okay now, he has friends. He's only one year behind in tenth grade.

"I'll make it up," he told her.

"I'm so proud of you. You're a smart guy," she replied.

They talk about school and friends.

"Every day I wake up and think *when is my mom coming back?*"

She swallows the lump in her throat. "We'll see . . ."

"Mom, I'm sorry. I was not myself. Now I know: *Helbrans kidnapped me.*"

At last. His allegiance to Helbrans is broken. "When did you . . . ?"

"When I was in France. I knew when I was there, I knew they didn't care about me. They were just using me to testify for Helbrans."

She reports Shai's new life to Steve and Larry.

"I want you should know how bad turned into good. I saw him on television. I got from my sister the video," she tells Steve.

"Hold on a second, I'll put this on speaker phone, I want Larry to hear it." He buzzes Larry to come into his office.

"What did Shai say?" Larry asks about the video. "Did he name names?"

"It comes out a little bit at a time," she tells them.

"He's not religious anymore, right?" Steve asks.

"No. He's doing normal things, I'm so happy."

"Will you go back to Israel?" Steve's question is gentle.

A long thoughtful pause. "I don't know. I love him very much. But if I go back, would it be his best interest?" She is thinking out loud. "I can't ask him to move in with me. He got two more years in high school. It's very important to study hard and finish. If I go back, I'll see him weekends, not he should move in with me. He lost a lot. He has to have his teenage years to enjoy and be normal."

"We're really happy for you, Hana," Steve tells her.

"I was crying four years, turning every night six, eight times, one side to the other side. But I never lost faith in God. I prayed to God. *Make him safe. He should have a warm winter coat.*" She pauses. "So now he's safe with Michael. You know," she brags, "after school he goes every day to the library. He's safer in Israel," she sums up. "In the United States . . . who knows?"

Steve hangs up and leans back, his hands laced behind his head. "I have a lot of respect for her. Her attitude is healthy."

Larry scratches his beard. "The process failed. The system failed. It took Hana Fhima to let them know you can't get away with it," he is focusing on the case. "That's the warning the hasids got: *You can't get away with it.*"

"Yup," Steve nods. "There's another side. What they did was a desecration. They justified kidnapping. It's dangerously close to what's-his-name? Rabin's assassin. He justified murder."

Larry jabs a finger in the air. "They broke the law."

The *Bergen Record* runs an article entitled "Look Who's Turning Fifty."

Dwarfing small photos of Donald Trump, Susan Sarandon, Sylvester Stallone, Candice Bergen, and President Clinton is a big blowup of lawyer Steve Rubenstein tooting his saxophone.

Susan throws him a big bash. Gifts are piled high. Funny gifts. Gag gifts. Expensive gifts. Practical gifts. Among them, a happy birthday card from Hana.

After the last guests clear out, he rereads it, hearing her words dipped in her Israeli accent: *I want the truth to come out. It's important people should see what the hasids did to Shai.*

On the bottom of the card, she has written: *Thank you for everything you did. Hana.* He grins at the funny way she makes the capital H of her familiar signature.

He slides the birthday card into his top drawer.

A card to save.

# 52. THE TRANSCRIPTION

**H**ana holds the sheaf of pages Alan Vinegrad sent her.

Across the top on page one it says *Translation/transcription of interview with Shai (Fhima) Reuven which appeared on Channel 2 of Israeli television*. She has heard it in Hebrew. Now she has it in English: Shai's words.

Quickly, eagerly, she reads the interviewer's introduction to the audience. How Shai Reuven, after four years with the ultra-orthodox, is speaking for the first time on television. How Hana sent him for bar mitzvah studies with Rabbi Helbrans.

*This was a mistake*, she comments. The rabbi secreted the boy deeply within the world of New York *yeshivot* and despite the work of the New York police and later the FBI, Shai was smuggled to Paris and from there to Holland and Luxembourg and then by ferry to London and by plane to Canada. From there, back to New York under fictitious identity. About six months ago he was transferred to a yeshiva in France. Two months ago he contacted his father in Arad.

"Father, take me home," said the seventeen-year-old youth who had left Israel when he was eleven, the interviewer explains. A month ago he landed in Ben Gurion Airport. Now he is here in the studio, for the first time facing the television cameras.

*Interviewer:* Hello Shai. I saw in the newspapers on the day you arrived you were still with a skullcap and sidecurls. Tell me about the day you removed the sidecurls.

*Shai:* I arrived home and I told my father they brainwashed me. So I want to finish with everything. So I took off the sidecurls and that's it.

*Interviewer:* Shai, let's backtrack four years. You arrive at

Rabbi Helbrans's yeshiva and you ask to remain there, right? at least for two weeks.

*Shai:* Yes.

*Interviewer:* What captivated you? What attracted you?

*Shai:* That's the power of the religion. That they have this power. I don't know, they, they told me a lot of things and brainwashed me. For example, if you return to your mother, you will, will go to hell, all kinds of things like that.

*Interviewer:* I'm holding here a letter. Did you compose these sentences?

*Shai*: No, no. They wrote me this and I only copied it for the handwriting.

*Interviewer:* Tell me about the daily routine at the yeshiva, how does it function?

*Shai:* One gets up at three in the morning. Goes to the ritual bath and begins to study until six and then one starts to pray.

*Interviewer:* At some stage did you tell them, "Enough, I want to go to my mother?"

*Shai*: Yes, I said it. But eh, I would say it and after a few minutes I would change my mind because I was afraid. They would instill me with fear. For example, if the FBI and the Mossad will catch you, I will be placed in an insane asylum in Israel and the country is Zionist and all kinds of brainwashing that . . .

*Interviewer:* Zionist and what?

*Shai:* Zionist and takes people away from religion. They will forcibly place you in a kibbutz, in an insane asylum, all kinds of things like that.

*Interviewer:* Did they also tell you that awaiting you, I don't know, hell, heaven, things like that?

*Shai:* If you return you will go to hell and you will burn. There is some book from which they would teach me a lot. It was Spirits Tell. All kinds of reincarnations of souls and that kind of hell. I was fearful of leaving.

*Interviewer:* You were really afraid?

*Shai:* Yes.

*Interviewer:* What is the character of this Rabbi Helbrans? Tell me about him. What kind of person is he?

*Shai:* I don't know. He is a person, he has a great ability to persuade. And he has a lot of delusions, that he talks with evil spirits, angels, all kinds of things like that.

*Interviewer:* This education that you are telling me about, you call it brainwashing, is it done only in pleasant ways?

*Shai:* He works using only pleasant ways. They never hit or things like that. Only there are punishments. There are punishments.

*Interviewer:* For example?

*Shai:* If a student comes to the Rabbi and tells him, "Listen, I did this and that," and it's considered an infraction, so he tells him, "You will receive three lashes or three hundred lashes." And then what do they do? They tie him with handcuffs to the table, they spray tear gas in his face, they take a belt and hit him on the back, all kinds of things.

*Interviewer:* Are these things you saw with your own eyes?

*Shai:* I saw it with my own eyes.

*Interviewer:* But you did not personally undergo it?

*Shai:* No, I did not.

*Interviewer:* Shai, you arrived in France for the first time with a passport which wasn't yours. Right?

*Shai:* Yes.

*Interviewer:* And then they caught you. How did you get back to the United States?

*Shai:* I was, they placed me in a closed institution. I ran away and I contacted a friend and told him: "Listen, I have to get out of here." So he rented a car and brought a passport and we went to Belgium, from Belgium to London, from London to Canada, from Canada to the United States.

*Interviewer:* All of this alone, as sixteen-year-olds. Under false identity?

*Shai:* Yes.

*Interviewer:* At all the airports through which you pass, at all the stops along the way, you use a different name?

*Shai:* With other passports, yes.

*Interviewer:* Who gave you the passports?

*Shai:* That's the hasidim. It's no problem arranging for a passport over there.

*Interviewer:* No problem arranging a passport with a different name and a different photo?

*Shai:* No, it's not a problem.

*Interviewer:* And at the end you arrive back at the yeshiva. Until what?

*Shai:* Until I noticed that they deceived me.

*Interviewer:* When you arrived for the second time to that same yeshiva, Or Yosef, in France?

*Shai:* Yes. It was the third time.

*Interviewer:* And what, you arrive at what conclusion?

*Shai:* Then I sat there. I saw it was not required to study. No one calls, no one shows interest, no one is sending money. I have to work to earn money. So I said that, I came to the conclusion that what help they gave me up to now was only in order to testify at the Rabbi's trial.

*Interviewer:* That's the trial in which he was charged with kidnapping you?

*Shai:* Yes.

*Interviewer:* Which, at the end he went to jail.

*Shai:* Yes, yes.

*Interviewer:* But before that you still in fact testified in his defense at the trial.

*Shai:* Yes.

*Interviewer:* And then you were returned to France and suddenly you come to the conclusion and when you are no longer needed . . .

*Shai:* Then eh, they don't care any more. I saw they don't care whether I am studying or not studying. Where I am. Within twenty-four hours, we took a trip through five countries and no one even knew of it.

*Interviewer:* And then you contact your father.

*Shai:* Yes, and I told him, I want to return. I've come to the conclusion I want to return.

*Interviewer:* But after this conversation you changed your mind again.

*Shai:* No, I didn't change my mind. Someone heard I talked with my father. So immediately the rabbis arrive. "What did you do, you spoke with your father. He will come here and he will take you." And once again they began with their talks and that night I was in Geneva, in Switzerland, having come from France. I called my father and he told me the easiest place to bring me to is Israel from France. So I convinced them. I told them, "No, I'll return and I'm still kosher and I will not go and so on," I returned and we did it quietly.

*Interviewer:* You are already a month in Israel.

*Shai:* Yes.

*Interviewer:* You smoke, don't you?

*Shai*: Yes.

*Interviewer:* You already lit up a cigarette on the Sabbath?

*Shai:* Yes.

*Interviewer:* You were not fearful that the sky will fall down?

*Shai:* No, I wasn't afraid.

*Interviewer:* Might you perhaps still be a religious man some day?

*Shai:* No. I don't think so.


Hana holds the pages against her chest. They warm her. This is the evidence. The truth what happened to Shai from thirteen to seventeen. Every word written down. What Steve and Larry call *the vindication.*

Where is the videotape? She cannot get enough of him.

She finds it on the bookcase and slides it into the VCR to watch again. Sits down on the sofa with the pages of transcript in hand. She will read the words in English and watch as he speaks them in Hebrew. Catch something maybe she missed. Be surrounded by Shai. His voice, his face, his gestures. His words in Hebrew coming from the television. His words in English printed on the pages. She turns the volume higher, her eyes darting from the television to the page. Devouring him.

Shai's true words. What in court he couldn't say, he was scared of them, he was under their spell. It proves how their witnesses lied in court in front of Judge Owens. How their expensive lawyers covered it up. How they hid Shai with false passports. How they were willing to commit crimes. How they were sure they could get away with it.

But now Shai says the truth on television. He's not scared of them anymore. He took back his soul.

She watches it to the end and slides the photocopies back into the manila envelope, noting the return address from Brooklyn is the U.S. Department of Justice, U.S. Attorney's Office/EDNY. "The United States Department of Justice," she murmurs with satisfaction. It's official.

She sits down on the sofa, the envelope a warm blanket on her lap. A soft smile shapes her lips. How handsome he looked on television. How nice he talked. How smart and grown up. Will the truth what happened to Shai save the next child they try to kidnap? Will it stop them? Will the big lawyer from New York, Gerald Shargel, win the appeal to free Helbrans? What will be when another hasidic rabbi kidnaps a boy and pushes him through airports with phony passports?

She stands up and gazes out the living-room window. Parked outside on the street is her used two-door Mazda, so far it's working. If Shai was here, she'd hand him the keys, so much joy and confidence she has in him now.

But what else can she do for him? Car keys are not enough.

So maybe he's better off with Michael. He has grandparents in Israel. A father and two half brothers. He visits her sister and brother. All around him now he has family and friends.

"What's best for him," she murmurs, longing to hug him.

# 53. PASSOVER

It is the middle of March. A mixture of blinding blizzards and bright sun-drenched days in the sixties have taken the kids from hooded winter jackets one day to short-sleeved cotton shirts the next day.

On this dark winter night, Hana sits alone on the sofa with one small lamp on. The children are asleep. The apartment is quiet. In a few weeks will be Passover. And in America comes soon the daylight saving time. The clocks jump ahead and the days grow long and full of light. The children will be outside playing. It will be spring. Life will be easier.

This Passover will be again no Shai. But you still have to do it right. Make the Kiddush and recite the blessing over the matzoh. *This is the bread of affliction which our ancestors ate in the land of Egypt.* A little in Hebrew, a little in English. Tell the story what we tell again and again, every generation.

She gets up to find the Haggadah Rabbi Weinberg gave her. She flicks on the kitchen light and sits down at the table to read a little bit to herself. *May God Who is merciful bless this home and all homes everywhere. May He bless this table. . . .*

She turns it over, face down, her thoughts turning to Shai.

Stroking the cover of the Haggadah, she feels a calmness fall over her. Hears the sound of her own breathing, ticking out beats of time.

The story describes four sons. The wise son. The wicked son. The simple son. And the young son who does not know enough to inquire. Shai, he was three of them. Now, thank God, he is the wise son. He understands what happened to him and he is free. So this Passover, the celebration of freedom is for us something special. *"Shai is free,"* she says softly.

She pushes her chair back and stands up to find the lace table-cloth. From the bottom drawer of her dresser, she takes it out and places it folded on the kitchen table, stroking the cloth with her fingers. From the back of a kitchen cabinet, she pulls out her candlesticks. A little polish and they'll shine. The children must have a nice seder.

I will say, *"This is the matzoh of hope."* I'll hide the afikomen and they'll run around the apartment looking for it. The one who finds it, I'll give a reward. The same every year.

And Shai? She is stroking the tablecloth. *One day we will be reunited, my son.*

With a shredded heart, Hana goes to the living-room window. She looks out at the inky starlit sky. She gazes at the luminous moon, absorbing its glow. Her eyes fall across the silky ribbons of moonlight.

She warms herself in the steady silver light.

*Look up, Shai. It's your moon, too.*

# EPILOGUE

On June 17, 1996, a four-judge panel of the Appellate Court denied Rabbi Helbrans's appeal. However, in the interests of justice, the court reduced his four-to-twelve-year sentence to two to six years. Rabbi Helbrans left Woodbourne Correctional Facility for a work-release program in Monsey, New York. In May 2000, he was deported back to Israel with his pregnant wife and six children.

On June 20, 1996, Bergen County Legal Services presented awards to Steve Rubenstein and Larry Meyerson. Each plaque says:

IN GRATEFUL APPRECIATION OF COUNTLESS HOURS
OF EXCEPTIONAL SERVICE GRACIOUSLY AND SELFLESSLY
GIVEN FOR THE BENEFIT OF THE PUBLIC, THE
ADVANCEMENT OF THE LEGAL PROFESSION AND THE
STRENGTHENING OF OUR COMMUNITY

On July 28, 1996, Shai Reuven flew to the United States to attend his brother Osheri's bar mitzvah on August 8 at Temple Beth Haverim. While staying with his mother in Maywood, he decided to live with her and attend high school in New Jersey.

Hana Fhima and her three children returned to Israel, as did Shai. He lived there for five years, sometimes with his mother and sometimes with his father. Now 22, he lives in Monsey, New York, and says he was not kidnapped or brainwashed. His parents don't agree. "So we let it alone," he says.

# SOURCES

I began working on this project in February 1995, when I met Hana Fhima and her lawyers Steve Rubenstein and Larry Meyerson at the Glenpointe Marriott Hotel in Teaneck, New Jersey. They asked me to consider writing a book to tell Hana's story. Larry sent me a huge package of newspaper and magazine clips that followed the events in the *New York Times*, the *Daily News*, the *New York Post*, *New York Newsday*, the *Bergen Record*, the *Star Ledger*, the *Rockland Journal News*, the *Jewish Standard*, *New York Magazine*, and others. In some articles, Hana posed for photos with her family. Later, Hana sent me Israel's *Maariv*, which covered Shai's return to Michael with photos taken in Michael's apartment. This was translated from the Hebrew by Bracha Weisbarth at the Waldor Library.

Throughout 1995 and 1996, I interviewed Hana, Larry, and Steve. I interviewed Hana in her home in Maywood and at court appearances which I attended with her. We talked on the phone frequently as each new piece of material unfolded. At one point, she was so dispirited, she phoned me to ask if I knew a deprogrammer for Shai, but I couldn't help her. In March 1996, she mailed me the translation/transcription of the interview with Shai which appeared on Channel 2 of Israeli television.

I interviewed Larry and Steve many times. In a major blizzard, I foolishly drove to their law offices in Oakland to run tapes. When I drove back on Route 287, it was dark, the roads were icy, and I could hardly see through the windshield. We talked on the phone back and forth throughout the writing of this book. I am deeply indebted to Hana, Larry, and Steve.

Other people I interviewed in person or on the phone were: Rabbi Milton Weinberg; Elaine Meyerson, Larry's wife; Captain Bill Plackenmeyer, NYPD; Rabbi Aryeh Zaks; Lieb Waldman, Zaks's father-in-law; attorneys Mitchel and Ben Ostrer; Judge Thaddeus Owens, Brooklyn Supreme Court; Ronnie Schwartz, his assistant; Alan Vinegrad, U.S. D.A., Eastern Division; Michael Vecchione, D.A.; Steve Lieberman, *Rockland Journal News*; Jack Sherzer, *Patriot News*, Harrisburg, Pa.; Pete Shellen, *Patriot News*, Harrisburg, Pa.; Sheriff James Kralik, Rockland County; Police Dispatcher Jean Iacono, Ramapo P.D.; Officers J. W. Read, Ken Jonston, and M. J. O'Halloran at the Rockland Sheriff's Headquarters; Nona Fried, Customs Officer; Nanette Cantwell; Livingston Police Captain Lee Schroeder; Judge Birger Sween, Family Court, Hackensack, N.J.; Mr. Goldman, Monsey, N.Y.; Mrs. Teller, Monsey, N.Y.; Gerald Shargel, attorney; Stanley Neustadter, Attorney; Skordinski, Rosen, and Caruso, three officers at Woodbourne Correctional Facility; Acting Superintendent Robert Hanslemair, Woodbourne Correctional Facility; David Willby, Canadian Customs, Niagara Falls; Michael Langone, Ph.D., Editor, *Cultic Studies Journal*; William Goldberg, M.S. W., A.C.S.W.; Marcia Rudin of Cult Awareness; and Bernice Devooght of Canadian Customs Project Return.

Some of the material came from my observations as I visited locations depicted in the story. Most valuable were: the courtroom of Judge Thaddeus Owens in Brooklyn Supreme Court; the courtroom of Judge Birger Sween in Hackensack Family Court; the NYPD station house office of Captain Bill Plackenmeyer in Brooklyn; Eric Smith Middle School in Ramsey, N.J.; the town of Monsey, N.Y.; Hana's apartment in Maywood; Alan Vinegrad's office at The U.S. Department of Justice in Brooklyn; and the border crossing at Niagara Falls. I visited Woodbourne Correctional Facility twice, but I struck out each time. I was not permitted to speak with Rabbi Helbrans.

Some people followed up our interview or phone conversation by sending me documents that were invaluable as sources. Gerald Shargel, Alan Vinegrad, Michael Vecchione, Paul Rooney, Joyce David, Michael Langone, and Bernice Devooght of the International Project Return at Canadian Customs all provided me with useful material.

Many people were extremely kind to me and sent me documents of the trial which ran about 2,500 pages. I took much of the jury trial directly from these documents. Many librarians gave me their attention and helped me find what I needed. Eleanor Friedl at Fairleigh Dickinson University's Library, Bracha Weisbarth at the Waldor Library, and librarians at the Ruth Rockwood Memorial Library were resourceful investigators, patient, professional, and amazing.

However, this does not cover all my sources. Some people asked not to be named and I have honored their request.

Elaine Grudin Denholtz

# INDEX